W9-BJB-003

small business *guides*

effective marketing

Levi's

small business *guides*

effective marketing

PETER HINGSTON

A Dorling Kindersley Book

Dorling Kindersley

LONDON, NEW YORK, SYDNEY, DELHI, PARIS,
MUNICH, and JOHANNESBURG

Project Editor Mark Wallace
Senior Art Editor Jamie Hanson
US Editors Gary Werner, Margaret Parrish
US Consultant Stuart Gittleman
DTP Designer Julian Dams
Production Controller Michelle Thomas

Managing Editor Adèle Hayward
Senior Managing Editor Stephanie Jackson
Senior Managing Art Editor Nigel Duffield

Produced for Dorling Kindersley by
Grant Laing Partnership
48 Brockwell Park Gardens,
London SE24 9BJ

Managing Editor Jane Laing
Project Editor Jane Simmonds
Project Art Editor Christine Lacey
Picture Researcher Jo Walton

First American Edition 2001

00 01 02 03 04 05 10 9 8 7 6 5 4 3 2 1

Published in the United States by
Dorling Kindersley, Inc.
95 Madison Avenue
New York, New York 10016

Library of Congress Cataloging-in-Publication Data

Hingston, Peter.
Effective marketing / Peter Hingston.
p. cm. -- (Small business guides)
Includes bibliographical references and index.
ISBN 0-7894-7197-3 (alk. paper)
1. Marketing. I. Title. II. Series.
HF5415 .H515 2001
658.8--dc21

00-065660

Colour reproduction in Italy by GRB Editrice
Printed and bound by Mondadori in Verona, Italy

see our complete catalog at

www.dk.com

Contents

Introduction

Marketing is the process of identifying a target market, defining what that market needs, and organizing a viable and profitable means to meet that end. The complex mix of activities that makes up marketing is central to every business, large or small, new or established. Marketing techniques are relatively straightforward to learn, and creating and carrying out a marketing strategy can be the most enjoyable part of running a business. Not all of your great marketing ideas will work, and you will have disappointments, but they should be balanced by the successes and by the excitement you will feel when you make a big sale or close a tough deal. You will also have the satisfaction of running a professional business.

Effective Marketing takes you through the whole marketing process, starting with the basics of your initial market research, and moving on to pricing and distribution – two interrelated areas that are hard to get right – and how to create an image for your business. Different methods of advertising are

scrutinized, along with the techniques of public relations and promotion. Selling strategies are discussed in detail. Also included is information on analyzing your sales data and dealing with different trading conditions. The final section of the book is an up-to-date guide to all the legal matters likely to affect you in the marketing of your small business. There is also a glossary of key terms, plus suggestions for useful contacts and further reading.

Effective Marketing is suitable for the self-employed (sole proprietors), partnerships, and corporations, and for all types of business, including service providers and manufacturers. It is also suitable for both a new business and one that has been in business for some months or years. Time is precious when you are running a business – this book can be read from cover to cover, or you can dip into the relevant sections as you need them. If you do only a half of what you read in this book, you will probably be ahead of many of your rivals.

Due to the many complexities involved when starting or running a business, you would benefit from taking sound professional advice before making any important decisions.

PLANNING Your Strategy

The marketing process involves balancing a wide range of activities. Market research is the cornerstone and, if carried out thoroughly and conscientiously, should result in a viable and purposeful business, guiding you with basic practicalities such as setting the correct price, choosing the optimum form of distribution, and projecting the right image. These elements can be brought together into a marketing plan.

STARTING YOUR MARKET RESEARCH

Market research is an essential intelligence-gathering and interpreting activity. Before you launch a new venture, your research will help you to learn if your business idea is viable. Once a business is up and running, research will help you to optimize your sales, seek new areas for expansion, and detect threats from competitors or other quarters. Market research can be thought of as having three parts: analyzing the market, observing the competition, and assessing your project. Analyzing the market is covered in this chapter, observing the competition on pp. 18–23, and assessing your project on pp. 24–9.

The constant changes in technology, society's habits, politics, and the business environment offer both opportunities and constraints. Every recession and every boom creates new situations – some good, some not so good for businesses. Superimposed on these varying conditions are regional differences.

Market research is the means to notice the opportunities and monitor the changes. Because market research may not appear to be essential to the day-to-day running of a business, it often drops down the list of priorities. However, just a few hours spent finding out more information about what your customers think of your existing business or what your competitors are up to could lead to a marked improvement in your sales.

Some Key Marketing Concepts

Before starting on your market research, it is useful to understand a selection of marketing concepts. Developed by marketing professionals, these concepts may be of varying use to you, but can provide interesting and thought-provoking ways of looking at and analyzing the data that you collect as part of your market research.

MARKET SEGMENTATION

The term "market segmentation" describes the discipline of considering the total possible market in much smaller segments or parts. A

CASE STUDY: Doing Initial Market Research

HAMISH WAS AN expert boatbuilder, specializing in fast, lightweight fiberglass dinghies, which he built with the help of two staff. He wanted to launch a new range of dinghies. First he did some desk research using the internet and going back through recent issues of various yachting, sailing, and racing magazines to see if his hunch that there was a niche for his new dinghy might be correct. He also discussed his ideas with a number of carefully selected past customers who were experienced dinghy sailors and whom Hamish felt could keep his ideas confidential. At the annual international boat shows, Hamish made a particular effort to visit the stands of each of his main rivals to try to learn as much as possible about their future plans before starting to formulate his own.

THE MARKET RESEARCH PROCESS

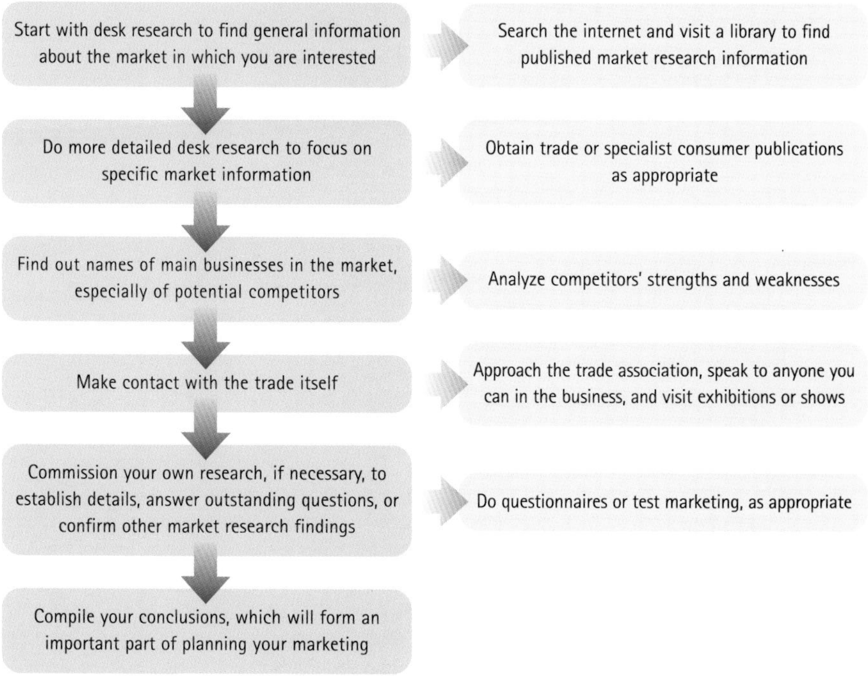

Step	Action
Start with desk research to find general information about the market in which you are interested	Search the internet and visit a library to find published market research information
Do more detailed desk research to focus on specific market information	Obtain trade or specialist consumer publications as appropriate
Find out names of main businesses in the market, especially of potential competitors	Analyze competitors' strengths and weaknesses
Make contact with the trade itself	Approach the trade association, speak to anyone you can in the business, and visit exhibitions or shows
Commission your own research, if necessary, to establish details, answer outstanding questions, or confirm other market research findings	Do questionnaires or test marketing, as appropriate
Compile your conclusions, which will form an important part of planning your marketing	

market segment is a group of buyers with similar needs. In other words, the discipline makes you think more clearly about who your customers are. Your scarce resources of cash, people, and time need to be focused on that part of the market where there are the best sales opportunities.

For instance, if you own a specialist shop, you might think that the potential market consists of every person living within a radius of so many miles. In fact, the real market is more likely to be much smaller, being people of a certain age range and income group, and those living or working close to your shop, or who travel past your shop. If you were a manufacturer or importer supplying protective gloves for a particular industry, your initial research might indicate many likely companies that would need to purchase these for their workers. When you started to approach these companies as part of your research, you might find that in some the work practices mean that the workers do not wear the gloves provided, so the companies have little need for new gloves; in others the workers might need to buy their own gloves; others might be part of a larger group that buys its gloves in bulk. In this case, the actual market is much smaller than that indicated by the initial research.

Find a need, then fill it – this is the key to a successful business

It is vital to understand just who constitutes your typical customer. You might also need to know where your customers live, work, or play. Without this knowledge, your whole marketing approach will be too imprecise to be very effective. Understanding market segmentation is even more important when considering the launch of a new project. Here you are trying to locate that niche in the market that has a demand for your product or service, is big enough to support your venture, and is not already dominated by competitors. Thorough market research is the only way to establish the boundaries of your market segment accurately.

For market research purposes, consumers are often grouped into a number of socioeconomic classes or into types of neighborhoods, which may be indicated by their zip code. These classifications are a means of naming different broad groupings working on the assumption that people with similar jobs, incomes, or living in similar places share characteristics in their lifestyles and spending habits.

Use your agility as a small business to keep ahead of your larger rivals

COMMON ERRORS WHEN DOING YOUR MARKET RESEARCH

1. Speaking to everyone except the actual potential buyers.
2. Failing to notice warning signals, because you are convinced your project will work.
3. Asking loaded questions, the answers to which just confirm your ideas without revealing the interviewee's thoughts.
4. Ignoring the fact that often 20 percent of the customers provide 80 percent of the turnover.
5. Assuming that you will compete effectively just because you have set your prices lower.
6. Underestimating how long it can take to enter a market and take a reasonable market share (it takes years, not months).
7. Failing to recognize the strength and the potential reaction of the competition.

MARKETING MIX

The marketing mix is made up of the "four Ps":

- Product (or service)
- Place (location and distribution)
- Price
- Promotion.

These four elements all need to be right for your business to succeed. Success comes as a result of striking the right balance between these four factors; concentrating on just one will get you only part of the way.

MARKET LIFE CYCLE

For new ventures, you need to know if the market you are entering is expanding, contracting, stable, or very dependent upon another market, which itself is changing rapidly. Markets tend to start slowly, expand rapidly, then plateau, or sometimes decline. The timescale of the whole process varies radically from market to market. Businesses that offer a new product or service early on when the market is expanding often do much better than those that come along later in the life of the market, but the early entrepreneurs are exposed to greater risk.

PRODUCT LIFE CYCLE

Like markets, products have life cycles. The traditional approach is to say that all products have a finite life, which is in three basic phases: growth, maturity, and decline. While this may be broadly true, it does not enable you to predict how long each of these phases might last. Some products have a very short life, while others keep selling for decades in barely changed form. Others still manage to undergo a mid-life metamorphosis and therefore keep selling well for some time.

Products during the growth phase usually need more nurturing in terms of time and marketing budget, and may not be very profitable as a result. Products in the mature phase should be profitable and relatively stable.

RESEARCHING THOROUGHLY
Market research involves exploring numerous avenues, from websites on the internet, to reference volumes in libraries, to asking questions of potential customers through a questionnaire.

The problem comes in detecting at what point maturity becomes decline – you might see a drop in sales, coupled with a gut feeling that the product is becoming dated. By now, you need to have new products in the pipeline to replace the declining product. Note that a declining product can still be very profitable, and the period of its decline can be several years.

Analyzing the Market

The first part of the market research process, analyzing the market, provides an inside picture of the industry, the trends nationally and locally, and an understanding of the needs of potential customers. The market is those people or businesses who might be your customers. The international situation will also be relevant if you are involved in exporting (see pp. 47–50).

LOOKING AT THE WIDER PICTURE

First look at the national situation. Many industries are described fully in market research studies (see p. 186), and copies of such reports can be read in large public libraries. The internet is a rich source of information – try government websites as a starting point. Other sources of market research information are relevant trade magazines, trade associations, and their shows and exhibitions. Your local library should be able to give you the names of relevant trade magazines and the addresses of the appropriate trade associations. From these you can find out details of exhibitions.

BEING AWARE OF TRENDS

Keep up to date with the business pages in newspapers and read relevant current affairs magazines. Copy, print out, or cut out useful information and start to compile a file. Continue adding to it, as it will help you to keep abreast of how trends change over time. Beware, however, of excessive media coverage given to a temporary trend. In such cases dozens of firms will pop up in response to the media signals, but it is unlikely that the actual market size is large enough, or that the demand (if it existed in the first place) will be sustained for long periods. Rely on an overview of your own market research to guide you.

Even if your business does not need a national-sized market to sustain it, national trends can have a significant effect at a local level. Look at the stage your market is at in its life cycle – the way to do this is through desk research. There may also be legislation in the pipeline that could have a major effect on your plans. If in doubt, contact the relevant trade association for information.

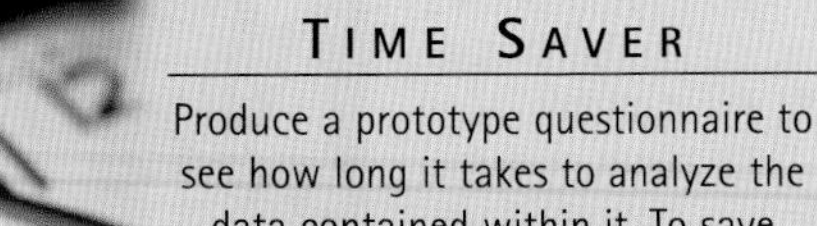

TIME SAVER

Produce a prototype questionnaire to see how long it takes to analyze the data contained within it. To save time, you might change the number of open-ended questions and add more multiple-choice questions, which are quicker to analyze. You might also use one sheet for several interviewees, if you can find a layout that allows you to do this.

LOCAL RESEARCH

Once you have built up some knowledge of the national situation and relevant trends, you need to find out much more about the industry on a local level. To this end there is no better source of information than the industry itself. Speak to the sales representatives of your likely suppliers – they can provide good information if asked the correct questions. Try to find out from them about consistent long-term sellers as well as what is popular right now. For a new venture, contact your local business development unit, and ask if they can put you in touch with someone who is working in the same business but located in a different part of the country (so that you would not be in direct competition).

PRODUCT OR MARKET LED?

Historically, many businesses were what is now called product led; that is, they focused too much on their products or service and expected customers to buy what they could supply. These businesses would tend to have little knowledge about their customers and some might even keep them at arm's length. They would also react to events rather than anticipating and planning for them. Today businesses are predominantly market led; they are proactive and sell what the customer wants. This is a more successful situation, and can be achieved through spending more time thinking about and researching the market, rather than just focusing on products or services.

YOUR TARGET MARKET

Next you need to consider the "target market" – the section of the population that could potentially use your product or service. Aim to define in detail who your customers are, their needs, and what benefit they will derive from using your product or service. A number of them are obviously surviving without what your business offers at present, so why will they want to use your business in the future? Also, are there enough potential customers within reach of your business?

At this point, you need to be clear whether your customers will be other businesses (trade), or whether you will sell direct to the general public, or both. Business customers generally have larger budgets and different requirements, such as the precise date by which a service must be completed, or specific details relating to the design of the packaging. They also expect credit, whereas a private customer is usually prepared to pay immediately, which can have a significant effect on your cash flow.

If your target market is business customers, first prepare a list of some or all of the businesses that may be interested in your product or service. Get their names from the Yellow Pages, or a similar directory, then find out the name of the best person in the firm to approach. Contact them and find out their views on what you have to offer.

In contrast, if your target market is private customers, trying to find out who will buy what from you is much more difficult. In this case, start by asking people already in the same business (where they are not direct competitors) for their views and advice. The next step is to speak directly to likely customers, and the most thorough way of doing that with the public is with a questionnaire.

Using Questionnaires

A questionnaire is the best way to find out about the needs, views, and habits of local customers in a structured way. Follow five golden rules to compile effective questionnaires:

1. **KEEP IT SHORT AND SIMPLE** Ask yourself what is it you are really trying to find out. Concentrate on the most important questions and avoid any fringe issues. There should be no more than five to 10 questions. A multiple choice or yes/no format is best as it is both easier to answer and quicker to analyze.
2. **AVOID LOADED QUESTIONS** This is best illustrated with an example. If you were considering buying a local shop, you might ask householders in the appropriate district their views to assess if the business would be viable. A question such as "Do you buy anything from your neighborhood shop at present?" would be reasonable. Asking "Would you use a neighborhood shop if it were more convenient than the large discount stores?" is a "loaded" question, and invites a positive reply. It is very easy to fall into the trap of asking such questions. Also, try to avoid emotive or exaggerated phrases in the question. Be aware that, out of politeness, people often give the reply that they think you want to hear.
3. **MINIMIZE OPEN-ENDED QUESTIONS** The purpose of the questionnaire is to pose specific questions that you have thought out carefully so that the answers allow you to draw firm conclusions. The danger of an open-ended question (such as "Do you think small, neighborhood shops are a good idea?") is that it could lead to a long debate. There is, of course, value in open-ended questions: the responses can reveal useful and relevant factors of which you are unaware. The best plan is to start with questions that have straightforward answers and to make one, perhaps the last

ASKING QUESTIONS

When you have compiled a questionnaire, use it to ask your potential customers for their opinions. If you are going to ask the customers personally, rather than by mail or other indirect means, choose a location where your target customers are likely to be.

question, an open-ended one.

4 **APPROACH THE RIGHT PEOPLE** Finding the right people might involve door-to-door interviews, phone interviews, or, if you are doing the survey in the street, stopping only those people who you think might use your product or service (such as those who seem to be within a certain age group). There is little to be gained from asking someone who is unlikely to be a customer. If you plan to mail the questionnaire to people, include a stamped self-addressed envelope, and give them some incentive to complete the form – such as a coupon – otherwise you are likely to receive few replies. If possible, try to choose places where your likely customers congregate. For example, if your business sells children's clothes, you could visit local schools and playgroups (with permission from the owners), or visit the downtown shopping area or nearest shopping mall on a Saturday morning.

COMPILING A QUESTIONNAIRE

It takes time and careful thought to put together a questionnaire that will provide you with enough of the right sort of information in the right form – data that you can use as part of your market research.

You do not need to know the name of the person you are asking, but it may be useful to include data on their age and sex. When you have compiled your questionnaire, try it out on a couple of friends to check that there are no ambiguities or loopholes.

SAMPLE QUESTIONNAIRE: POOR EXAMPLE

This questionnaire is from a newspaper wanting to increase the number of local retailers who use its classified advertisements. As some of the questions are unclear, the results are likely to be inconclusive.

QUESTIONNAIRE FOR RETAILERS

Q1 What is your attitude to advertising, and where do you advertise?

Two questions are asked, and the first one is too open; there is no question about how often the store advertises

Q2 Do you use classified or display advertisements?

Two questions are asked, and there is scope for an ambiguous answer

Q3 What emphasis do you place on displays?

This question is imprecise: does it mean window displays, interior displays, or display advertisements?

Q4 How do you try to compete with the big department stores and discount stores?

Although this is a rather nosy question, which people might not answer, it may provide useful information for the newspaper's advertising salespeople

5 APPROACH ENOUGH PEOPLE The more people you ask, the more accurate your survey results will be. Try to ask at least 50 to 100 people; more if possible. You can use a fresh questionnaire for each person for ease, or try to cover several people on one sheet for speed.

ANALYZING THE ANSWERS

Once you have gathered a reasonable amount of useful, representative data, you need to analyze it. Try to quantify the data into percentages where possible, although do not assume that your results are totally reliable or not subject to change. The data you produce from a questionnaire can form an important part of your market research. Be as objective as possible when analyzing it; avoid simply looking for any answers that support your ideas. If you have included any open-ended questions, look out for and note down any themes and suggestions that emerge from the answers given – they can often lead you in a direction you had not previously thought of.

The introduction stresses benefits to the reader

This question defines precisely what is meant by "regularly"

This request allows for the compilation of a precise list of the competition

This question, along with the next one, will provide clear data on the percentage of people who use each type of advertisement

An open-ended question enables advertisers to add the aspects that are most important to them

This question will provide information about the motivation of advertisers

QUESTIONNAIRE FOR RETAILERS

Would you please take the time to complete this short questionnaire. By doing so, you will assist us in our continuing efforts to provide you with a quality service that meets your precise requirements.

Q1 Do you advertise regularly (at least monthly)? ☐Y ☐N

Q2 Please list which newspapers or magazines you advertise in. ....

Q3 Do you use classified advertisements? ☐Y ☐N

Q4 Do you use display advertisements? ☐Y ☐N

Q5 What factors do you try to emphasize in your advertisements? ....

Q6 Do you use advertising to compete with the large department stores and discount stores? ☐Y ☐N

SAMPLE QUESTIONNAIRE: GOOD EXAMPLE

This questionnaire is an improved version of the example opposite. Here, the questions have been phrased clearly, and broken down into small segments. The answers should be simple to quantify.

OBSERVING THE COMPETITION

Close observation of actual and potential competitors is a critical part of your market research, and can provide a great deal of useful, and possibly vital, information for your venture. If your business is not yet in operation, your competitors are doing today what you plan to do tomorrow, and you can see how well their approach works and perhaps improve on some of their weak points. Once your business is up and running, knowledge of your competitors is essential, as they may be taking measures, such as cutting prices, that could seriously jeopardize your business.

When you are planning a new venture, it will almost certainly involve operating in a market where there are competitors. You need first to find out exactly who your competitors are, and then build up a picture of their business and their likely response to you.

Finding Out Who Your Competitors Are

Techniques for pinpointing competitors are fairly simple, but vary according to the size of the market in which you intend to operate.

LOCAL COMPETITORS

If your new project is based in one area, with a target market that is predominantly local, there are several avenues of research you can follow:

- **DIRECTORIES** Consult the Yellow Pages or any similar local trade or business directories. Between them they will list virtually every business operating locally. You then need to check out each relevant entry.
- **LEARNING ABOUT THE AREA** If your intended business is in the retail sector, walk along the streets in the area where you are thinking of opening, and mark on a street plan the name and location of any

CASE STUDY: Learning About a New Competitor

ANN AND MARK published a niche fashion trade journal that was well established and profitable. One day Ann had a call from one of their advertisers to say that they had been approached by someone trying to sell them advertising space in a new magazine to be launched in competition to Ann and Mark's publication. Later, another customer sent them a copy of a letter that they had received from the new magazine's publishers announcing the forthcoming launch. This gave company details, which Ann and Mark could investigate to see who was behind the venture. They also acquired a media pack that told them what the new magazine would look like, its launch date, its advertising rates, and so on. They therefore improved their own publication slightly (by increasing the number of pages and adding a high-gloss cover) and they secretly brought their next issue publication date forward to just before the new magazine's launch to act as a "spoiler". They also mounted a charm offensive with all their current advertisers to help ensure their continuing loyalty.

COMPUTER SOFTWARE SHOW

An international fair, such as this computer software show in London, can be a good area for market research, depending on the norms of your trade and whether you are planning to compete abroad by exporting. It is possible to gain a good overview of trends and to investigate specific competitors.

competitors. At the same time, look for locations that suit your needs, perhaps with plenty of passing business. Ask real estate agents with local knowledge if they know of any business similar to your proposed venture that is also looking for premises in the area at the moment.

- **ASKING SUPPLIERS** Ask your proposed suppliers' sales representatives which other businesses they supply in your area. Note, however, that if they are willing to give you information about other businesses, they are equally likely to inform others about your plans.
- **ASKING CUSTOMERS** If possible, ask some of your potential customers whom they buy from at present (you could include a question to this effect if you are compiling a questionnaire; see pp. 15–17). The answers might point out businesses that you would not have previously considered to be your competitors. For instance, an outdoor clothing retailer might be surprised to learn how many of their well-heeled customers are in fact buying their field coats at bargain prices from discount stores.

REGIONAL OR NATIONAL COMPETITORS

If the new project is more regional or national in character, then other research strategies are required; in particular:

- **TRADE EXHIBITIONS** Attend the relevant trade or consumer exhibitions. Talk to as many people as possible. Take notes. Here your competitors are at their most vulnerable – their goods are on display and you can usually walk straight into their booths. However, since these companies are operating in a fiercely competitive environment, they are likely to be taking some defensive measures: their price list may not be on display, and their latest products may either be hidden or only a dummy example will be displayed.

- **SPECIALIST PUBLICATIONS** Read the relevant trade and specialist consumer press and try phoning and asking to speak to one of the editorial staff. These staff are usually very knowledgable and may not mind talking to someone for a few minutes. Prepare several questions in advance, but realize that you will probably be expected to explain who you are and why you are calling. Editorial staff may be interested in knowing more about your new venture, as it could be newsworthy.
- **LIBRARIES** Visit a public library and ask for any directories for your proposed business sector. There are so many directories available that, not surprisingly, there are even directories of directories. Some general directories list manufacturers or retailers, often giving names of buyers and other key personnel. Some give maps of main shopping streets and shopping centers. Most directories are updated annually, so ensure you are reading the most recent edition.
- **INTERNET** Try an internet search using appropriate keywords. You might be surprised at the diverse number of sites that this search reveals. If you are planning to do business online, it is worth investigating the results of your search in detail; if not, investigate the top 10 or 20 matches.

DISCOVERING NEW COMPETITORS

If you are already in business, you will usually be aware of existing competitors, although it is most important to keep an eye out for new competition, either in the form of completely new businesses, or existing ones that are starting to make inroads into your territory. If you obtain early warning of a potential competitor's plans, it is easier to make their market entry more difficult.

So how do you get the earliest possible warning of a new competitor planning to enter the market? One of the best sources of information is trade gossip, since the new business will, at some stage, have to start talking to the same suppliers and customers as you. Trade publications can also be good indicators, especially the vacancies columns; the new firm may need to recruit specialist staff at a very early stage, probably prior to starting in business.

Remain on the lookout for new competitors once your business is established

In a retail context, if a shop unit becomes vacant near yours, phone whoever is selling it to find out as much as you can (the seller is only likely to give you information if you show an interest in the vacant unit yourself). In a manufacturing context, look out for new businesses at trade exhibitions and notice any advertisements by new companies (particularly in the trade press). Sometimes loyal customers will tip you off that they have been approached by a new competitor.

NO COMPETITION?

If you have conceived an interesting business idea and found there are apparently no competitors, you might think that you will be first in the field and your business will be a great success. However, in this situation, which is not uncommon, the fact that nobody is doing what you plan to do might indicate that there is an insufficient market for a viable business.

If there is indeed a gap in the market with good potential, it is fairly unlikely that you are the only person who has spotted it, and others may be working on rival plans. Gathering information from the sources given above should help you to receive an early indication of the nature of their activity.

Gathering Information About the Competition

Once you have located a competitor, there are a number of techniques you can use to learn more about their business:

- **DIRECT OBSERVATION** Where practical, sit outside your competitor's premises, perhaps in a car, and watch the people or vehicles coming and going. You need to do this at different times, on different days. This observation can reveal the general level of activity of the business. If there are vans making deliveries and pick ups, you may also learn the names of suppliers and customers (conveniently written on the sides of the van).
- **ANNUAL REPORTS** If a competitor is a publicly traded company, they are obliged to file annual and quarterly reports and other notices, which are available for free on several internet services, including the U.S. Securities and Exchange Commission.
- **USING A SERVICE** If the competitor is in the service sector, try to use their service. If that is not practical, ask friends to phone as though they were potential customers, to get information on prices or on how soon any work could be done (that might reveal how busy the competitor is).
- **CHECKING A SAMPLE** If the competitor is a manufacturer, try to buy, rent, or borrow a sample of their product and check it out, noting strengths and weaknesses. How does it compare with your own product? Note, too, any patent or registered design markings, since these should be respected.
- **WRITTEN INFORMATION** Obtain a competitor's sales literature and price lists whenever available, by writing or phoning to request information, or at exhibitions where the competitor has a stand.
- **ADVERTISEMENTS** Photocopy or cut out each competitor's advertisements. These not only give details of the product or service they are offering, but may also give details of prices. More importantly, they reveal how your competitors are marketing themselves – which customers they are trying to attract, the features they are emphasizing about their product or service, the image they are trying to project, and any special inducements they are offering, such as low-interest financing deals, or quick deliveries.
- **PUBLISHED ARTICLES** At your local public library, look through appropriate newspapers or magazines where there might be articles on your competitors. Make a photocopy of any you find.
- **CUSTOMERS** If you get the opportunity, speak to past customers; this can often be most revealing.
- **INTERNET** Check a competitor's website, if they have one.

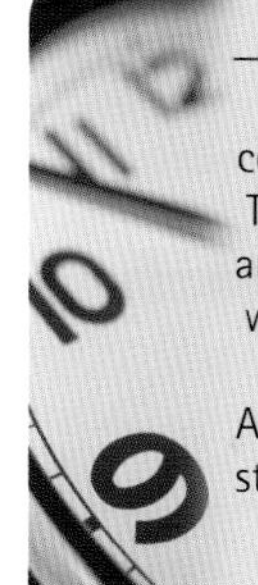

TIME SAVER

Buy a few shares in any large companies that are your competitors. This is a quick and easy way to keep an eye on them; as a shareholder you will be sent their annual reports and other interesting information. Although the data is historical, it will still be useful. In addition, the annual report usually announces the company's future plans.

The easiest way to keep track of the market research information you are gathering is to keep a small file or folder for each competitor. Into each folder you can put copies of their sales literature, price lists, press cuttings, advertisements, and any other notes you may have made as a result of observations, testing out products or services, or talking to customers. Keep your file up to date once your venture is up and running.

LEARNING FROM COMPETITORS

Although you need to research all your likely competitors, focus your main attention on the particular competitor who is the market leader.

They are likely to have been in business for some time prior to your starting your new venture. They will be ahead of you, as they will already have refined their product or service, made mistakes, gone down blind alleys, and eventually found better ways of running their business and of marketing and selling their product or service.

Assessing the Situation

When you have gathered plenty of in-depth information on your competitors, you are in a position to take an overview of the market and your potential position within it. If

DATA ON COMPETITORS
Prepare a checklist of information on major competitors at least, and on every competitor if you have time. Fill in as many of the categories as you can, adding any other relevant details.

COMPETITOR ASSESSMENT CHECKLIST

Business name ....

Business address ....

Phone number .... Fax number ....

Email .... Website ....

Publicly traded company, partnership, or sole proprietor? ....

Are they part of a larger group? ....

Year started in business ....

Names and locations of other branches/subsidiaries ....

Names of the proprietors/directors ....

Names of other key staff ....

Relevant details from their annual reports

....

What do they do? ....

Technical description of their products/services ....

Do the products/services have any special features? ....

What are their prices ? ....

What aspects do they stress in their sales literature? ....

What aspects do they stress on their website? ....

What advertising do they do? ....

What other promotions do they do? ....

What are their sales methods? ....

Assessment of their strengths and weaknesses ....

Proposals for most effective ways to enter into competition

....

Include the sales manager and marketing manager if applicable

Include annual reports details only for publicly traded companies

Describe their business in full

Include only products or services similar to yours

Include where they advertise and what they stress in their advertisements

Include incentives, discounts, credit terms, and guarantees

you are operating in a particularly competitive field, or if you feel under threat from a competitor, look through your research regularly to analyze the strengths and weaknesses of your competitors, and take the time to compile an assessment checklist; an example of a checklist is shown opposite.

When taking an overview of how your business, product, or service will enter the market, consider whether it will increase the size of the market (quite common with new products or services) or whether it will succeed only at the expense of existing competitors, who will lose market share to your business. If you think you will be expanding the market, it means you think you will attract customers who have not chosen to use your competitors – so why should they now want what you are offering? If you are trying to muscle into an existing market, how will you win customers from your rivals?

ANTICIPATING RESPONSES

When you start a business, there is a serious risk of a counterattack from existing businesses – they are unlikely simply to open the door to you. Techniques they might use to damage your business include:

- dropping their prices to engage you in a price war
- poaching your key staff
- interfering with your sources of supply
- criticizing your venture when speaking to mutual customers or the trade press
- stealing your customers
- taking legal action against you.

It is hard to anticipate the level of response from competitors. Most established companies react with some hostility to a new business if they think they are going to lose customers. In some cases they overreact and in others they are surprisingly inactive – perhaps they simply underestimate the threat.

In any event, if they try to attack your fledgling enterprise you are unlikely to win unless you have enormous resources behind you. A good survival strategy may be to adopt a low profile, and present as little threat as possible to a larger and more established rival – at least until your new venture becomes established. Competitors are an ongoing fact of running a business; for more details on how to deal with different types of competitors, see pp. 171–5.

ASSESSING YOUR PROJECT

Whether you are starting a new business or initiating a major development in an existing business, after you have carried out exhaustive market research you will need to make some sense out of a huge amount of information, some of which might seem to be contradictory. It is essential to analyze this information methodically so that you can find out the answer to the fundamental question: Does anyone want what I am selling? If you do not carry out an assessment in an objective and rational manner, you may rely too much on your own feelings and desire for success when making business decisions.

You can assess the viability of a new project by subjecting it to four tests, each of which is from a different perspective:

1. the financier's test
2. the market researcher's test
3. the market's test
4. your own test.

Before you can consider your project as likely to be a viable and worthwhile venture, it would need to pass all four tests.

Undergoing the Financier's Test

A financier is unlikely to invest in a project unless it has a good chance of being profitable. The test a financier might carry out on the viability of a new small business therefore provides important insights into its financial soundness. If you are funding the project yourself, you should still carry out this test – after all, it is your money at risk. A financier would look at the following four key aspects of a new business proposal:

- project management
- market entry
- profit margins
- project longevity.

PROJECT MANAGEMENT

Do the managers or proprietors of the project have a balance of skills and experience? The skills and experience in question cover marketing, sales, finance, and administration, plus any industry or technical expertise. In a small business this knowledge may be vested in only one or two people, but most financiers would prefer there to be a team. Teams are valued for a number of reasons: the team members are more likely to have a range of complementary skills, whereas a sole player is bound to have some weaknesses; should one person become ill, the project is more likely to continue if there is a team in place; with a team there are several people, rather than just one, who can invest in the business.

FACT FILE

Make your market research and preparation particularly thorough if your new project takes you into unfamiliar territory (in terms of technical, geographical, or market area). The risks of entering a new field are considerable simply due to the many unknowns ahead.

CASE STUDY: Carrying Out Test Marketing

AFTER MANY MONTHS of preparation, Carey and Melissa were ready to test their new natural perfumes. They had carried out focus group testing but wanted some wider feedback before committing themselves to full production. They approached several department stores and tried to persuade the stores to let them carry out in-store demos. Due to the existing cosmetics suppliers, this was not possible, so the pair rented a vendor's handcart at a major shopping center. This gave them an excellent opportunity to do test marketing and they soon found out which perfumes were popular, which they should drop, and which price points were the most acceptable. They also discovered that over 80 percent of their customers were buying their perfume to give as gifts, and therefore their packaging had to be greatly enhanced to make the gift look extra-special.

MARKET ENTRY

A financier would prefer a new project to have difficulty entering the market. This seems contradictory – why should anyone want the market entry to be difficult? The answer lies in the simple fact that, as soon as your business starts and appears to others to be successful, it will encourage imitators. These imitators cause a dilution of the potential market and raise the possibility of price wars. It is therefore a great advantage to have a project that is not easy for others to copy. There are a number of barriers that can discourage (or even prevent) a new competitor from copying your idea, including:

- specialist skills or knowledge (technical, creative, or otherwise)
- patent protection
- licenses (a project may operate under license granted by an overseas company that is the leader in its field – the license effectively stops competition)
- contracts with the biggest likely customers.

Note that a high initial investment is not, in itself, a natural barrier to others.

PROFIT MARGINS

The financier is looking for the potential for high profit margins. What this also means is that the business should enjoy good positive cash flow, have funds for future development, and should still survive if margins are eroded by unforeseen events. Just what constitutes a "high" or "low" margin is difficult to say in general terms, since it depends on many factors. Refer to the information on pricing (see pp. 30–39) and seek advice from your accountant.

PROJECT LONGEVITY

At the planning stage, project longevity is not often considered, since small businesses tend to place more emphasis on short-term results. Longevity in this context simply means a project that, once launched, is likely to continue to be competitive and profitable for a number of years without substantial change or need for further investment. This justifies the initial investment to launch the project. Thus "trendy" business ideas are discouraged, as are those that rely on a large number of external factors outside your control, such as currency exchange rates, which can fluctuate.

Doing the Market Researcher's Test

A market researcher would seek to answer three specific questions:

- Does the project appear to be viable? (And, if so, what assumptions are being made about what the business is likely to achieve?)
- What detailed form should the project take to match the market's requirements?
- Are there any discernible trends?

To assess as objectively as possible the large amount of market research information gathered and to answer these questions properly, you should try to put the salient points on one piece of paper. In this condensed form, the information can be assimilated and it is easier to read through in one sitting.

PROJECT VIABILITY

Everyone thinks their business idea is a good one and is going to work. It takes the cool, dispassionate look of a market researcher to assess if this is indeed the case; it is not easy to judge likely success, since the market can respond unpredictably. For example, potential customers might express enthusiasm for the concept, but ultimately not place an order.

However, the more research that you do, and the closer that research is related to what you plan to do, the more likely it is that you will obtain meaningful results. Where a new project is not innovative, it is easier to assess its likely chances; as the level of innovation increases, the harder it is to judge from market research alone – some test marketing may be called for.

PROJECT DETAILS

Even if the market research indicates that the project is likely to be viable, there will often be many details that need to be worked out. Research should help to resolve these details. For instance, the concept might appear to be viable, but the proposed business name might be receiving a poor reaction, or the research might indicate the need for a business to be located in one particular place, or reveal that the viability is dependent on winning a long-

LOOKING AT DIFFERENT TRENDS

TYPE OF TREND	CHARACTERISTICS	POINTS TO CONSIDER
INDUSTRY	Relates to statistical information about your industry	Although information is historic, it should indicate any trends over time
ECONOMIC	Relates to statistical information about the local or national economy	A key trend to look for in this category is changes in the spending power of your target market
TECHNOLOGICAL	Relates to advances in equipment, software, or completely new innovations	Effects of these trends vary widely from an almost immediate revolutionary effect to a long-term change
COMPETITORS	Relates to changes in competitors' prices, products, or tactics	Any increase in activity by competitors may be bad for your business
SALES	Relates to analysis of your own sales trends once you start in business	Sales figures recorded over time are one of the most important trend indicators you can have
WEATHER	Relates to both seasonal and long-term variations (such as global warming)	Weather and climate changes can affect tourism, sports, outdoor businesses, and many others too

term contract with a particular customer. These details can make the difference between a business succeeding or failing.

TRENDS

None of us tend to be very good at forecasting the future, and the further ahead we look, the more difficult it becomes. From a small-business standpoint, looking even one year ahead is difficult enough, but it is worthwhile making some effort in this respect. Market research should provide most of the clues. Trends to note are covered in the table opposite.

Use test marketing as a link between "having the big idea" and launching a full-scale venture

Testing Out the Market

Test marketing involves putting your product or service out into the marketplace in a limited and provisional way in order to assess the market reaction at an early stage before you are fully committed to the project. It is not always necessary or possible, but can be very useful, especially where your other market research is inconclusive, or where the investment required is such that you want some positive feedback from the marketplace before going further. Test marketing can also provide useful, possibly vital, feedback on details of your product or service, but it has the disadvantage that it may reveal your hand to a competitor. In some test marketing an element of bluff may be required, particularly if you have not yet opened your business.

Test marketing is not just relevant to a completely new product or service; it may also be relevant to assessing the suitability of a change being contemplated for an existing product or service, such as new packaging, a new pricing structure, a store revamp, or a new image. It is therefore a very common practice in both large and small businesses and takes a number of forms.

ADVERTISING

This is the simplest way for nonretail ventures to check market response. You place a single advertisement or perhaps a series of advertisements as if the product or service were actually available (even if you are not quite at that stage) to see what reaction the advertisement produces. Your ad must not be misleading and should not request any cash, but may simply invite a response for more information. The main limitation of this method is that you will receive minimal feedback unless people take the trouble to contact you; the advertisement therefore needs to be particularly stimulating. You may just get a silence, from which it is difficult to draw useful conclusions.

SAMPLES

If you are making a product that is to be sold to the industry, you could take samples to potential buyers, or exhibit them at a trade show and take orders before committing yourself to full production. This practice is common in the fashion and gift industries, where buyers are used to placing orders many months before receiving the goods. In some cases it may be possible and useful for a potential large customer to try out a sample product at no expense. This allows the customer to assess the product and provides you with valuable performance data.

MAILSHOTS

A mailshot is a letter that is sent to a potential customer detailing your new product or service and requesting a response that would indicate their interest in what you have to offer. This can be an effective technique, especially if the customers are businesses and the letters are addressed to named individuals. Rather than sending out letters in a random, untargeted way, spend time creating a quality mailing list (see p. 55); this will also be of ongoing value once you have started in business. For national coverage, you can rent such mailing lists; a local one is probably best created yourself from existing contacts, directories, and your market research. Ideally each letter should be individually addressed, dated, and signed. Keep the letter short and easy to respond to. Where you are writing to a consumer, include a stamped self-addressed envelope for their reply. The more targeted the letter, the better the likely response, but you may still need to follow up by telephone to obtain the information you are seeking.

Focus Groups

Focus groups are often used by businesses whose customers are the general public. Selected people from the target market (actual or potential customers) are invited to form a focus group and attend a meeting, where they are shown prototypes of new products or samples of new packaging, or a new service is fully described. They are then asked prepared questions, usually starting with closed questions and moving to more open-ended ones, always keeping the subject in close focus. There is some open discussion, which is controlled by a moderator to prevent a dominant person from influencing others. All responses are carefully recorded, often on video, for later analysis. The function of the focus group is to give individuals a chance to express their own opinion about your project – group consensus is not the objective. Participants are often paid, and good light refreshments are made available. You can organize a focus group yourself, or ask an outside company to do so. The latter method produces a more professional result and distances you from the discussion, but is costlier.

Leaflet Drops

A version of the mailshot, leaflet drops are less personal and used on a larger target audience. Leaflets describing your product or services and giving contact details can be distributed to the general public via their mailboxes. Leaflet drops could also be used for local trade customers. To spread your net wider, leaflets can be inserted loose into newspapers or magazines (where they are called "inserts").

Exhibitions and Trade Shows

Another way to judge market reaction is to rent a stand at a suitable exhibition or trade show. This method is particularly useful because, unlike most other options, you receive immediate feedback from potential customers. This can be crucial in helping you to fine-tune your product or service, establish prices, or conclude that there is an inadequate market. Appearing at a trade show does, of course, reveal your venture to other businesses, some of whom could become

Delivering Leaflets

Having leaflets distributed manually is a good way to convey details of your product or service to households within a limited area. Delivery of leaflets as inserts in a publication allows for wider coverage.

competitors in future, or try to copy aspects of your idea. For more details on exhibiting at a show, see pp. 153–7.

PILOT STUDY

When you are producing a product or service that you hope will have a national market, one form of test marketing is to try it out first in one small area. This trial is usually called a "pilot" and should include advertising in the selected area. If the pilot is successful, the product or service can be rolled out nationally with more confidence.

Ensure you have an escape route planned in the event of trouble

Carrying Out Your Own Test

At this point it is wise to consider the project's potential impact on your lifestyle and on any existing business you run. Every new project will have its ups and downs, which may have direct consequences for the proprietor and any dependants.

LIFESTYLE

The lifestyle implications of how you choose to make a living can vary enormously and will be with you for the whole project. Lifestyle effects should be taken into account at an early stage, before you are saddled with debt, leases, stock, staff, and so on. Questions to ask yourself include: "Where do I want to be in five years' time?"; Does this new project help me to achieve that?"; and "Do I want all its problems?" A useful exercise is to make two columns on a sheet of paper, one listing those aspects of business that you like, and the other listing those that you dislike. Will the new project increase the "likes" or "dislikes"?

BUSINESS STABILITY

Unfortunately all too many sound businesses collapse due to the launch of a new project that went wrong. A new major project can develop completely unforeseen problems, and even well-known companies may teeter on the verge of bankruptcy when a project runs into trouble. You should therefore pause to consider a worst-case scenario, quantifying the likely impact on the business if everything went wrong.

If the new project runs into problems it will make at least two major and immediate demands – management time and money. If there is an original business, it may not be able to sustain the loss of those two precious commodities, in which case the whole business will be jeopardized. What might have been a perfectly healthy original business could fail.

On a more positive note, the new project could produce spin-offs or utilize unused capacity in the existing business. It might even take off to the point where the original core business is simply allowed to decline and the new project becomes, in time, the principal activity of the business – a type of metamorphosis that is a feature of many successful businesses.

Assessing the Test Results

If your project has passed all four tests with flying colors, that is a good sign, but does not in itself guarantee success. A more common scenario is that the project will pass some tests easily, just pass others, and perhaps fail one – this situation is more challenging to assess. Certainly if the project fails any of the four tests, that is a sign that you need to look at it again very carefully. Each of the four tests is arguably of equal value, though the effects of failing some will differ from those of others. If you are able to make alterations to a project so that it will pass all four tests, that is worth pursuing. Otherwise, it may be simply a matter of judgment as to whether or not the project is worth taking further.

PRICING

Your prices send out important marketing signals, establishing the position of your products in the market, and contributing to the overall image of your business. It is essential to get your pricing right. If you price too high your sales will suffer, and if you price too low your profits will suffer. In addition, once you have set your prices it may not be possible to adjust them readily if you find they are wrong. As you gain experience your pricing will become more accurate, but all businesses need to check their prices regularly since rising costs and inflation can erode profits in real terms.

A key element of working out pricing is understanding your costs. Once you know your costs, you can use them as an element in the pricing calculation. Two types of costs are relevant here:

- **FIXED COSTS** Also known as overhead, these refer to business expenditure, which is basically constant or fixed irrespective of the level of revenue. Rent, taxes, most salaries, and insurance are examples of fixed costs.
- **VARIABLE COSTS** Also known as direct costs, these comprise expenditures, which vary directly in relation to the level of business – for instance, the cost of raw materials.

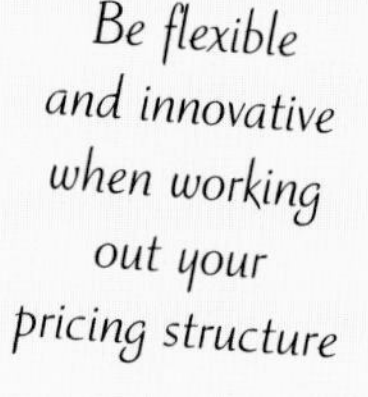

The price you choose for your goods or services needs to meet your fixed and variable costs, and make a surplus (your profit) on top. This is the minimum you need to make from your sales to stay in business. To cover fixed costs it therefore makes a good deal of difference whether you sell one item or 100 per year, or provide a service for one day or 100 days, since the entire fixed costs have to be recovered on those sales. Dividing the fixed costs by one, 100, or whatever, obviously has a huge impact on the end price. As a result, you need to be very cautious in predicting your likely sales in terms of units sold or billable time.

Fixed costs must always be kept to a minimum since they can float upward if left unchecked and may soon overwhelm the profitability of a business (see pp. 37–9). Businesses are usually better at controlling their variable costs. For example, when a supplier raises their prices,

CASE STUDY: Calculating a Competitive Rate

LIZ WANTED TO come up with a rate for her consultancy work that she would charge, with expenses added on top. First she calculated what her core operating costs were to run her small office, including her full-time secretarial assistant, plus a reasonable salary for herself. When she worked this out, it came to a daily figure that was lower than other similar consultancies were charging and did not allow for contingencies. Liz felt that this rate would make her work seem less attractive to potential customers, who might think the rate was cheaper because her work was of lesser quality. She had excellent qualifications and experience, so concluded that she should charge a similar rate to others. She subsequently found this to be acceptable to her clients.

MONEY SAVER

Be cautious about pricing your product on the assumption that you will be operating at full production all the time, for that is most unlikely. If you are working on your own, to work out a labor cost, charge at least what you would have to pay an employee to do the same work.

most businesses take notice and, where the rise is unjustified, they will challenge it or find a new supplier.

UNDERSTANDING MARKUPS AND MARGINS

A markup is the amount added to the cost price to reach the selling price; a margin is the amount of profit you are making on an item. The calculation for a markup is:

$$\text{Markup (\%)} = \frac{\text{(selling price - cost price)}}{\text{cost price}} \times 100$$

The calculation for a margin is:

$$\text{Margin (\%)} = \frac{\text{(selling price - cost price)}}{\text{selling price}} \times 100$$

Markups and margins vary from industry to industry, and in different parts of any supply chain. Learn the norms for your business; the only way to do this is to ask the industry, either through a trade association or contacts. Beware of a common error: sometimes people say their markup is 200 percent, meaning that they buy for one price, and sell for double that price. In fact, this is a markup of only 100 percent.

DISTRIBUTION AND PRICING

How you distribute your product can make a great difference to your pricing. The main options are selling direct to the customer, using an agent on commission, or distributing through a wholesaler or retailer. Each method is appropriate to a particular industry; ensure you know the markups of the different distribution stages relevant to you so that you can work out your "end-user" price to see if it is competitive. Some people, when starting a business, begrudge using wholesalers or retailers since they feel they will take too much of the overall profit to be made on an item. However, selling direct to the customer takes both time and effort on promotion, neither of which is cheap. It might be better to sell indirectly via wholesalers or retailers, who already have the outlets and the customers.

BASIC PRICING FOR WHOLESALERS AND RETAILERS

A straightforward way to price a product for wholesale or retail purposes is to use the following equation:

Selling price per unit = net cost price + markup

For example, if you buy an article for $4.65 net, and if the typical industry markup is 85 percent, the selling price would be calculated as follows:

($4.65 + 85%) = $8.60

There are several other points to consider:

- You may consider rounding the price up or down to a figure (such as $8.50, or perhaps $8.99) that sounds more appealing to a customer.
- Keep your prices in line with those of your competitors.
- Check that your cash flow forecast reflects your markups, in terms of the relationship between the sales figures and the inventory/raw materials figures. For example, if you are using a 100 percent markup, your inventory/raw materials figures should be about half the value of the sale figures, or you will be understocking or overstocking gradually.

BASIC PRICING FOR MANUFACTURERS

If you are a manufacturer, a straightforward calculation to price a product is:

Selling price per unit = (cost of raw material + direct labour + overhead contribution) + markup

You can calculate the elements in this sum in the following way:

COST OF RAW MATERIALS This should be relatively easy to calculate per item, but do remember to allow for wastage.

DIRECT LABOR This is the realistic cost of employing staff to make the units. Staff costs should include about one-third as much again on top of the wage to allow for Social Security, workers' compensation premiums, unemployment insurance taxes, paid vacations, and so on. If you are self-employed, do not price your own labor costs cheaply – if you do, and you take on staff in the future, you will either have to raise prices or take a drop in profits to cover the extra cost.

Price to achieve the maximum profit possible

MARKUP Insert a known markup that is appropriate for your particular industry into the pricing equation (see p. 31) to obtain your selling price; you can then make slight adjustments to the final price as necessary. The markup needs to provide a small surplus (say five to 10 percent) to provide funds for future expansion, new product development, or simply to save for any future contingencies.

OVERHEAD CONTRIBUTION This considers the overhead (fixed costs) of the business, which obviously have to be supported by the production. To work out the overhead contribution per item, use the following calculation:

$$\text{Overhead contribution} = \frac{\text{total overhead}}{\text{total production}}$$

An important point to note is that this calculation assumes that everything that is produced is subsequently sold.

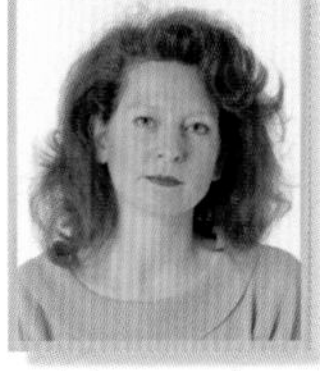

CASE STUDY: Working Out the Unit Price

ELLEN IS self-employed, making children's garments. The raw materials cost $10 per unit (allowing for wastage), and each item takes one hour to make, so in a 40-hour week she might make 35 such items (allowing for downtime, time spent on administration, and so on). The labor cost is $500 – equivalent to what it would cost to pay an employee to do the job – plus one-third extra for paid vacations, sick leave, and so on. So the direct labor cost would be:

$$\frac{\$500 + \$165}{35} = \$19 \text{ per unit}$$

Assume total overhead comes to $8,000 a year, and total annual production is 1,680 items (for 48 weeks' production, allowing for some vacation). The overhead contribution is:

$$\frac{\$8{,}000}{1{,}680} = \$4.76 \text{ per unit}$$

Finally a markup is added of 10 percent. The selling price, therefore, is:

$$(\$10 + \$19 + \$4.76) + 10\% = \$37.14$$

Ellen might choose to sell at more or less, depending on the competition and the market.

BASIC PRICING FOR SERVICES

The pricing of services is usually based on hourly labor rates plus material costs. For consultancy or freelance work, this is usually called "fees plus expenses." Service businesses often give a quotation, which is their price for doing a job (see p. 34).

CALCULATING HOURLY LABOR RATES

$$\text{Hourly rate} = \frac{(\text{total overhead including all wages}) + \text{markup}}{\text{total likely productive hours}}$$

First of all, find out the typical going rate for what you are planning to do. If you plan to employ anyone, allow an adequate hourly wage for them out of the amount you are planning to charge, making allowance for downtime and profit. Work out overhead and an appropriate markup. To calculate your productive hours, assume you (and any employees) will be productive (doing work for which you can charge) for, say, 75 percent of the working week. The actual figure may be lower. Being productive for 75 percent of the time means that in a typical 40-hour week you will only be charging for 30 hours, but having to pay your staff for 40. The remaining 10 hours are absorbed in getting sales, doing paperwork, and so on. Do the calculation, and insert that figure into your cash flow forecast. If the cash flow forecast figure looks good, and your labor rate is about that for the industry, that is a good start. If not, see what you can realistically adjust.

MATERIALS These are usually charged "at cost," but charging the price you paid ignores the time you take to locate the materials, the cost of travel to pick them up, and so on. So most businesses define "at cost" as the retail price; they purchase the goods at industry or wholesale prices, giving themselves some margin.

CASE STUDY: Working Out an Hourly Rate

PAOLO AND GEORGE run a small car servicing and repair business as a partnership with no employees. Their overhead is $25,000 per year, and their basic working week is about 50 hours. They calculate that they can do productive work for 40 hours (administration and cleaning taking up the balance of time). They take four weeks' vacation per year and, when possible, draw $50,000 a year each. The equation, assuming a 10 percent markup, would then be:

$$\frac{(\$25{,}000 + \$50{,}000 + \$50{,}000) + 10\%}{2 \times (40 \text{ hours} \times 48 \text{ weeks})} = \$35.80$$

The hourly rate is very dependent on them achieving a full 40-hour productive week with no time lost. In practice they also make a useful profit on the spare parts being installed.

CASE STUDY: Looking at Different Options for Charging

CAROLINE IS A graphic designer who wants to freelance. She plans to work on her own from home and to visit clients as necessary to get work and to discuss projects. She calculates the minimum hourly rate she must charge to provide an adequate "wage," and to cover any overhead she has. She needs to allow for time lost due to traveling, getting work, and administration. Any materials used she will charge at cost. She may be able to quote her hourly rate for some jobs, while in others she may be given a budget to work to or asked to quote an overall price. Her difficulty in the latter situations would be estimating how long the job might take. She plans to keep a time log, and at the end of a fixed-price job she will use it to calculate the actual hourly rate she achieved; this will help her with future estimates.

Estimates and Quotations

Service businesses, and some manufacturers or suppliers who make or supply items to very exact and individual specifications, usually operate by providing customers with an initial estimate, which can be verbal or in writing. An estimate is the approximate price for carrying out a job and may be open to negotiation and change. It is prudent at this stage to ensure you emphasize the word "estimate" to avoid any misunderstandings. An interested buyer will then usually ask for an itemized quotation in writing. Unlike an estimate, a quotation is a fixed price and, if agreed, forms the basis of a binding contract between the two parties.

Use a standard layout for both your estimates and your quotations to ensure you include all necessary details, and always take the time to look at previous quotes to a client before submitting a new one so that you can keep the basics consistent.

QUOTATION

If you have to do a large number of quotations, it can be useful to have a standard template so that you can fill in the relevant details. Always put the date on the quotation and make clear for how long it is valid. Be clear about exactly what is covered in the quotation and include your payment terms.

10 Sellers Lane
Any City, Any State, ST 54321
Tel: 212-555 4321

Mrs. S. Nixon, Manager
Excellent Products Inc
Unit 3, Industrial Park
Any Town, Any State, ST 12345

June 21, 2001

Dear Mrs. Nixon,

WINDOW GATES - QUOTATION

Thank you for taking the time to meet me yesterday. I now have pleasure in providing you with a quote to supply and fit window security gates for your factory unit.

QUANTITY	Four windows, all to the rear of the premises.
SPECIFICATION	Mild steel expanded mesh as per sample left with you. Gates to be attached to window surrounds by one-way security screws.
PRICE	$623.00 + tax. This quotation is valid for 30 days.
TERMS	Payment is due 30 days from date of invoice.
GUARANTEE	We guarantee our workmanship and materials for 12 months.

If you have any questions, please do not hesitate to call me. I look forward to hearing from you in the near future.

Yours sincerely,
Paul Wilson
Sales Manager

Quantity and specification are described in detail

Length of time that quote is valid is shown

Payment terms are made clear

Variations on Basic Pricing

The various pricing equations covered in the previous pages are generally called cost plus, since they are based on your costs with a profit margin added. These methods of pricing are relatively simple and straightforward to calculate and to use, and they can provide the baseline for all your pricing: you know that if your prices are lower than these basic prices, you may be operating at a loss, and if your prices are higher, you are likely to be making a reasonable profit.

Many businesses will be able to set their prices using a simple cost plus equation. Others will find that additional, more complex factors come into play, including the effects of competition and the demands of the market, which will affect their prices.

PRICING BACKWARD

A variation of cost-plus pricing, pricing backward should perhaps be called price minus. It occurs when you supply a product or service to a major customer who dictates what they are prepared to pay. You then need to attempt to work backward to see if you can meet their specified price. To do this you need to start with your basic cost plus calculations, varying the elements to see if the tough demands of the customer can be met and still leave you room to make some profit. If you find their specified price is lower than the minimum viable price you can work out, either your costs are too high (see p. 39), or their low price may be a negotiating gambit (see pp. 157–9), or you may just not be able to do business with them because their proposed price is unrealistic.

MARKET-BASED PRICING

When following this pricing method, your prices attempt to reflect market conditions. You set your prices at what the customer is prepared to pay – in other words, what the market will bear. This method is quite common in many different industries. In general, if you price low (in relation to market prices) you hope to increase volume sales and thereby achieve a certain annual profit. Alternatively, if you price high, you may make fewer sales but end up with the same profit.

In practice it is not that easy to work out the exact price to opt for, since buyer interest naturally wanes as the price rises. You can try to establish the market price as part of your market research by close examination of rivals' prices (which effectively set the market price), and by a thorough understanding of what motivates your customers to pay a certain price for that type of product or service. In any event, you still need to do a cost plus calculation to cross-check that you are making a reasonable profit.

If there is no competitor already setting a market price with a similar product or service, it is much harder to assess just what customers

DOS AND DON'TS OF PRICING

- ✓ Do put a realistic price on a product or service.
- ✓ Do make sure you include all the costs in your pricing calculations.
- ✓ Do take into account the true value of your own time.
- ✓ Do compare actual costs incurred on a job with the invoiced price.
- ✓ Do react quickly but thoughtfully to a competitor changing their prices.

- ✗ Don't forget to increase prices in line with inflation.
- ✗ Don't make the price hard to find in your sales literature.
- ✗ Don't price low just to get the work.
- ✗ Don't discount too much, too often.
- ✗ Don't think the customer is concerned only with the price.

are prepared to pay. Since competition tends to force down prices, if you have no competitors and a good-quality product or service, you may be able to start high and reduce your price if need be. Look at the table below for further guidelines to help you decide which market-based price to set for your product or service. In some cases, test marketing is likely to be required (see pp. 27–9).

PREMIUM PRICING

Being able to supply a product or service at a premium price is only possible when demand far exceeds supply and the product or service has a degree of exclusivity that means it cannot be copied readily, or the work required cannot be done by someone else. Premium pricing is characterized by long customer waiting lists. Being a sole player with a premium-priced product or service is an open invitation to a new competitor to price below you with a similar product or service that may be better, or simply promoted more strongly, than your own.

Phone an employment agency to get an idea of going labor rates when pricing services

SENDING THE RIGHT SIGNALS

While covering all the costs of your business, including production or providing a service, is an important element in calculating a price – one you should never lose sight of – there are numerous other factors you need to take into account. For instance, your selling price can send an important image signal to your customers. In the absence of other indicators, people will judge the quality of a product or a service by its price. Hence, when they are faced with making a choice, they will often conclude that the more expensive product or service must be better. Similarly, they may not purchase an item because the price seems too cheap, and they will think there must be something wrong with it.

Your prices will also run into psychological price barriers, such as \$1, \$5, \$10, \$20, \$50, \$100, \$500, \$1,000, and so on. It is a good idea to keep your price to just below one of these price barriers.

CHOOSING A STRATEGY FOR MARKET-BASED PRICING

CHARACTERISTICS OF PRODUCT OR SERVICE	POSSIBLE STRATEGY
NOT INNOVATIVE, READILY COPIED, WITH FEW COMPETITIVE ADVANTAGES	■ The only option is to penetrate the market slowly with limited promotion so as not to alert potential competitors. ■ Set a low price to prevent being undercut.
INNOVATIVE BUT READILY COPIED	■ Achieve market penetration rapidly to achieve domination in a short space of time by using a large promotion and a low price. ■ To merely skim the market with a high price, aim for quick sales with a large promotion. You may then need to change to a lower price before rivals enter the market.
INNOVATIVE AND NOT READILY COPIED	■ In this almost ideal situation, you can price high and either skim the market with a limited promotion or penetrate the market more deeply with a larger promotional budget.

Note that it is illegal for manufacturers or suppliers to fix retail prices, and that retailers can choose to price as they wish (see p. 178).

PRICING WITH PRODUCT LIFE CYCLE

The stage a product or service is at in its life cycle (see pp. 12–13) can affect its price. Generally speaking, the price during the growth period will be a matter of overall strategy (see the table, left), although you may set a special launch price to get sales moving. During the mature, established phase, the price will remain fairly constant, rising in step with inflation. In the declining phase, which can take many years, the price is gradually dropped to clear the remaining stock.

DIFFERENTIAL PRICING

Tactical or differential pricing involves altering some prices at certain times or for certain groups, such as students or senior citizens – for example, there may be a regular discount for seniors on a Wednesday afternoon. By their nature, some of these special prices will be permanent; others may vary on a daily or weekly basis. The reductions can be for either short-term or special reasons, usually to boost sales, clinch a sale, or combat competition. Differential pricing can be very effective, especially in fast-moving business areas, such as retailing. Care needs to be taken that your pricing policy does not confuse or alienate some customers, so there must always be a reason for altering prices or giving one category of customers a better price than others.

PRICING A RANGE OF PRODUCTS

When you have a range of products or services to offer, it is tempting to perform a detailed pricing calculation and to come up with one markup that you apply universally. This may make the arithmetic easier, but it is better to price every product or service individually to permit each to be correctly positioned in the marketplace and achieve maximum profitability, as each will face its own rivals and constraints.

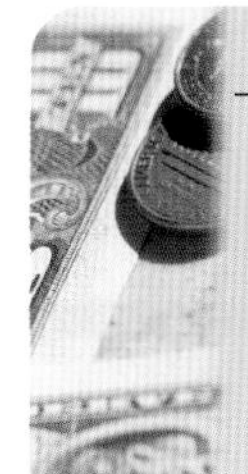

MONEY SAVER

Reduce bank charges on business checks (and therefore reduce your overheads) by using your personal credit card where possible. Pay off those business items on your card statement each month using one business check.

Keeping Your Own Costs Low

To ensure that you are making the maximum profit, to enable you to drop your prices if necessary, and for the sake of good business sense, it is essential to keep an eye on your own costs, both fixed and variable, and to keep them as low as possible.

WHAT IS THE REAL COST OF MAJOR BUSINESS PURCHASES?

In addition to watching your overheads, you need to think carefully about all major purchases you make. Investment in your business is essential from time to time, but there are choices you can make that minimize the costs to you.

A good illustration of a new business purchase that can be bought cheaply or expensively is a car. If you look at the list price for a new car, you will find a figure quoted that, in a business context, is completely different from what the car will actually cost you. The cost to you requires a complicated calculation. If you are buying the vehicle with cash, the cost will include the loss of interest on that money had it been invested (which is not insignificant over the life of a vehicle), plus the depreciation in value of the car over time, plus the running costs, minus capital allowances, and minus any expenses allowable for tax. If you lease the car, or finance part of the cost, you need to alter the calculation accordingly – there will be interest to repay in addition to the sum borrowed. A further complication occurs depending on the status of your business and whether you or the business owns the car. If you operate as a corporation and the vehicle is company-owned, the vehicle is regarded as a perk and taxed accordingly. If you are in business as a sole proprietor or partnership, it is taxed differently.

Most vehicles have a similar lifetime, so a $20,000 vehicle will not be worth much more than a $10,000 vehicle after 10–12 years. What this means is that you will have lost nearly twice the amount of money if you buy a more expensive vehicle. Even over a shorter period of time (as most people do not own a vehicle for its whole life), the depreciation of the more expensive vehicle will be higher, though the rate of depreciation especially in the early years can differ markedly from model to model. Depreciation is not just an accounting term, but a real and tangible cost to you. Leasing is an alternative to buying, with different implications again. Vans are treated differently for tax purposes and may be more economical to purchase than a car, if they are suitable for your needs. For other major purchases, think of reliability, tax allowances, and depreciation, but also of technological relevance – will an expensive new item soon be superseded by new technology?

The table opposite will give you numerous ideas about areas of your business to watch and in which you can make savings.

Watching Your Profits

Finally, the aim in pricing correctly is to maximize your profits. There are only three ways to increase the profits of a business:

- to reduce costs
- to raise prices
- to increase sales.

A mere one percent improvement on all of these (that is, reducing costs by one percent and raising both prices and sales by one percent) can make a big difference to your overall profit figure. Try it yourself with your own figures, and you should find your profits increase by much more than three percent; more so if your profitability is currently low.

BUYING A NEW CAR

A Mercedes is an example of a major business purchase – look into all the alternative ways to pay, or consider leasing, before making your decision.

CHECKLIST FOR MINIMIZING OVERHEADS AND OTHER EXPENSES

This ten-point checklist is for you to work through, in your own time, reviewing each category of costs with the sole aim of reducing your core operating costs. To motivate you in this quest, remember that each $100 saved is equivalent to $100 instant profit.

Advertising and promotion ☐

Review the response (in terms of estimated sales) from your current advertising. Do not be surprised if it is insufficient to cover your advertisement costs. Consider focusing more on promotion and PR – these may achieve better results and for a lower cost.

Business premises ☐

Costs of renting or owning property can be a major overhead. Are you making efficient use of space? Could you operate from smaller premises? Are you gathering data to challenge your next rent review? If you rent, once your business is established, consider buying premises: buying can be an investment (provided you buy wisely); renting is merely an ongoing expense. Calculate what size of mortgage could be paid with what you currently spend on rent.

Finance ☐

Review your borrowings (if applicable). Excessive stock levels are one cause of high borrowings. Generally an overdraft is the cheapest way to borrow money commercially. In the long term, consider aiming to be financially self-sufficient – that is, to have no outstanding loans.

Heat and light ☐

Review your energy costs for the past year. We insulate our homes, but seem less interested in doing this for our workplaces, even though they are often large and poorly insulated so therefore wasteful. Consider increased insulation and the use of time clocks and thermostats to help reduce these costs.

Insurance ☐

Review your current insurance coverage to check you are not overinsured (but equally be sure you are not underinsured), and get alternative quotes. Consider using an insurer who is used to your particular type of business, as they can usually quantify the risk better than a general insurer, and therefore offer a lower premium.

Phone bills ☐

Review your recent phone bills. These are almost always larger than necessary. Consider trying to reduce the number of long, chatty calls by using emails or faxes. Also consider alternative phone companies and minimize costly mobile phone usage.

Purchasing ☐

Review your purchasing procedure (or create one). Consider approving all major purchases yourself. If you decide to delegate this function, do so under strict guidelines with definite limits and controls in place. Staff have different priorities from proprietors, and this can be reflected in their purchasing decisions.

Staff ☐

Review your actual staffing needs. Wages will usually be your largest overhead. Take on staff only when you have to, and minimize staffing by investing in automation. Eliminate all unnecessary work and simplify work practices. It may be better to have one high-caliber employee who needs less supervision than several of lesser ability. More mature and experienced part-time staff can be particularly worthwhile. Try to increase productivity by tight control, comprehensive job descriptions, proper training, and realistic incentives.

Travel ☐

Review your travel costs if you or your staff have to use trains, planes, or hotels. Consider researching the different fare or tariff options, as considerable savings are often possible.

Vehicles ☐

Review your requirements carefully when you come to change your present vehicle(s) or if you think you need an extra one. Consider which way to finance your purchase, since there are big differences in costs, especially when maintenance is included. Take impartial advice, perhaps from your accountant.

FIGURING OUT YOUR DISTRIBUTION

Distribution – the route your product takes from you to the end-user – is an important link in the marketing process. If your distribution is erratic or inefficient, you may fail to sell in adequate amounts. Choosing the best distribution options is an ongoing challenge that confronts almost every manufacturer, importer, and wholesaler. Distribution is also relevant to businesses that regard themselves as being in the service sector but that have a tangible product to sell, such as computer software companies. Franchising is also covered here, and is applicable to many service businesses.

There is no simple yet ideal distribution channel, since each has its own complications, advantages, and disadvantages. Manufacturers sometimes resent the markup that wholesalers or retailers put on their goods, while wholesalers complain about erratic or delayed deliveries from suppliers and the extended credit retailers often take. Some small manufacturers and importers feel tempted to market their products directly instead of via wholesalers and retailers, but the cost of this can be prohibitive. A business may use a variety of methods concurrently or may use different methods in different geographical areas. Shown opposite are different distribution options.

> *Try out several distribution methods to find out the best for you*

MARGINS

Depending upon the distribution method you choose, the margins on products can vary dramatically from a seemingly paltry 5 to 15 percent, if you are an intermediary (importer or wholesaler), to considerably more if selling direct. But, almost invariably, those distribution options that have

CASE STUDY: Trying Different Distribution Options

PAUL HAD DESIGNED an innovative car alarm and made a sample batch. His problem was how best to market the device. He first offered it to a large car accessory retail chain, but the buyers there seemed unable to make a decision. He then considered selling it by mail order using advertisements in automobile magazines. He selected two magazines and booked small color ads. With a professionally taken photo and artwork, the ads looked appealing. Meanwhile, one of the two magazines did a review of car alarms, and, since he had sent them a sample, his was included in the review with favorable comments. However, the response to Paul's ads was disappointing, and he had to conclude that a car alarm with innovative aspects, even at a reasonable price, was not going to sell this way. Perhaps too many cars were already equipped with alarms or immobilizers as standard. After 10 months, an East Asian car-maker contacted Paul via his website and, after long negotiations, they agreed to install the device as standard in some of their model ranges.

CHOOSING YOUR METHOD OF DISTRIBUTION

DISTRIBUTION METHOD	RELATIVE SETUP COSTS	POTENTIAL MARKET COVERAGE	PROBABLE MANAGEMENT WORKLOAD	LIKELY MARGINS (not overall profitability)	POINTS TO CONSIDER
SELLING TO RETAILERS	Low	High	Low	Low	This is a suitable route for many manufacturers to take.
SELLING BUSINESS-TO-BUSINESS (NONRETAIL)	Low–Medium	High	Low	Variable	Selling direct is a suitable route for those who make parts or supply equipment or systems for other businesses.
ONLINE SELLING (VIA A WEBSITE)	Low–Medium	Possibly worldwide	Medium	High	A favorite for many businesses, either on its own or with other distribution methods.
EXPORTING	Medium	International	Medium	Low	This is only appropriate for businesses with a product that has international appeal and can withstand the higher costs of exporting.
DIRECT SELLING	Medium–High	Possibly high	Medium–High	High	A specialized option, this is only appropriate for products with a wide appeal.
SELLING BY MAIL ORDER OR DIRECT MAIL	Medium–High	Possibly high	Medium–High	High	Although "getting rid of the middleman" is tempting, it is often difficult and costly to do successfully.
FRANCHISING	High	Medium–High	High	Medium	A popular approach, this requires substantial capital and an experienced management team.

the higher margins also carry proportionally higher overheads, so the actual profitability of the different methods is often not dissimilar. You should therefore consider more than simply profit margin when deciding on the distribution channel. Usually what constitutes an optimum channel for distribution is one that has the capacity to take a reasonable volume of goods from you at a reasonable margin and is also likely to be dependable.

LOOKING AT ALTERNATIVES

An alternative to arranging your own method of distribution is to enter into a joint venture with another company. For example, you might approach a company that has a large sales force, selling to buyers similar to your own, but whose products are not in direct competition. Another example might be to tag on to someone else's mail-order catalog or to share the mailing with your own leaflet. These methods are not always feasible, of course, but are well worth thinking about. If none of the different ways of distribution seems obviously the best, a degree of trial and error may be needed. Although you may start with one particular distribution channel, you might be able to experiment with others and combine several methods.

AVOIDING CONFLICT OF INTEREST

If you are combining methods, you need to ensure that any new channel is not going to make you lose your original customers. For instance, if you were selling to retailers and then decided to launch mail order too, it might

USING AGENTS

Many small businesses that cannot afford to have their own sales staff use agents who sell on commission. These are self-employed salespeople who usually carry several noncompeting product lines. The agent merely takes orders, with the delivery, invoicing, and chasing bad payers normally being the responsibility of the supplier.
Finding good agents can be very difficult. Agents sometimes appear dilatory, their efforts seem minimal, and their paperwork may be incomplete. However, from an agent's point of view, the 10 to 15 percent commission they earn on the sales from a small business can often amount to very little. Furthermore, some of the companies that they represent do not deliver the goods ordered or, worse still, do not pay the commission due to their agents.

Select agents with care, preferably on recommendation. They need to have contacts, industry experience, and should not carry so many lines that they cannot look after your products adequately. Give agents your full backing and support (as though they were partners in your business) and monitor their work carefully. Commission is normally paid on the net sales (after discounts), and is due when invoiced rather than when the customer pays. Ensure that all these details are covered in a written agreement. This agreement should include the following points:

- **COMMISSION** Cover the commission to be paid, precisely how this is calculated, and when it is due.
- **TERRITORY** Define the territory in which the agent can operate. In particular, it needs to be agreed upon if commission is earned by the agent on those sales within the area that are not taken by the agent – normally commission is due on all sales made from a given territory.
- **AUTHORITY** Define the extent of the authority of the agent to negotiate different prices or delivery terms.
- **TERMINATION** Agree on the period of notice that will be required on both sides, in order to terminate the agreement.

lead to the retailers losing customers. Some retailers might cancel or reduce their orders as a result. A solution to such a problem might be to offer slightly different products for mail order than those being sold retail, or, if the products must be the same as those sold retail, you could ensure that they are sold at a similar price to the one at which the retailers are selling them, and then add to it any post and packing charges.

Aim for your product to sit on the shelf for as short a time as possible

Another conflict of interest can occur when you supply one business and are approached by a rival business which asks you to supply them as well. In some trades it is common practice for a supplier to sell to almost anyone who can buy their products, irrespective of competition between their customers. In other industries, customers tend to be supplied on a more exclusive basis. Ensure that you know your own industry's norms.

Whenever you plan to embark on a course of action that is likely to upset (or even lose) existing customers, it is obviously prudent to take their likely views into consideration.

Selling to Retailers

If you have a product that is suitable for mass retail sale, you can try to interest retail buyers directly. Alternatively, you might try to interest a wholesaler in your product. However, this route is becoming less common because there are fewer wholesalers than there used to be, and increasingly retailers want to buy direct from manufacturers to obtain a better price.

What will a good retail buyer be looking for? Most importantly, a buyer wants items that will sell and continue to sell, ideally quite quickly. This means that a product must be attractive, have a wide potential market, be appropriately priced, and – the key point – offer something that is different from its rivals.

The product also needs to meet a whole range of other criteria: to comply with any regulations; to have attractive packaging; to be capable of display; to be handled without being readily damaged; and to be of appropriate quality. A buyer also needs a supplier to be reliable, to be able to meet orders, and to deliver full orders on time. Part deliveries or late deliveries are highly unpopular.

Overcoming Problems

For a retail buyer, especially one representing a large retail chain, the following aspects of buying from a new small business are undesirable and may prevent a sale.

- A small business is an unknown quantity – a buyer prefers to deal with existing suppliers.
- A buyer does not like small suppliers with a limited range of products.
- A buyer prefers suppliers to have distribution depots near to the stores being supplied.

How can you overcome each of these apparent barriers? First, since you are an unknown quantity, you need to convey the quality and professionalism of your organization (however small it is) and your products. This can be through your company name, literature, and qualifications, but is more particularly reflected in your actual products. If you already supply anyone, emphasize your good track record, particularly if you supply a large customer.

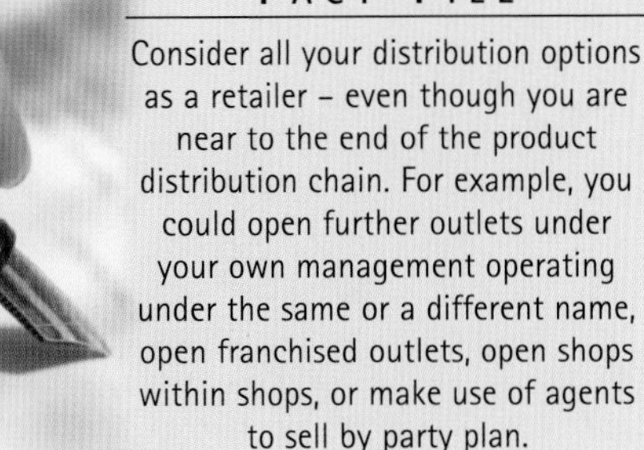

FACT FILE

Consider all your distribution options as a retailer – even though you are near to the end of the product distribution chain. For example, you could open further outlets under your own management operating under the same or a different name, open franchised outlets, open shops within shops, or make use of agents to sell by party plan.

Next, a buyer will only make the extra effort that is involved to deal with you, rather than an existing or larger supplier, if you have something completely original and highly worthwhile to offer. In your approach to a buyer, emphasize the unique and superior aspects of your product.

Finally, if you are located at some distance from a buyer, this may count against you, especially if your business is in a remote rural area. If necessary, you could approach retailers through a local contact or from a temporary office address that is closer.

Selling to Large Retail Customers

There is the potential for a mismatch between a small supplier and a large customer. Some large retailers look after their smaller suppliers very well, since they realize that it is in their own interests to do so. Others are not so careful. Weigh the risks and advantages carefully before entering into business with a large retailer – it might not be the best option for your business, at least to begin with.

Try again later if you are unsuccessful in a sale – buyers change frequently

The normal procedure for trying to sell to a large retail customer is first to find the name of the buyer responsible for your particular product range. Send them a sample with a cover letter. The package must look professional and the cover letter should be short, but give key relevant details, such as sizes, colors, prices (wholesale, not retail), and availability. You are unlikely to receive a response to this first approach.

Follow up with a phone call to the buyer, leaving a message if necessary. The aim is to arrange a meeting in which you can present your products and try to gain an initial order. The more professional buyers will usually respond, so this is a good indication of the quality of the organization with which you are dealing. Finally, you may be invited to the all-important meeting, which may be as short as 10 or 15 minutes. It really is make-or-break, since you are unlikely to get another chance in the near future. Preparation is essential, as is not arriving late.

A buyer may request numerous changes to your design or exact very difficult conditions. Even if you are given the impression that you are likely to get an order, you may be dismayed at how little the buyer is prepared to pay for what you have to offer. Frequently purchases are taken on a sale-or-return basis – if they do not sell they are returned to you in return for a full refund. Shipping and handling costs are invariably the responsibility of the supplier, so ensure that is factored into your calculations. Orders from large retailers usually specify a particular day or week for the delivery; take every measure necessary to meet such specifications, otherwise the retailer may immediately cancel the order and possibly penalize you for your failure too.

If you are a small business dealing with a large customer, that customer will usually represent a significant proportion of your turnover. This can be good business, and might indeed be invaluable to you, but it can also be worrying. Should they cancel orders or default on payment (both of which are quite common), it may cause your business significant harm.

Selling to Smaller Retail Customers

It is usually too difficult and time-consuming to visit large numbers of smaller retailers individually, but a good way of making sales is by taking a stand at suitable trade shows, where relevant small retailers visit to place orders. Many will tend to place tiny orders, but the price you will be paid is likely to be much better than the price offered for a larger order or by a larger retailer. This higher price will be needed in part to offset the higher shipping and handling costs per unit of sending out small

Fact File

To avoid plagiarism – where an unscrupulous buyer will take your idea and get another (home or overseas) manufacturer to make a close copy at a lower price – speak to your trade press or trade association before you make contact with buyers. The trade association usually knows who likely plagiarists are, and may be prepared to warn you.

orders. Small retailers also tend to be less fussy about terms and conditions, but they may be slow payers since they are often undercapitalized. If in doubt about their creditworthiness, ask for payment by credit card or payment in advance by pro-forma invoice.

Another point to consider is how to resupply the small retailer. Few of them will have the time to phone you once their stock is sold, so the onus is on you to chase them, either by phone or in person. The latter works better, but is costly in terms of your time and travel. In some cases, you could carry stock with you (in a van) and resupply the retailer there and then; this may be cost-effective, since you will then only need to make one trip.

An advantage in supplying many retail customers rather than one or two big retail chains is that your risk is spread. However, if there is a downturn in the economy, the small outlets tend to be the most vulnerable.

Selling Business-to-business

If you make parts (components) or equipment for other firms, or supply raw materials or complete systems for nonretail businesses, you will probably need to sell direct to them. The business customer is quite different from a consumer in many respects. Two key differences are that business customers usually have much greater buying power than consumers and that they expect to be given credit terms.

Finding the Right Approach

The normal procedure for trying to sell to non-retail businesses is first to locate some possible customers. This could be done in the first instance by some desk research:

- Look in the Yellow Pages or similar business directories at your library.
- Contact trade associations who publish lists of members.
- Use the internet by searching with appropriate keywords.

Once you have located possible customers, contact them to find the name of the person to whom you should write. Send them a personal letter enclosing any sales leaflets or brochures you might have. If your product is relatively cheap and small, enclose a sample with the letter. Follow up your letter about a week later with a phone call with the purpose of making a sales appointment.

If the products or raw materials you are supplying are appropriate only to a small number of companies, a slightly different approach is likely to be required. First, thoroughly research the relevant companies (using the same techniques used for competitors – see pp. 21–2). This will give you vital background information so that you can tailor your offering to meet their likely requirements. You can then write a customized letter to each one, which is more likely to receive a positive response.

An alternative approach is to take a stand at an appropriate trade show and try to attract the interest of the relevant trade buyers. It is unlikely that simply being at a trade show will bring sufficient sales on its own to begin with, but it will raise your profile and you will probably get some useful feedback. You might need to supplement this approach with a mailshot before the show and a telephone follow-up afterwards.

MARGINS

The margins on business-to-business sales can vary enormously from relatively low margins if supplying components or raw materials, to a medium level of margins if you are supplying equipment, and possibly quite high margins if you are supplying complete systems. Although you will be aiming to maximize your margins, check out the norms in your industry and use them as a guideline.

GETTING PAID

A major problem with many business-to-business sales is not receiving payment on time. The whole area of payment and credit requires great care, which needs to start with carrying out a proper credit check on a potential customer and, if you have any doubts, not offering credit.

If a customer's credit check does prove satisfactory but they turn out to be slow at paying, you need to instigate a formalized debt recovery procedure that slowly escalates from a polite phone call to numerous reminders verbally and in writing, to seeking legal advice and eventual legal action.

Monitor how many visitors your web site receives

MAKING THE MOST OF SELLING ONLINE

1. Put your telephone number on all your emails.
2. If you receive an order by email, confirm it as soon as possible by email.
3. Send an email informing the customer when the goods are despatched.
4. Put your return policy on your website.
5. Record how many people visit your website.

Online Selling

Some small businesses are established to operate solely on the internet; others sell online via their website simply to complement other distribution methods. The internet is used for selling all sorts of things; the main areas likely to be of relevance to new small businesses are niche consumer markets (where products are not available through shops) and business-to-business sales.

Note, however, that not every product is suitable for selling online. The internet market is growing and evolving rapidly, but current research seems to indicate that products that sell particularly well online include books, music, software, tickets, and financial products. As a small business, if you have an innovative product that needs some explanation to introduce it to customers, your product is unlikely to sell well online.

If your competitors are already selling online and you think that this method will benefit you, selling via the internet could be a distribution method worth using. How to create a website is covered on pp. 100–04.

WHAT TO INCLUDE ON YOUR WEBSITE

Essential information to put somewhere on your web ite is your full contact details, including your address, your phone and fax numbers, and your email address.

Ensure that you fully understand the procedures for performing secure online sales transactions, and their strengths and weaknesses. Not everyone wants to buy online, so consider offering the additional service of including a form on your site that the customer can download, complete, and then mail or fax to you to place an order. Find out the pros and cons of different methods of receiving payment (such as by credit or debit card) and what different fees you may be charged for each method – these additional and variable costs need to be taken into consideration, and if possible built into your online prices.

If you are selling products online, when you receive an order your business operates effectively as a mail-order business. For more details about how to run an efficient mail-order operation, see pp. 52–3.

Record how many visits your website receives for your own information, in order to monitor how well your site is doing. As a small business, however, it may be wise to keep this information private: bragging about the success of your website may attract competitors, while, if the site is not doing well, potential customers may be put off.

Exporting Your Products or Services

Exporting is another possible method of distributing your products. Exporting can either be done passively at a very low level, where you simply accept and fulfill orders from abroad, or you might choose to do it actively and try to build up your export sales to where they become a substantial part of your overall turnover. Exporting is a complex process: as a small business, do not consider going into exporting unless either you are well established in your home market (and thus financially strong), or one of the proprietors has worked in exporting before and already has the contacts and necessary experience.

Advantages and Disadvantages of Exporting

Advantages		Disadvantages	
Market Size	One of the biggest advantages of exporting is that the potential market is much larger than that of your own country.	High Costs	Traveling abroad to get orders is expensive in time and money. Shipping goods and agents' fees may also raise your prices.
Market Match	The product or service you are selling might suit certain overseas markets better than your own country's market.	Market Mismatch	Cultural differences can be such that a successful product or service in your own country might have little appeal elsewhere.
Diversification	Selling in markets beyond your own country provides a possible safeguard against a downturn in your own country's economy.	Regulations	You need to find out about local regulations. There may also be import restrictions or onerous duties.
Currency	Exchange rates can give you an advantage if your currency is weak against that of your customers, or a disadvantage if your currency is strong.	Shipping	Speak to a shipping agent at an early stage. Note that the expression "shipping" includes both trucking and air freight.

If you wish to enter exporting in a passive way, the main requirement is to ensure that you get payment. This is best done by credit card, or pro-forma invoice (so that the customer pays before you send the goods), or through your bank using a letter of credit. It is best not to indulge in giving credit until you have done business successfully with a particular company for many years and are convinced they will pay.

Active exporting is quite another matter and can represent such a major project in itself that it is more like starting a completely new business. It requires thorough market research of the target country and a full understanding of how business is done there – norms and processes may be quite different from those at home. There are significant differences, even between the English-speaking countries of the world, so do not assume that because you share a common language and similar culture that business is done the same way. You may also find that your product will require modifying to suit specific overseas markets. Determine whether you will require an import license for the country concerned, whether there are any import duties, and if you require an export license from your own country.

DISTRIBUTION OVERSEAS FOR MANUFACTURERS

Assuming your market research results are encouraging, you need to consider how best to approach the overseas market. Manufacturers have a number of options.

■ **AGENT** An agent will visit potential

TRANSPORTING CARGO

Air freight is just one of the possible means of distributing export goods. Although it is expensive, and best used for lightweight goods, it is a fast and efficient method.

customers and take orders on commission. (which is typically 10 percent). You then ship the goods direct to the customers and invoice them individually. You will therefore be responsible for getting payments. Finding a hardworking, reliable agent and controlling customer debt are the main problems. If the agent represents another (noncompetitive) company from your country, ask them for a reference. Agents often start with enthusiasm, but this can wane if they find that selling your product is going to take some perseverance, or they realize they are unlikely to earn much from your sales (being a new and small business).

Explore further possibilities in the market in your own country before considering exporting

- **DISTRIBUTOR** A distributor actively seeks and takes orders, but also holds stock of your goods. You therefore need only to ship them to the distributor (rather than direct to individual customers) and issue one invoice, saving both time and money. Using a distributor usually works better than having an agent, but the distributor will require a significant discount, and you need to ensure that your distributor is reliable and likely to pay you on time. One way to find a suitable distributor is by recommendation through your trade association or from other companies that they represent. Do try to get a credit rating for a new distributor, too. As with agents, distributors should not only sell your goods, but also provide important feedback from customers.
- **DIRECT SALES** Direct selling can be done by taking a stand at a trade show abroad or by visiting selected larger customers. Once you make a sale, you need to ship to and invoice each customer individually. Follow-up sales might be difficult or too expensive for you to undertake on a regular basis, but, if you have attended the trade shows and taken orders in the past, customers will expect to see you there.
- **ONLINE SALES** You may generate export sales if you have a website. For small sales to end-users or retailers, you could ask the customers to pay by credit card; this safeguards your payment.
- **COLLABORATIVE PROJECTS** A completely different approach to distribution overseas is to enter into some form of collaboration with a company abroad. This might take the form of you providing certain facilities or contacts for them in exchange for the overseas company providing the same for you.
- **MANUFACTURE UNDER LICENSE** In this case, an overseas manufacturer agrees to make and sell your product locally. You could supply them with parts, specialized tooling, or even the whole product in kit form. Alternatively, you may just get paid a royalty in return for the right to make your product. Manufacturing under license is complex legally and needs good professional advice. It is essential to check out fully the other party's track record, financial status, and integrity before entering into any binding agreement with them.

DISTRIBUTION OVERSEAS FOR SERVICE INDUSTRIES

For a service business, the options for distribution overseas depend very much on the type of business concerned. Sometimes it will be necessary to open an office or shop in the overseas country. Recruiting and supervising local staff can be a challenge, so franchising might be one possible solution (see pp. 55–7). Certain types of service business may generate good sales leads though their websites.

PAYMENTS

A key problem that faces many new exporters is not getting paid. Certain countries seem to be notorious poor payers, while others have the reputation of being excellent payers; obviously, individual companies differ. With a small purchase, you might insist on payment by credit card or payment in advance by pro-forma invoice. With the latter, ensure that you are not liable for currency conversion charges. For larger purchases, you could request payment by pro-forma, but this offers no protection to the buyer. The buyer is more likely to opt to pay by a letter of credit or other documentary collection instead; these methods of payment are handled through your bank and are relatively safe, but tend to be costly.

If you plan to offer credit to customers abroad, check references just as you would with any local customer, but do so with even greater attention to detail, get a credit rating, and do not take any chances.

In the event of nonpayment, use normal debt collection procedures – issue statements, follow up with a letter then phone calls, and finally consider visiting the customer abroad if the size of debt warrants it. Some customers assume that, because you are far away, they can simply ignore you. Arriving in person usually has the desired effect.

Direct Marketing

Direct selling, mail order, and direct mail are all examples of direct marketing – the wholesaler and retailer are cut out of the sales distribution chain and the manufacturer (or importer) sells direct to the end-user. Direct marketing uses the mail, the phone, email, direct-response advertising, and personal contacts to find its customers. It can be a suitable means to sell to both consumers and business customers. Direct marketing is increasing in popularity for many reasons, such as greater use of credit cards, more products

HOW IS DIRECT SELLING DONE?

Before becoming involved in direct selling, it is important to know the main types of selling, and how each of them works.

DOOR-TO-DOOR This type of direct selling usually operates with the salesperson leaving a catalog and returning a few days later, hoping to take an order and pick up the catalog. Success tends to rely on repeat business. Your salespeople need to knock on a lot of doors to make a living from their sales as they usually only receive about 20 per cent commission on sales.

PARTY PLAN Still sometimes called "Tupperware parties" after the company whose name is synonymous with this method of selling, party plan is a very popular form of selling and is used as almost the only method by some companies. The host, or more usually hostess, who is the salesperson or a friend of the salesperson, invites a group of friends to her home. The salesperson brings along samples, or has stock of the items, demonstrates the products, and then encourages the guests to place orders. Some people who sell in this way prefer to hold stock, while others take orders and collect the money only when they hand over the goods. Ideally, party plan selling does not require a hard sell; instead it relies on good demonstration and saleable products.

SELLING TO CONTACTS This method of selling is also known as "personal referral". Your salesperson finds the people who may potentially be interested in obtaining the product, then visits them and tries to make a sale. The key is for the salesperson to know a lot of people and to be prepared to approach them all. They might contact neighbors, friends, relatives, and fellow religious or club members. The downside is that not everyone likes to be on the receiving end of this type of selling and the salesperson can become unpopular and lose friends.

being available through direct marketing, mail-order businesses responding much more rapidly to orders, and also due to the growth of shopping on the internet.

DIRECT SELLING

Direct selling is where a manufacturer sells direct to the consumer; unlike mail order, these sales are made by personal contact. The manufacturers use self-employed salespeople, whom they call "distributors," "consultants," "demonstrators," or "associates," sometimes prefixed by the word "independent." Many products are sold by direct selling, including clothing, cosmetics, household goods, jewelry, books, and dietary or nutritional products. The term "direct selling" covers selling door-to-door, by party plan, or selling to contacts.

Direct selling companies often continue to grow and prosper, even during hard economic times when many other businesses are struggling for survival. The great majority of salespeople working for direct selling firms tend to be women working on a self-employed, part-time basis from home. To succeed at direct selling, an individual needs to be self-motivated and should enjoy selling. It also helps to be gregarious and know plenty of people who can be initial sales contacts.

NETWORK MARKETING

Some direct selling companies also operate a multilevel system of sales, in which a salesperson can recruit others and receive bonuses, depending on how well their recruits perform. This way of selling is known as network marketing (sometimes abbreviated to networking), or multilevel marketing (MLM for short). You sell the products to friends and contacts. One or two of them might think they can sell it to their friends, so they agree to become distributors. By recruiting them, you

PARTY PLAN SELLING
This form of selling, in which the salesperson invites potential buyers to his or her home to see the products and place orders, is ideal for more personal items such as underwear and makeup, but can also be used for a wide range of other goods.

earn bonuses that are dependent on their sales. If those new distributors recruit more people, you get a share of their sales bonuses, too, and on it goes as the network expands. The people who recruited you are called your "uplines" and the people you recruit are your "downlines."

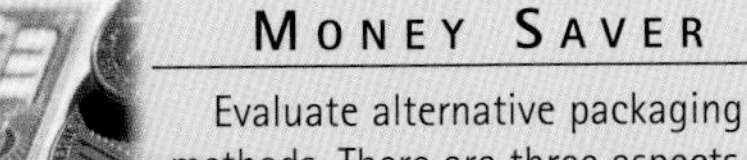

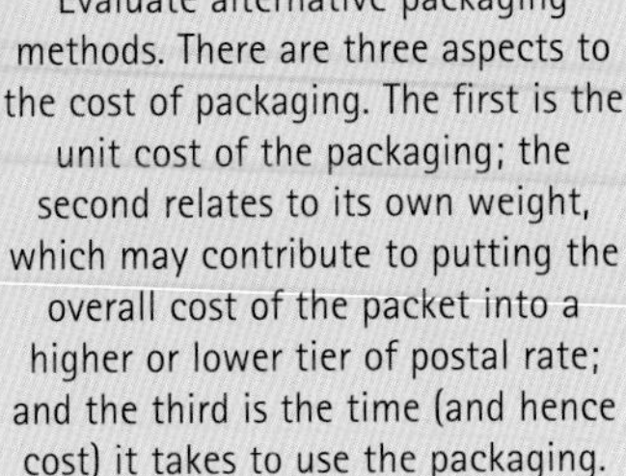

MONEY SAVER

Evaluate alternative packaging methods. There are three aspects to the cost of packaging. The first is the unit cost of the packaging; the second relates to its own weight, which may contribute to putting the overall cost of the packet into a higher or lower tier of postal rate; and the third is the time (and hence cost) it takes to use the packaging.

IS DIRECT SELLING RIGHT FOR YOU?

If you are considering using direct selling as a distribution method for your products, you need some experience as a salesperson for an existing direct sales organization to see what works and what does not. Although it costs little for someone to become a salesperson for a direct sales organization, that cannot be said for setting up the organization in the first place. To do the market research, develop and test new and unique products, produce sales procedures, and promote your new business will be a time-consuming and costly process. Although the sales tend to be done by self-employed distributors, your company would need a team to recruit these distributors in the first place. It should also be pointed out that such companies have a high failure rate, due to a variety of reasons from poor products to very high prices to being undercapitalized when they start up, but if your direct selling business does work the rewards can be enormous.

Offer nonretail goods to succeed in mail order as a small business

In the past some direct sales businesses have been accused of unethical practices. However, today many of the major companies belong to trade associations (see p. 184), formed to promote high standards of business practice and to ensure consumer protection. There is also specific legislation to comply with (see p. 181).

RUNNING A MAIL-ORDER BUSINESS

Mail order takes a variety of forms. In addition to the large, traditional family mail-order catalogs that cover clothing and most non-food domestic items, there are small specialist catalogs, sometimes called "specialogs," that focus on one popular selling area, such as clothing, gardening, kitchenware, gifts, books, or a particular hobby or sport. In the business world, there are numerous large catalogs, selling stationery products, industrial clothing, promotional gifts, office furniture, and other business-related items.

The internet has provided many businesses with the opportunity to display their products in their own online catalogs. People can browse these sites at their own convenience, and then place their orders by phone or on-line via secure order forms. Sales-orientated websites are a natural extension of printed catalogs, but have the advantages of being readily changeable, instantly accessible by a wider range of customers, and much cheaper to produce.

Another popular form of mail order is where a business "sells-off-the-page." Here, instead of producing a catalog, the business places an advertisement, usually offering one or a limited number of products for sale. This method can be very successful with the right product – those that seem to work include large items such as furniture, and fashions and small trinkets. Customers either place an order as a response, or send off for more information. This method often uses a fairly large (expensive) full-color advertisement or series of advertisements.

Mail order also has a role to play in providing replacements; for example, your engagement calendar, financial ledger, or calendar might have an order form at the end to enable you to send off for a copy for the following year. Similarly, when you purchase a piece of equipment, such as a vacuum cleaner, included with the instructions could be an order form to obtain replacement dust bags. This sort of mail order makes life easier for the customer and provides a steady and continuing income for the supplier.

If you are thinking of selling your own goods by mail order, it is important to understand what it is that motivates people to purchase by mail order. Also, certain products sell better by mail order than others. Given the option, most people would choose to buy retail rather than mail order in most instances. This is for many reasons: first, they can actually inspect and feel the goods; second, they can compare the goods with others, possibly from rival companies; third, they can take home the goods immediately; and, finally, they never like to pay for the "postage and handling," which is either charged extra or built into the price.

To counteract the preference for retail, mail-order firms need to provide some compelling reasons for buying through them. One factor might be that the products offered are simply not available in the shops. This explains the success of many of the "specialogs," which often show products unique to them; other firms have special lines in addition to their usual ones that are mail order only. Another factor is that mail order can give a bigger choice to some people, especially those in rural locations. Convenience also explains the use of mail order by businesses, particularly for stationery.

If you are planning to start a mail-order business, it is important to get the whole process of order fulfillment streamlined. Ensure that you always hold sufficient stock, take orders efficiently, and package up and despatch the goods quickly. The whole transaction should be a positive experience for the customer and it needs to be a priority to despatch the goods as promised, on time.

With mail order, there are also a number of legal aspects to consider (see pp. 178–81).

SELLING BY DIRECT MAIL

Mail order is essentially a passive sales activity, in which you react to an order placed by someone who has seen your leaflet, advertisement, or website. By contrast, direct mail is, as its name suggests, a more direct and more proactive form of selling. It consists of sending a mailshot, which can include a letter or a brochure or both.

Direct mail can be used for both consumers and business customers. Its strength (and weakness) lies in the quality of the mailing list on which the mailshot is based. Direct mail is therefore particularly useful for selling to your

Fold each leaflet carefully to fit neatly into envelope

SENDING OUT DIRECT MAIL

Although time-consuming to prepare and send, direct mail can be a well-targeted and relatively inexpensive way of marketing, distributing relevant sales literature to carefully selected people.

existing customers, whose details (including name, address, and buying preferences) you already have on record.

A direct mail letter is basically a selling document that is written to a targeted participant. In some instances it will encourage the recipient to react by placing an order; in others, for more complex products or services, it will be written with the aim of arranging a sales appointment.

It is claimed that a direct mail campaign can achieve an average response rate of some five percent, which, in advertising terms, is a very high response rate. Because of the precise nature of its targeting, direct mail should be a very cost-effective form of marketing. It has other advantages too, such as the almost instant response to the mailing, which is quantifiable, and the fact that most customers do not usually expect credit (unless the item being advertised is expensive).

Direct mail can be used on its own as a means of selling and distribution, or to back up other forms of advertising. Alternatively, you can use other advertising to boost your direct mail response.

DIRECT MAIL LETTER

This example of a direct mail letter does not aim to sell any products from the letter alone, but to persuade the recipient to agree to a meeting at which a sale may be made.

Letter is addressed to an individual, who is the decision maker

Opening paragraph introduces business succinctly

Credibility is established by partners' long experience

Penultimate sentence hints at risk if no action is taken (in other circumstances, a special price could be mentioned)

Next step (to make an appointment) is left in control of writer

10 Sellers Lane
Any City, Any State, ST 54321
Tel: 212-555 4321

Mrs. S. Nixon, Manager
Excellent Products Inc.
Unit 3, Industrial Park
Any Town, Any State, ST 12345

May 21, 2001

Dear Mrs. Nixon,

NEW RANGE OF SECURITY EQUIPMENT

This letter is to introduce our company, which has recently been set up . We are offering businesses a comprehensive service of advising, installing, and maintaining physical security equipment.

The two partners behind Secure Gates have, between them, over 20 years' experience in the security field, and have both worked for well-known companies in technical and managerial capacities.

Secure Gates specializes in gates, but can meet all your physical security equipment needs, such as locks, padlocks, roller shutter doors, etc.

I would welcome the opportunity to meet you to discuss your company's security equipment needs and to advise you on what you may require to meet ever more stringent insurance requirements. I shall phone you in the near future to arrange an appointment.

Yours sincerely,
Paul Wilson
Sales Manager

Mailing Lists

There are three ways of acquiring a mailing list:

- produce your own list
- purchase a list
- rent a list.

In certain special circumstances, there may be a fourth way: if your new venture is likely to promote sales of some other business's products, they may be prepared to give you a copy of at least part of their own mailing list.

If you compile your own mailing list, you will need a computer with suitable database software. You can list the names and the addresses of existing customers and supplement these with new ones by your own desk research using the Yellow Pages or similar local business directories.

The cost of purchasingor renting a mailing list is normally quoted in terms of a fee per 1,000 names. A common problem with bought and rented mailing lists is that they suffer from duplicates and obsolete names or addresses, so that some of the names and addresses you buy will instantly be useless.

Due to the time and effort necessary to maintain a good-quality mailing list, it is becoming more common to "rent" a mailing list. In this situation you never see the list; it is sent to an independent mailing house, which will stick the labels on to your envelopes. The owner of the list does not therefore risk it being copied and you can make use of the list for a much lower cost than outright purchase. For more information on finding business and consumer mailing lists that are available for rental, see p. 184.

Offering Franchises

Franchising, in which you allow someone else to use your business format, is an effective form of distribution. In business format franchising, you license someone to copy your business, under an agreement known as a franchise. In this agreement, you as the franchise-giver (or "franchisor") allow the other party (the "franchisee") to use your business name. You also train and assist the franchisee to set up their business and you provide ongoing support for them. The franchisee then runs a business that is a clone of your original one. For this, the franchisee has to pay you an initial fee, which can be quite substantial, and subsequently royalties.

As a method of increasing your distribution, the major advantage of franchising is that it allows you to expand your business rapidly, using the franchisees' capital, motivation, and commitment. Although your expansion may be rapid, it is not without its challenges. The ultimate profit that any franchisee can earn is

What You Should Offer a Franchisee

1. A business format that has been proven and is viable.
2. The use of a business name and, if necessary, a trademark.
3. An operations manual setting out procedures clearly and in detail.
4. Training in both industry and business skills at the outset, and subsequently as it is needed.
5. An exclusive territory that is large enough to support the franchisee.
6. Full support before, during, and after start-up.
7. Ongoing advice and guidance, including help when they have a problem.
8. Long-term market research to ensure that the business keeps up with changes in the marketplace.
9. A contract that clearly defines the rights and obligations of both parties.
10. Support in designing and placing advertisements of all kinds.

largely dependent on their own efforts, but they must ensure that they comply with the rigorous requirements of their franchise contract.

SETTING UP A PILOT OPERATION

Business format franchising is particularly suitable for retailing and local services. Before you can consider if your own business is suitable for franchising, you need to set up a pilot operation and prove the following points.

- **MARGINS** The business needs to have high margins and be very profitable. This usually requires premium pricing due to brand awareness. This is necessary because the franchisees have to create sufficient profit for themselves and, in addition, to afford to pay a royalty to the franchisor.
- **POTENTIAL FOR REPLICATION** The business format should be widely applicable. Should the pilot succeed, there needs to be many similar locations where the same business could succeed as well.
- **PROTECTABLE BUSINESS CONCEPT** The concept of the business needs to be protected legally or in other ways, ideally by patent, trademark, or using secret ingredients. This is to make it more difficult for a competitor to copy the product directly or compete on the same terms.

These are demanding requirements, but there is little point in considering franchising if your pilot does not meet all these points.

Assuming that you wish to go ahead with franchising, you need to create an operations

A POPULAR FRANCHISE OPERATION

McDonald's is just one example of a highly successful franchise operation that has spread rapidly and is able to make profits based on its strong branding and use of the same core products worldwide.

manual. This will probably require specialist help to compile. The manual lays down the whole format of how to run the business – it is the franchisee's guide and bible. In good franchise operations, the franchisor works in close association with the franchisee to ensure they make good profits and run a sound business. This is in your own interest, as you will want a royalty, calculated as a fixed weekly or monthly amount or a percentage (typically two to 20 percent) of the franchisee's sales. Note that this royalty is usually based on the franchisee's sales figure and not on their profits; this is a subtle but important point.

Ensure that the rights and obligations of both parties are described in a detailed contract that forms the basis of the close association between you and each franchisee.

Researching the Wider Market

It is neither cheap nor quick to set up a franchise. Once the pilot is up, running, and successful, you need to start the long process of researching the wider market, evaluating the competition on a national level, producing the franchise documentation, and eventually advertising to recruit potential franchisees. Your own legal, accounting, and professional franchising advice costs may be high by this time. Thereafter comes the need to find premises for each new franchisee (unless the franchise is home-based or mobile) and to advise them and commence their training prior to their launch.

Looking after new franchisees will be time consuming and demanding for your business, as they are likely to have all sorts of problems in the early stages. Many will be new to running their own business, and they will probably be well spaced geographically.

Many franchisors are members of the appropriate franchise associations (see p. 184), and there are various franchise magazines available and regular franchise shows held around the country. Several banks have specialist franchise departments. If you are seriously considering going into franchising, you need to read the publications, meet the bankers, and visit several shows to get an initial feel for the industry.

PROJECTING THE RIGHT IMAGE

You might think that image is something that only large corporations need be concerned with. In fact, every business, large or small, projects an image, whether or not it is consciously trying to, and this image affects sales. Creating the right image is therefore another essential element in your marketing strategy. Image permeates every aspect of your business and the products or services you offer, from the exterior of your premises, to the attitudes of you and any staff you employ, to the packaging of products. You need to give careful thought at an early stage to the image you would like to project.

Image can be thought of as the personality, or character, of a business and its products or services. It gives an aura that differentiates the business from others that are selling products or services of a basically similar nature. An image often relates to your unique selling proposition (USP) as a business. Projecting a positive image can add to the value of a product or service as perceived by the customer. In fact, if the right image is projected, it might just give a customer the confidence to buy from a small, and possibly still quite new, business.

To get an idea of the sort of image other businesses are projecting, ask yourself, for instance, where you would go to buy a cheap second car. Would you visit a large, main car dealer on a prestige site with carpeted showrooms and sales staff dressed in suits? Probably not – they are putting forward an upmarket image that implies what they are selling is more expensive than the car you need. Instead you might buy the car from a secondhand car dealer operating from a local site where the salespeople wear casual clothes. Here you would expect to find cheaper cars but would generally anticipate fewer guarantees with what you buy.

Another example to consider is where you buy your clothes: what is it that draws you to some stores in preference to others? Is it their convenience, their fashion style, their prices, the known brand names, the friendliness of the staff, the look of the shop, or a mixture of all of these factors? Think about how different clothes stores in the same area project different images to set them apart from each other and attract their target customers.

CASE STUDY: Choosing an Appropriate Image

MARCUS AND JAMES were planning to set up a men's shirt store. They intended to operate from retail premises in the commercial center of the city, and their target customers were male office workers. An upmarket image was deemed to be right, and the store would sell classic and designer shirts, all of well-known prestige brands. The storefront, exterior sign, and interior decor all had to project a male, upmarket image, so the store designers came up with an interior featuring dark wood paneling, wooden floors, and large wooden counters that had an old-world feel and gave the impression that this business had been around for a long time.

Deciding What Image to Project

Any image is a mixture of elements which, taken together, add up to make a unique blend. One core element of image is the price point at which the business is aiming; your decision on this will have a marked bearing on the other elements of the image mix.

There are basically three price-point levels, and they have the characteristics shown in the table below. There is no simple recipe for success in relation to price based on philosophies such as "we aim at the top end of the market since the customers have plenty of money to spend," or "all our goods are cheap, so everyone can afford them." Profitable business can be made at any price point, but, not surprisingly, the characteristics of a business aiming at the very top end will be completely different from those of another business aiming at the bottom. So it is important, even essential, to know at which end of the market you are aiming. You may aim some products or services at the top end, and others at the midrange or bottom end. Larger businesses may try to develop a range of products to cover all price points; other businesses focus their efforts on one.

Project the image that your potential customers expect

Generally a small business will wish to project one image that encompasses the whole business, including the products or services it sells. As that business grows, if it starts to sell products or services that require a different image from the one currently projected – usually because the product or service is at a different price point and is aimed at a different target market – the business may then start to build a different image for the new product or service. This is a good strategy, provided that the two images do not confuse likely customers: the two different parts of the business need to be treated separately for all marketing purposes.

Different image options are listed in alphabetical order on pp.60–63. The list is not exhaustive, but gives an idea of the more popular images and how they might be projected.

THE THREE PRICE-POINT LEVELS

PRICE POINT	CHARACTERISTICS	PRODUCTS	SERVICES	CUSTOMERS
TOP END	■ Exclusive ■ Prestigious ■ Upmarket	■ Designer label ■ Expensive brands ■ Very high quality	■ Supply high end clients ■ Selective ■ Personalized	■ Small in number, but they can afford the premium prices
MIDDLE MARKET	■ Value for money	■ Branded ■ Own label ■ Good quality	■ Very diversified	■ Large group, but many businesses competing for same customers
BOTTOM END	■ Cheap ■ Discount ■ Mass market	■ Unbranded	■ Limited to essentials	■ Large group, but spending power limited

Business Name

For a small business, particularly one that is relatively new, a key way to project a clear image is to choose a business name that reflects exactly that desired image. It is a simple, yet very successful, strategy. The name can also tell people what you do, and even hint at how well you might do it (by using words such as "quick," "express," and so on, where relevant).

For inspiration when trying to think of a business name, get ahold of a franchising magazine to see how the professionals do it, often in very competitive areas of the market. Look at your competitors, too, and list their trading names along with your comments. It may be best to choose a name that people can say easily, although a counter-argument runs that if you choose an unusual name that people have some difficulty saying to begin with, once they have mastered the pronunciation it stays in their mind more readily.

There are other factors to consider in specialized circumstances. If your customers are likely to find you by your listing in the Yellow Pages or other directories, consider a business name beginning with "A," or even "AA." If you are going to be an active exporter, check that your proposed name is not offensive or puzzling in the appropriate foreign languages.

Before you make a final decision on what name you are going to operate under, try it out on as many people as you can, and listen to their reactions. Note that a business name is the legal name of a business. For most businesses, this is the same as the operating name, but a business can choose to operate under a different name. There are legal restrictions governing the wording of business names (see p. 179).

Fact File

A tricky situation can occur where a business name that was ideal at one time becomes less so with the passage of time. This affects businesses of all sizes, and the usual remedy is to change the name partially or in stages so customers have time to get used to the new one.

Dos and Don'ts of Business Names

- ✓ Do consider using a name that explains what you do.
- ✓ Do think of a name that reflects your proposed image.
- ✓ Do consider using made-up words to make your name unique.

- ✗ Don't use a name that clashes with the name of an incorporated company.
- ✗ Don't choose a name that clashes with a registered trademark.
- ✗ Don't select a name that is the same as one with an existing web site.
- ✗ Don't use a name that could be confused with an existing business in your area or in your trade.

Cheapness

One of the most common images that businesses choose to project, cheapness can be conveyed by a "cheap and cheerful," or a "cheap but super value" appearance, an example of the latter being discount warehouses. There are many ways to convey cheapness, but they all stress price. The business name may also reflect low prices. Advertisements may stress factors that allow the price to be low, such as selling direct from the factory. Any premises or displays will project a no-frills, utility look.

Competence and Credibility

The qualities of competence and credibility are highly relevant when you are selling expertise – either in terms of your products or services. Such expertise could embrace artistic, professional, or technical areas of business. Manufacturers of high-tech products, designers, consultancies, and business-to-business operations would all be suitable examples where image should reflect competence.

Competence can be conveyed in a number of ways. If the proprietors or directors have suitable professional qualifications, these could be shown after their names on letterheads or leaflets. Membership in relevant trade associations could also be mentioned. If a business has been in operation for several years, credibility can be gained by stating how long it has been established. If the business already has prestigious client companies (such as local government or national companies with well-known names) you may be able to mention this fact. You may need first to obtain the permission of the organizations involved if you are planning to mention their names overtly.

Competence and credibility can also be reflected visually in leaflets or brochures by photos of your premises (obviously only if they are impressive) or photos of staff doing the type of complex or technical work in which your business is involved.

CONVENIENCE

Convenience is a factor you can offer in several ways. Your business can be convenient in terms of location (near to your potential customers); by staying open for extended hours; by offering customers an "everything under one roof" service (also called a "one-stop-shop"); or by providing a convenient delivery/collection service. Such convenience is often projected in the name of the venture or by the use of a prominent slogan, such as "24-hour service" or "1-hour service." To get the message across, your image has to shout a bit, so signs, advertisements, and so on need to be bold. A subtle approach is uncommon.

CUSTOMER SERVICE

These two words are frequently mentioned, but far less often met in practice. Of course, every business should consider customer service as one of their principal objectives, for no satisfied customers equals no repeat business. In practice, you can consciously project a friendly, caring image. For instance, staff members could use their first name rather than simply an initial with their last name when signing letters; advertisements and brochures might show pictures of contact people looking welcoming and smiling; the business entrance and premises (be it an office, shop, or workshop) should look inviting (this applies also to industrial units, which are too often very uninviting). Such efforts all help to project a positive image. Even the wording used in letters, advertisements, and leaflets can be made to sound more friendly and personal. In such literature you might also highlight aspects of your business that are customer-care-orientated – for instance, by nominating a member of staff as the customer contact person and making them readily available.

OFFERING SOMETHING DIFFERENT
The delivery of a weekly box of organic vegetables is an example of a service that differentiates one business from others. Convenience and quality are part of the image.

An important element of customer service is the use of the telephone. While what you say and how you say it is important, it is also vital that phones are answered speedily. A small business with an office that is often not staffed needs an answering machine or mobile phone, since lost calls are likely to mean lost business.

The final (and perhaps the most important part) of building a reputation for customer service is to provide staff training to convey the importance of making every contact with a customer helpful and pleasant.

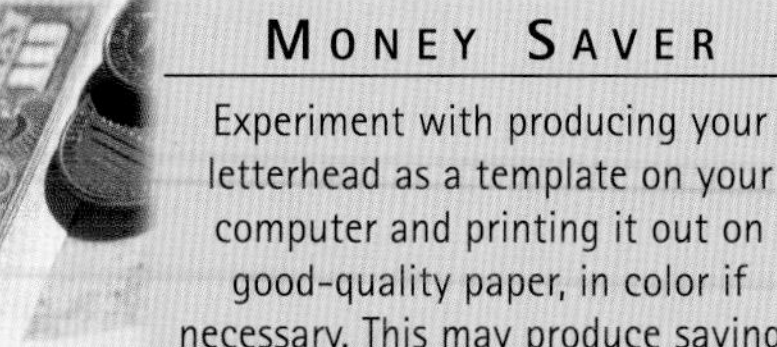

MONEY SAVER

Experiment with producing your letterhead as a template on your computer and printing it out on good-quality paper, in color if necessary. This may produce savings over having headed paper printed up professionally, or can be useful as a stopgap if details such as phone numbers change.

DESIGN AND FASHION

Any business that operates by selling its design or creative expertise (in the widest sense) needs to align its image with its products or services. An important aspect of design- and fashion-orientated images is perceived to be their attention to detail, and their awareness and creation of new looks. A dull, boring image would be a huge letdown. A fashionable image is likely to reflect styles or designs in vogue, which will naturally become obsolete in a relatively short time. A fashion- or design-oriented image will therefore require more frequent revamping than others.

EXCLUSIVITY

Think of the image of an upmarket car. One of its attractions is that there will be few others like it on the road. Exclusivity may be the appropriate image if you are producing a small-volume, high-value product or service. See also Prestige, below.

INTERNATIONAL CAPABILITY

A small business aiming to win overseas contracts or sales, or perhaps trying to acquire an agency from an overseas company, would obviously benefit from portraying this image. Simply adding your country name to your address block on letterheads, cards, and so on is a good start. If you are dealing with one specific country, a neat touch is to include the full phone dialing code from that country to your business. Also, if dealing with countries that speak a different language, a few words translated into their language is an effective way of indicating you really do mean business. If you have a contact, agent, or representative abroad, you might print their address and contact details on your stationery too.

INTIMACY

Some nightclubs, hairdressing salons, beauticians, cocktail bars, and clothing stores may choose to reflect an image of intimacy. Subdued lighting, subtle decor, hushed sounds, and a general feeling of being enclosed can create such an impression.

NATIONAL CAPABILITY

If operating on a national scale it could be helpful to indicate this by including words to that effect in the company's name. If you have several bases around the country, your stationery might list their details as well as those of the head office.

PRESTIGE

Prestige can be an important image angle if you are trying to sell your products or services to large organizations or wealthy or aspiring customers who prefer to deal with a well-established company. Prestige can be conveyed by a suitable choice of name, address, style of letterhead, brochure, and finally decor, if clients need to visit you.

PROFESSIONALISM

Many service businesses need to project a professional image. This can be done in quite a straightforward manner, by efficient telephone answering, a prompt response to any inquiries, and neat and orderly paperwork. If you have to meet customers, a stylish appearance, promptness, and a no-nonsense, sensible approach to tackling any problem all help with conveying a professional image.

QUALITY

Another concept that is much quoted, less frequently achieved, quality should be an essential ingredient of most business images. It can be projected in a number of ways, depending upon the business sector in which you are operating. Manufacturers may stress quality in terms of dedicated quality control staff and procedures they use, and compliance with the appropriate ISO or other relevant standards. Service-orientated businesses may reflect quality in terms of well-known (and dependable) brand names they use or sell, or quality-conscious business customers they deal with. Even the standard of letterheads and promotional literature reflects the thought given to overall quality in a company. In fact, general attention to detail is an essential part of a quality image. Comments from satisfied customers (identified by their full, real name) can also help. Simply stating that you are concerned with quality does not impress many buyers.

Inform all your staff of the image you are aiming to project

RAPID RESPONSE

A business may choose to project the image that it can provide a rapid response to a customer's requirements. Typical examples include a quick car-tire and exhaust change center, an instant print business, or an emergency plumbing/electrical repair service. Such an image is very often reflected in the name of the business, and all of their advertising reflects the quick, instant, or rapid response they can achieve. It is also vital to make phone numbers obvious in any communication, brochure, or advertisement. You could also highlight your phone number in the phone book and any business directory, such as the Yellow Pages. Ensure that there is always someone available to take the calls as advertised; list a mobile number if necessary.

RELIABILITY

There are two areas of reliability – the reliability associated with machinery, and the reliability of a business in terms of it doing what it promises to do. Some of the ways of trying to project this image are similar to those described under Quality, above, with the added point that reliability, by its very nature, needs to be proven over time. After suitable time has elapsed, it is worthwhile stating that you have achieved certain reliability targets. Excellent guarantees (that actually work when put to the test) can also provide customer confidence.

SIZE

To some customers, the size of the organization they are dealing with is important. Size can be conveyed on a letterhead by, for instance, listing the number of retail outlets you have or the number of partners or directors in the firm. Promotional literature could mention the size of workforce, annual turnover, or the production capacity, as applicable.

Encouraging Customer Recognition

There are many ways in which to brand your products, services, and every visual output from your business. Having a coherent visual image can become an important tool of marketing, as long as the customer associates this image with desirable qualities.

LOGOS AND BRAND NAMES

A logo is a unique symbol (or device) by which you hope customers will identify you and your product or service. It can be a vital part of your image and, by clever design, can also say something about your business. However, it usually takes a long time (and, in the case of the consumer market, a large promotional budget) before customers start to recognize logos.

The design of a good logo usually requires a professional graphic designer – an amateur design tends to look just that. A logo can be as simple as the name of your business, always written in the same, distinctive way, or it can include a shape or image. Before you consider asking a designer to produce a logo, you need to have a very clear idea as to what image you want the business to project. Ask the designer to show you several design suggestions. Once a logo has been produced, the artwork can be reused many times in brochures, advertisements, packaging, and so on.

A brand name is the name by which a product and its designer or manufacturer is recognized. The brand name, often used on a label or packaging, is not always the same as the company's name. If a company's products are diverse, it may not be possible for the firm to have a name that covers its different products, so the use of different brand names may help its marketing.

For logos and brand names, where the customer base is relatively small (up to a couple of hundred), the majority of customers will soon get to know any logo and/or brand name you use. In that situation logos and brand names can therefore be useful tools. However, when you are dealing with a consumer market of many thousands of customers, the chances are that the majority will not recognize your logo or brand name for quite some time unless you have a very substantial promotional budget. Once your brand name becomes recognized, however, it is a very valuable marketing tool, since people tend to buy brands they already know and have used before with success.

BRANDING

Virgin goods and services are one example of successful and widely recognized branding, with the distinctive colors and writing being seen on items as diverse as cola, airplanes, shops, and mobile phone services.

SIGNAGE

Signage is a practical necessity in some shape or form for most businesses. Making your signs clear and professional is another way to reinforce your image. Signs must be functional in that they are easy to read, giving the information that the reader seeks.

There are four contexts in which signage is important. First, there are signs directing potential customers to your location. People need to know you exist, and then they need to find you, so direction signs are an important

advertisement for your business. If you have a logo to put on the sign, it can make recognition by customers quicker. Next there are signs at your location, such as a shop sign, the sign at an industrial unit, or the sign by the entrance door of an office. Signs can also be useful if you are carrying out work at a temporary location; for instance, if you are laying a carpet at a hotel or cleaning store windows. A mobile sign forms a free advertisement and can incorporate a safety message too, if necessary. Finally there are, in some businesses, signs within a business, perhaps in a showroom or on products.

Spend time on your packaging design – good packaging sells

SALES SLOGANS

A sales slogan is a short and catchy message that can be used in advertising, on letterheads, leaflets, invoices, in radio commercials, and so on. As a sales tool, slogans usually reflect the unique selling proposition of the business, and so they are an attempt to encapsulate the image the company tries to project about itself. It can be difficult to think up an effective slogan – try having a brainstorming session, then try out the favorite alternative on friends.

Getting the Packaging Right

The design and manufacture of packaging for products has become a very sophisticated industry in itself, and is a key component of creating an image. Although you might first think of packaging in terms of consumer products, good and attractive packaging is also very important for business-to-business purchases; even the humble wrench is likely to come in a presentation bubble pack. The process of designing the packaging often runs parallel with the design of the product – each has a bearing on the design of the other. If necessary you can consult specialist packaging designers.

Packaging has to be attractive to a would-be buyer, compete with other products, perhaps on the same shelf, and meet a number of additional requirements:

- **ATTENTION GRABBING** It has been estimated that the average supermarket shopper scans just over 4 feet of shelving from top to bottom in one second. From a crowded shelf, the packaging therefore has to catch the shopper's eye and let them know instantly what its contents are, without any ambiguity. It is impossible to generalize about what makes an item eye-catching. However, it is important to have an understanding of the situation in which the item will be sold. For example, in the design of a book jacket, the spine is of key importance, since it may be the only part of the product showing on the bookshelf.

- **DISPLAY** Packaging needs to reveal the attractive features of the contents. This can be achieved by numerous methods, such as the use of clear windows, cutouts, or a rigid bubble in the packaging. In many retail situations, the size and shape of the packaging is important to enable the products to fit onto standard display shelving and allow the retailer to stock a dense concentration of goods. Some products are usually hung from metal bars or display racks – the packaging design has to allow for this. Most products require bar-coding too, and, in all cases, the packaging must protect the contents from harsh handling by shoppers. If you supply major retailers, show them a dummy of any proposed packaging to get their comments at an early stage.
- **BUSINESS IDENTITY** The packaging must reinforce the image of the company and, according to your strategy, either fit in with any other products the company produces, or differentiate a product so that it is likely to appeal to its target market.
- **LEGALITIES** In certain industry sectors, such as food, toiletries, and toys, the labeling has to contain important, legally required information. This needs to be allowed for as part of the packaging design process.
- **ENVIRONMENTAL CONSIDERATIONS** Waste generated by packaging is a major ecological problem. Increasingly, manufacturers need to respond to pressure from conscientious buyers for more biodegradable, reusable, minimal, or recyclable packaging; such packaging may also be a key part of your company image. If you do use such packaging, make sure you let your buyers know it.
- **STORAGE AND TRANSIT** The packaging needs to protect the contents while in storage and during transit. Its physical dimensions and shape have to allow it to fit inside any external cardboard carton that may be needed to ship the goods in bulk.
- **PRICE** The packaging can amount to a large proportion of the unit cost of an item. Be sure to research the options and their costs fully. Try to think laterally; you may be able to come up with something original or better than other comparable products also on the market.

FACT FILE

Once you have created initial sample dummies of your packaging, you need to assess the design. The only way to do this properly is to place it in context alongside competing products. For instance, ask a retailer if you can try your dummies on their shelves; place it on low as well as high shelves and ask the retailer's opinion. This technique is known as comparative packaging.

TRADITIONAL PACKAGING
Using glass jars and bottles to package food, such as jam, or beverages, is an effective way of both displaying and protecting the product.

REDESIGNING PACKAGING

Giving your packaging an overhaul can be a very cost-effective way of improving and refreshing your image. While there are obviously design and origination costs, these are onetime costs and the end result can last for years. Consider redesigning your packaging if the existing design is starting to look dated. Alternatively, if you are launching a new product or service, you could redesign the packaging of existing products at the same time to update the look of the whole range.

Putting the Image Together

Every external manifestation of a business contributes to its image – the letterhead (and how letters are written), business cards, brochures, order forms, invoices, advertisements, website, business name, address, logo, brand name(s), sales slogans, packaging, premises, exterior signs, interior decor, company vehicles, staff clothing, even the size and style of check book. These are all tangible factors. The intangible aspects, such as how a receptionist greets visitors, how the telephone is answered, and how sales staff handle customers, are also important. To make the most of the image you project, it is obviously sensible to coordinate all the contributing aspects to enable colors and themes to be uniform. Ensure that you communicate to staff the image you would like them to project, and the thought behind it.

On a large scale, this is known as corporate image. Even on a small scale, it makes sense to spend time and effort to coordinate all aspects of your image. Consistency is an important point; if the approach is one of cut and paste, the only image projected will be one of confusion. The achievement of a distinctive image is not an overnight job, but, done correctly, a small business can project an appealing and effective image with little extra expense, just through some thought and effort. If you are just setting up in business, you have an ideal opportunity to think about all the aspects that contribute to image from the start. If you are up and running, set aside some time to look at your existing image (and ask for others' opinions about it), then start to make improvements. If you have a clear vision of the image you want to project, you can make numerous small changes that add up to a transformation of your image.

PLANNING YOUR MARKETING

A marketing plan is the culmination of your market research. It is a document setting out the objectives of your marketing, and how you plan to achieve them. Such a plan is most useful once you have started in business, when you need a way of focusing on your marketing strategy, its budget, and the results it is producing. A marketing plan is about more than simply marketing – it encompasses the direction in which the business is moving, and forecasts future sales levels. It is also a method of investigating aspects of the business that have not been as successful as planned, and looking at other aspects that may be more profitable in the future. The launch of a new project is another area in which the marketing needs careful planning; this is covered on pp. 73–5.

A significant characteristic of a successful business is the degree of planning that it carries out. Many small businesses do very little planning, usually because the proprietors feel they do not have the time, or they may think that because the business is small they have a good grasp of what is happening. However, a business that does little or no planning is often one that reacts to events rather than one that creates its own opportunities. There may also be a lack of sense of direction, or the business may tend to stop and start with different strategies. Such businesses also seem to suffer more unexpected problems and lose time in crisis management.

REFINING YOUR BUSINESS PLAN

A business plan, produced before a new business is started, usually with the aim of raising financing for the business, tends to

CASE STUDY: Combining Marketing with Long-term Goals

HENRY WAS A skilled carpenter. His business with Ed, a salesman, to make and sell sunrooms, had been in business for six years. In that time, the business had grown to include over 20 staff and a number of salespeople around the country. During the rapid growth period, their planning was essentially short-term, but now that the business was more established Henry and Ed felt it was time to do more long-term planning. Over many months they discussed several options – to continue to grow the business organically, to diversify, or to grow by taking over another similar firm. The option they chose would have a major impact on their marketing strategy. Eventually they realized they had to put the options down in writing to help clarify their thoughts.

With some additional desk research and help from their accountant, it began to be clear that their best option was to grow by acquisition. With this in mind, they decided to keep their marketing as it was until they had found a firm to buy, but to start reserving funds and begin initial planning for a marketing push for when they were ready to relaunch as a larger operation.

focus in detail on the first year of operation, and includes sections on market research and advertising and promotion. This plan determines the initial direction of the business. If you are starting a new business, it is vital, as part of the process, to consider your marketing in detail, and include as good a strategy as possible in your business plan.

A marketing plan can be thought of as a specialized and refined version of a business plan. It carries on from where the original plan ended, which is generally after the first year of business; you can, in fact, start making your marketing plan after a few months, as soon as you have built up some figures. Since the marketing plan is based on actual trading results, it should be much more accurate than the business plan.

TIME SAVER

Sell more to existing customers – it is easy to forget that this is the quickest and usually the easiest method of increasing your sales. Looking for and promoting your products or services to new customers takes considerably more time, money, and effort.

BENEFITS OF A MARKETING PLAN

Time spent on planning your marketing is worthwhile financially, since it can indicate which sales avenues are more profitable to pursue. It also counteracts the tendency in new small businesses to chase every avenue for sales in the belief that this will result in a large turnover in a short space of time. Even established small businesses who have never formalized their marketing strategy will benefit from producing a marketing plan as a way of distilling their experiences and exploring new directions.

Put great effort into planning – the more you plan, the better the results

Unlike your business plan, which was probably seen by a number of people, such as your bank manager, your accountant, and perhaps other business advisers, the marketing plan can be an entirely private document for your eyes only. However, it may be appropriate to discuss it with your key staff, so they know in which direction the business is going.

The marketing plan you produce should not be done, filed, and forgotten. Just as with your original business plan, it provides a route map for you and your business, and should be referred to and updated regularly (at least every few months). This will allow you to focus on marketing in a practical way, and to see what progress you are making, if your various predictions for sales avenues are materializing, and if you have remembered to implement all your good ideas.

CONTENTS OF THE PLAN

The main topics that a marketing plan covers are:

- **WHERE YOU ARE** The plan may indicate which aspects of your business are more profitable than others and hence should be promoted more strongly in the future; it could also show which activities have been unprofitable or barely profitable and so should be abandoned or altered in the future. Where you tried something that did not work out quite as expected, the plan can record what you think you did wrong.
- **WHERE YOU WANT TO GO** Details in this section may include the opportunities that you see for your business and the potential threats from market changes, competitors, and other sources. Taking these, along with the knowledge of what has been successful up to now, you can plan your objectives for the future.
- **HOW YOU MIGHT GET THERE** The plan can lay out a marketing strategy that is intended to achieve your objectives over a set period of time.

ELEMENTS OF A MARKETING PLAN

SECTION	WHAT TO INCLUDE	COMMENTS
PART 1: THE PAST YEAR	A brief calendar of the past year, highlighting the main events, including both successes and failures.	■ Use the overview provided to look at how past trends might continue into the future.
PART 2: OBJECTIVES	Give an objective, or several objectives. These could be in terms of turnover, number of sales, or customers, or you could set quantifiable marketing goals (such as opening a new shop).	■ Phrase your objectives as a short statement. ■ Be modest with your goals – their achievement will act as a motivator. ■ State any assumptions you make.
PART 3: PRODUCT/SERVICE	A brief summary of what the business is doing today and a description of its products or services.	■ The act of writing this down makes you think more objectively, and can put some problem areas into perspective.
PART 4: NEW PRODUCT LAUNCH	Describe the readiness of the project, the timing of its launch, and what launch publicity you are planning.	■ Include as much detail as possible, and a timetable if necessary.
PART 5: MARKET RESEARCH	Include a few lines or paragraphs on the salient points of the most recent market information.	■ Include the industry's own predictions for the coming year, plus comments on your key accounts and competitors.
PART 6: PRICING	Summarize your latest pricing calculations.	■ Record the prices of your competitors at the same time.
PART 7: SALES PLAN	A lengthy statement on how the sales are to be achieved to meet the targets mentioned in Part 2 above.	■ Review your distribution, sales responsibilities, monitoring, and sales strategies.
PART 8: ADVERTISING, PROMOTION, AND PR	Specify, in detail, what advertising, promotion, and PR you are planning for the year ahead.	■ This is a key part of the plan and may therefore represent quite a large proportion of the document.
PART 9: BUDGET	A calculation of how much the marketing budget should be for the forthcoming year.	■ The budget will relate directly to likely advertising, PR, and other promotions, specified in Part 8.
PART 10: CASH FLOW FORECAST	Include a cash flow forecast for the year ahead.	■ Ensure the cash flow forecast for your business is consistent with your objectives, pricing, and budget outlined in this plan.

The actual contents of the plan can be flexible and will depend entirely on your particular business, its circumstances when you write the plan, and how you prefer to do your planning. Some common elements and suggestions are detailed in the table opposite. As for the physical form of the plan, it could be a file on your computer, a printout, or just some hand-written notes – whichever suits you.

One key advantage of detailing all your marketing activities in a single plan is that it helps to ensure that the different aspects of your marketing are not carried out in isolation. The most successful marketing strategies complement and reinforce each other. For example, if you get a good response to your website, it is essential to build into your plan a sufficient capability to follow it up properly; otherwise, the expense and effort that went into creating the website could be wasted.

Budgeting for Your Marketing Activity

It may seem a difficult task to work out how much to budget for your whole marketing activity, all the more so for a new or recently established business with little or no trading record. The method of calculating your budget contained in the table below provides some guidelines for working out how much you might spend, taking into account certain factors. The starting point of five percent is

HOW TO WORK OUT YOUR BUDGET

Start with a typical annual marketing budgetary figure of five percent. For each factor in turn, work across the table, adding or subtracting percentage points depending on your own situation. If the factor is not relevant to your type of business, proceed to the next factor.

TABLE FOR ESTIMATING THE MARKETING BUDGET

FACTOR	ADD 2% FOR EACH APPROPRIATE FACTOR	5% (typical figure)	SUBTRACT 1% FOR EACH APPROPRIATE FACTOR
AGE OF BUSINESS	New	Young	Established
AGE OF PRODUCT	New	Young	Established
INNOVATION LEVEL	Very innovative; customer needs educating	Some innovative details	None
PREMISES/LOCATION	Remote; low profile	Not remote or prime	Prime; high profile
CUSTOMERS	Consumer	Consumer and business	Business
AGENT/DISTRIBUTOR NETWORK	None	Limited	Good coverage
COMPETITION	Hostile	Benign	None
SPECIAL FACTORS	Yes – more need to promote	None	Yes – less need to promote

based on a percentage of forecast turnover; this is a common way of expressing a marketing budget. So a budget of five percent on a forecast turnover of $100,000 would indicate that you need to spend around $5,000 on marketing, to encompass advertising, promotion, and PR, but excluding the direct costs of salespeople. This baseline of five percent is not set in stone and will vary from industry to industry, but is a useful marker for a small business.

Keep projects on schedule by good planning

Modifications are likely to depend on factors specific to your own business, such as how new your business or its product or service is, where your premises are located, the type of customers you are aiming at, and so on. For example, you would need to spend more on marketing if you were a new business selling an innovative product to consumers. You could spend less if you were an established business with a good distribution network and little competition.

The method of tailoring a budget to your needs (outlined in the table on p. 71), is purely a guide to give you an indication of the sort of factors you might consider. Your final decisions should be interpreted in the light of your own circumstances. Whereas the factors in the table have all been given as plus two percent or minus one percent, you may consider that one or more factors as they apply to you should have larger figures applied. The special factors that may create a need for greater or lesser promotion include anything that you intuitively feel will affect your marketing budget. This might be your strategic objective – if you are planning to increase sales targets more than usual, your marketing budget is likely to need a little extra investment. The case studies on this page illustrate two situations in which this method of calculating a marketing budget has been used.

CASE STUDY: Working Out a Budget for a Shop

EMMA RECENTLY OPENED a shop selling children's clothes located in a town center site (but not a prime location) with benign competition. To work out her marketing budget, starting with five percent of her forecast turnover, she calculated as follows:
Age of business: new – add two percent
Age of product: not relevant
Innovation level: not relevant
Premises location: not remote or prime
Customers: consumers – add two percent
Agent/distributor network: not relevant
Competition: benign
Special factors: none.
Emma therefore planned for a marketing budget of approximately:
5% + 2% + 2% = 9% of her forecast turnover.

CROSS-CHECKING YOUR FIGURES

To check the figure you calculate for your marketing budget, consider the different marketing activities you may need to undertake – advertising, promotion, and PR – and make a list of those you feel are necessary to achieve your sales targets. Then work out likely costs. By being specific – working out typical advertisement sizes, where to advertise, and how often, for example – you can see how much each method would cost.

Add up all the figures for the different marketing activities you ideally would like to pursue, compare the total with your provisional budget, and then adjust both your plans and the budget accordingly.

ENLISTING OTHERS

Your budget for marketing can be increased dramatically with some cooperation from other interested parties. For example, a retailer may receive support from a supplier who agrees to pay a proportion of the cost of advertisements if their product is the only one shown, their brand name and/or logo is clearly seen, and,

CASE STUDY: Working Out a Budget for a Manufacturer

BEN RAN A small design firm, two years old, in an out-of-the-way location. He was about to launch a new product for the oil industry. The company had a number of distributors, and there was no direct competitor. To get an idea as to how much he should budget for marketing the new device, the calculation would be as follows:
Age of business: young
Age of product: new – add two percent
Innovation level: very – add two percent
Premises location: not relevant
Customers: business – subtract one percent
Agent/distributor network: good coverage – subtract one percent
Competition: none – subtract one percent
Special factors: competition anticipated – add two percent.
Hence his marketing budget should be about: 5% + 2% + 2% - 1% - 1% - 1% + 2% = 8% of his likely sales of the new device.

usually, they have approved the advertisements before printing. Other marketing cooperation could come from neighboring retailers or non-competitor firms taking joint advertisements or creating joint leaflets. For instance, a fabric supplier may help a garment manufacturer's advertisements, or a printer, graphics studio, and bookbinder may produce joint leaflets.

INVEST IN MARKETING

All marketing activity should be seen as an investment in your business and not just a cost burden, or an afterthought tagged on at the end. Advertising, promotion, and PR should not be done just when there is some spare money, and shunned when business is booming (so that there is no perceived need for marketing) or abandoned due to lack of funds when business is slack.

Just as an investment of any kind must show a return, so your marketing must produce quantifiable results. There is no point in putting even small sums of money into one particular line of your campaign when it shows no tangible results. This would be simply squandering your money. Where possible, start by doing a test run of a particular marketing method and, if that does not work, try something else until you find what works for your own business. For more details on analyzing your sales data to assess the impact of your marketing, see pp. 162–7.

Planning a New Project Launch

When considering the launch of a new project, you need to decide just when and how you are going to enter the market. Planning your market entry requires even more precise and detailed thought than an overall marketing plan.

CHECKING THAT YOUR PROJECT IS FIT AND READY

In your enthusiasm to see your new project become a reality, and to start making sales, timescales may be truncated. The possibility of problems arising can be either ignored or glossed over. There is usually little provision made in terms of time or money for contingencies. Surprisingly few projects are

FACT FILE

To survive, many businesses need to have significant ongoing advertising and promotion of their product or service. This is particularly true of innovative products sold direct to customers. Consider how this marketing cost affects your pricing – proposed marketing and pricing can be interdependent.

LAUNCHING A NEW PRODUCT

At this launch, information about the sunbed and the company is clearly displayed, staff are present to answer any questions, and the product is demonstrated.

fully organized with all staff trained and the necessary backup (documentation, procedures, spares, inventory, and so on) in place at the moment of launch. What usually happens is that there is a heroic struggle that focuses on launching the project on time. Not only is this very wearing to all concerned, but the newly launched project is now vulnerable. This vulnerability can be to a competitor's counterattack, to customer disappointment, or simply to low sales because of lack of promotion, insufficient inventory, underdevelopment, inadequate staff training, or any number of other reasons. To avoid, or at least reduce, this last-minute rush and resulting vulnerability requires planning.

Keep your plan flexible so that you can include last-minute changes

TIMING

One of the most important matters to consider when doing any business and marketing planning is the timing. Most small businesses simply launch their new project as soon as it is ready, even if this is clearly not the optimum time. For example, specialty shops that open in January or February miss the important Christmas season, while manufacturers whose new products are launched too late to appear at a key trade show miss a major opportunity to promote their product to its target market. The urge to launch as soon as you can, even if the timing is poor, is understandable and often overwhelming: there is the desire to generate cash flow and get ahead of competitors. If the timing is not good, however, the whole project may be jeopardized.

In terms of market entry, the timing aspects to consider include seasonal changes (choosing a time when the customer is ready to buy rather than being led by when you are ready to supply), and the likely reaction of your rivals, who may try to thwart your launch. Where a product rather than a service is concerned, other aspects to consider include the lead time of producing and fully testing the new product, and producing adequate stock to meet hoped-for initial demand. For a service business, staff training can be critical. Where new premises come into the equation, again much time can be spent finding suitable premises and then negotiating lease or purchase details.

CREATING YOUR PLAN

One of the simplest planning tools is a wall chart with the key deadlines marked. You can then work backward to fill in what needs to be done in order to meet the deadline. Allow for a contingency at each stage so that one delay does not put the whole project at risk. Bear in mind, too, that you are more likely to be able to control processes within your business than those you are having done externally.

TIME SAVER

For complex planning where timescales are tight, use critical path analysis. Establish those activities that are time critical to the project being completed on time. You can then see which activities can be done at the same time, and which are dependent on others being completed. Modify your plan as needed.

GAINING MAXIMUM PUBLICITY

The launch of a new product or service is a major marketing opportunity that should not be missed. Use your plan to ensure that your marketing plans dovetail with your own launch dates. The objective is to gain the maximum publicity (or exposure) for the new venture so that your potential customers are made aware of it as quickly as possible. Obtaining this publicity at the right time, either by free means via media coverage, or by advertising or distributing leaflets, or by running sales promotions to kick-start early sales, requires considerable orchestration.

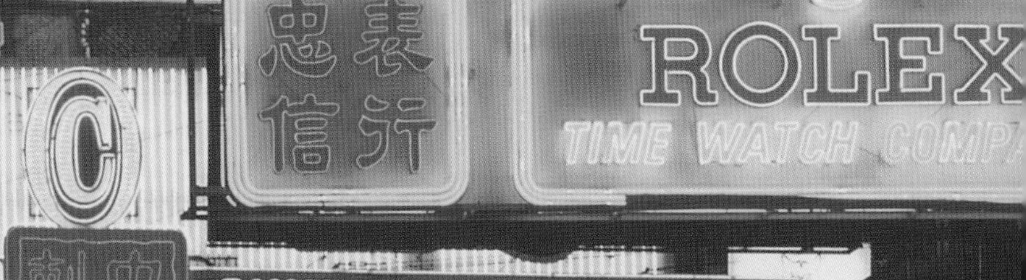
Cook
Bureau de Change
忠信表行
ROLEX
TIME WATCH COMPA

中国刺綉
CHINA PRODUCTS CO.
中国·香港でのお土産は是非当店で

ADVERTISING

Although marketing is about much more than advertising, getting your advertising strategy right is an important factor in your overall marketing campaign. Advertising through various media, including your own leaflets and brochures, is usually the principal means of informing potential customers about your services or products.

ADVERTISING BASICS

Advertising is likely to form a major part of your overall marketing strategy. You need to take an analytical approach to decide your objectives in advertising; these objectives will determine exactly where and when you advertise. There will inevitably be an element of trial and error: advertising can and does work in the right context for some people, but fails for others. This chapter looks at why, when, and where to advertise; the next chapter (see pp. 88–105) looks at how to produce effective advertisements and monitor the results. Together they provide the information you need to advertise successfully.

Assuming your market research concludes that there is a genuine market for the product or service you are planning to advertise, there are five main elements to a successful advertising campaign. These are:

- defining the objectives of the advertising
- timing it right
- choosing the correct media
- designing effective advertisements
- monitoring the results.

Part of the marketing process is learning what does and does not work for your business. A lack of success with advertising over a period of time can be for a number of reasons, such as little market interest in what is being offered, not enough technical and design expertise employed in creating the advertisements, an insufficient budget for a proper advertising campaign, or poorly targeted placement of advertisements.

Resist pressure from salespeople – make your own decisions about where and when to advertise

It is vital, therefore, to put considerable thought into each stage of the advertising process, from the decision to advertise for a certain reason, to checking the final text. Too many small businesses, once they decide to place an advertisement, pay scant attention to looking at different ways for the advertisement to convey its message, how it is designed, where in the publication it is likely to appear, and so on. It is therefore hardly surprising that the results may be disappointing.

CASE STUDY: Planning an Advertising Strategy

AMANDA WAS PLANNING to launch a specialist car magazine, to be published solely on CD-ROM. In addition to the significant challenge of creating an interesting publication that would be sufficiently different from the many other rival (printed) car magazines, she had the problem of advertising the magazine so that sufficient numbers of people would be interested in ordering a copy and, ideally, subscribing. She decided that she would promote it on her new website and take advertisements in selected printed car magazines that would also be read by her likely target readers. She negotiated a discount on these advertising costs by offering hypertext links to these magazines' own websites from her site and free advertisements for those publications on her CD-ROM. Amanda found that her advertising costs would be substantial in relation to her overall start-up costs and she also felt she would need to continue to advertise heavily for some time.

Why Advertise?

You can have a desirable product or service to sell at an attractive price but, at the moment it is launched, your potential customers will know nothing about it unless you have taken the trouble to inform them. Even once your product or service is launched and selling, you need to continue to let potential customers know about what you are offering because almost all businesses have a turnover in customers due to natural wastage. In almost all cases, making prospective customers aware of your existence and what you have to sell requires advertising and/or promotion.

Some small businesses may have no need to advertise at all, relying instead on other promotional means (see pp. 118–37) to achieve their objectives. But a key advantage of advertising over other forms of promotion, such as sending out press releases (see pp. 121–6), is that you can control what is being said and where and when it is being said. This can be very important indeed.

Often an advertisement is placed with the general objective of helping sales. You need to be much more precise than that. Although the long-term idea may be to increase sales, the immediate objective of each individual advertisement can be quite different. For example, consider the situations in the table on the right. Clearly, a different type of advertisement is needed in each of these different instances.

DIFFERENT ADVERTISING OBJECTIVES

SITUATION	OBJECTIVES
NEW BUSINESS, PRODUCT, OR SERVICE	To create potential buyer awareness; to assist your salespeople who are on the road; or to encourage retail visitors.
EXISTING BUSINESS, PRODUCT, OR SERVICE	To increase sales by attracting people to visit you; to assist salespeople; or to encourage a direct response.
DIRECT MAIL	To achieve a sales response or to find sales leads.
CHANGE OF ADDRESS	To let customers know how to find you.
EXHIBITION/SPECIAL EVENT	To encourage people to visit your stand or other organized event.
BUSINESS EXPANSION	To recruit new staff or sales agents.

When to Advertise

Many small businesses advertise when they are ready, rather than timing the advertisement to match when the customer is likely to wish to buy. In most businesses, even if the business goes on at a reasonably constant rate throughout the year, there are better times for selling, when prospects (prospective customers) are more likely to become buyers. Advertising during off-peak or out-of-season times may be cheaper, but will often bring disappointing results.

The timing of an advertisement often needs to be a compromise between a number of factors. You may wish to advertise the launch of a new product or service, or the opening of new premises, but the timing may not coincide with when potential buyers are in a buying mood. A further problem is that the media you choose will have their own inflexible timescales and, in some cases, they require notification of placing an advertisement weeks, sometimes many weeks, in advance. Compromises that suit your own timing are usually possible, but the key to finding the best timing is planning.

PLANNING AN ADVERTISING CAMPAIGN

Note the need to plan a campaign, rather than simply planning an advertisement – one solitary advertisement, unless brilliantly executed, will rarely achieve a satisfactory response. Placing a single advertisement is an error frequently made by inexperienced advertisers in the belief that almost everyone who sees the publication or hears the radio commercial will notice the ad and act on it.

One natural objection to the idea of having a series of advertisements is the cost, but it is better to plan several smaller advertisements than to spend your entire budget on one big advertisement. Most advertising media offer series discounts but, if you are trying a publication you have not used before, you ought to consider starting with a limited number of advertisements to see what the response is like before committing yourself to a longer series of advertisements that will earn you a discount rate.

COMMON MISCONCEPTIONS ABOUT ADVERTISING

1. Assuming that a successful advertisement needs to be large, glossy, and in full color.
2. Thinking that to advertise means placing a solitary advertisement in a publication once in a while.
3. Confusing advertising with promotion – advertising is a slower, ongoing process.
4. Avoiding advertising in case you will be unable to cope with the expected rush.
5. Thinking that advertising is a waste of money if past experiences have been unsuccessful.

A response to a new advertising campaign is likely only if the potential customer has a need for the product or service at precisely the time of seeing or hearing the advertisement. It is for just that reason that small businesses offering domestic services, such as plumbing, electrical repairs, carpentry, roof repairs, and so on, need to do almost continuous, low-level advertising (such as classified advertisements). In any trade sector, with regular advertising, an ongoing awareness can be built up that may influence a later buying decision.

REINFORCEMENT

The first time a potential customer sees or hears mention of a new business, product, or service, they are likely to forget it almost instantly unless the advertisement has some immediate relevance and impact on them. If an ad does have an impact on first sight, the effect is sometimes called resonance. If the prospect then sees or hears another mention of the same business soon afterward, there may be reinforcement in their mind of the business name or the relevant product or service.

Each time the person is exposed to a mention of the business, product, or service, the process of reinforcement, or growing awareness, continues. It helps if there is a theme (visually or verbally) running through all the advertising (and any other promotions) so that they will be linked together in the person's mind. An awareness of branding and the use of a consistent logo also adds to the effectiveness of your advertising (see p. 64).

This reinforcing combination can be achieved in a number of different ways by backing up one line of advertising or promotion with another: editorial articles backing up advertising; recurring advertisements in the same publication; advertisements in different media that the same person might see or hear; an advertisement backing up a leaflet/brochure that the person has received; an advertisement reflecting a local shop-window theme; an advertisement backing up an appearance at an exhibition, and so on.

	PRODUCT	LEAFLET	MAGAZINE AD
APRIL		Meeting with printer	Book advertising space
	Mock-up ready to photograph		
		Draft leaflet text	
	Check photographs		
MAY		Leaflet to printer	Submit advertisement
		Check proof	Magazine deadline
		Collect leaflets	Check proof
JUNE	Initial production run starts		Magazine out/Submit advert
			Magazine deadline (same ad)
JULY			Magazine out

SIMPLE PLANNER

In this example, a manufacturer is launching a product and wishes to advertise in two consecutive issues of a monthly magazine. The advertisement is inviting the reader to send off for a leaflet, so that also has to be worked into the plan so it is produced on time.

PLANNING YOUR TIMING

To assist in planning, a simple calendar planner or chart, as shown above, may help you with the inevitable juggling you will have to do. Start with the time you wish to run the advertisement (perhaps to coincide with the launch of a new product), and then work backward, finding out when the advertisement needs to be booked to appear at the right time, and how long it will take you to prepare the necessary text and images. If the advertisement is planned to coincide with another of your marketing initiatives, such as a brochure, press release, or launch ceremony, work this into your plan, too. Creating a detailed plan in this way will help you to plan your own time effectively – and to chase up those who are working on the product, advertisement, or other relevant items for you.

Where to Advertise

The choice of where to advertise is seemingly unlimited, but for any specific business the number of places where the advertising will be effective is in fact much more restricted. The best media to choose are clearly those where the readership or audience most closely matches your target market, and those that are suited to the target market's buying habits.

Choosing an Advertising Method

Method	Cost	Advantages	Disadvantages
Direct Mailshot Letter	Low	■ Targeted audience ■ High response rate (two-five percent)	■ Time-consuming to locate or produce a good mailing list
Small Poster	Low	■ Large readership ■ Long life	■ Limited locations ■ Message must be short to make an immediate impact
Mailbox Leaflet	Low	■ Can be partially targeted	■ Low response rate ■ Post office distribution is most effective but increases the cost
Website	Low/ medium	■ Potentially huge audience ■ Full color, sound, and some animation possible	■ Difficult to stand out in the crowd
Directories	Low/ medium	■ Ad life is one year ■ Allows comparison with competitors ■ May have wide circulation	■ Can only make changes annually
Direct Mailshot Leaflet	Low/ medium	■ Targeted audience	■ Response rate is variable ■ Time-consuming (but less so than direct mailshot letter)
Ad in Local Paper	Medium	■ Local audience ■ Can repeat often ■ Supporting editorial is possible	■ Readership much larger than your target market
Ad in Trade Publication	Medium/ high	■ Targeted ■ Editorial often possible ■ Publication can have long life	■ If publication is relevant, none, except price
Ad on Local Radio	High	■ Wide audience	■ Ad time very brief so needs repeating frequently
Ad in National Magazine	High	■ National audience ■ Color may be available	■ Editorial unlikely ■ Need to book months ahead

Read publications carefully to work out what sort of reader the journalists are writing for and who the other advertisers are targeting. For other media, think about who is likely to see the ad – an ad on the back of a bus is obviously likely to be read mainly by drivers.

It is possible to have a match with your target market but a mismatch with its buying habits. For example, some trade or association directories might match a market, but if buyers do not naturally refer to these directories, an advertisement (or paid-for entry) there would be a waste of money.

Your business also needs to be suited to the type of response likely to be generated by an ad in a particular medium. Although it may be good for the ego to see your full-color advertisement in one of the national newspaper weekend supplements, it could be a waste of money if your business has only one retail outlet and no mail-order facilities or other means of national distribution.

NEWSPAPERS AND MAGAZINES

A bewildering array of publications is available. It is worth spending considerable time researching the magazines, trade publications or newspapers that are most likely to reach your target market.

Some less common methods for advertising that may also be suitable for certain small businesses include transportation advertising, in which you place advertisements on the sides of buses or taxis, or posters on the escalators of subway stations or inside the trains themselves. You can advertise on the tiny space available on parking meters or the backs of tickets, or the very large space afforded by a movie screen. Another medium is the billboards around the edge of a sports area or field, such as a football field. Look around the catchment area of your business, and build up a list of all the locally available advertising spaces.

To find out which advertising media might work for you, try asking other people in your industry for advice. You need to strike a

TARGETING YOUR ADVERTISING

CUSTOMER TYPE	CUSTOMER DISTRIBUTION	LIKELY ADVERTISING OPTIONS	
CONSUMER	Local	■ Local newspapers ■ Mailbox leaflet ■ Posters ■ Buses, taxis	■ Local magazines ■ Local radio ■ Yellow Pages (or similar)
	Regional/national	■ Regional or national newspapers ■ Website	■ National consumer magazines
TRADE	Local	■ Yellow Pages (or similar) ■ Direct mailshot	■ Special feature in local newspapers ■ Buses, taxis
	Regional/national	■ Trade publications ■ Direct mailshot	■ Trade directories ■ Website

balance and form your own opinions, however – following blindly what your competitors are doing is not necessarily correct, but equally if no competitor is using the medium you are considering, ask yourself why. The table above helps to narrow down the potential choices.

FINDING OUT ABOUT DIFFERENT PUBLICATIONS

To find out the names of relevant publications, visit your local library or ask your trade association. Once you have identified a number of interesting publications, the next step is to phone their advertising departments and ask for a media pack. It is also useful to ask for their advance features list, which will give details of special feature articles they are planning, one of which may be exactly appropriate to what you are selling.

The media pack normally consists of a copy of the publication, a rate card, and details of the publication's circulation. The rate card gives all the advertising costs (or rates), technical data (such as the exact size of advertisements), and their business terms.

CIRCULATION AND READERSHIP

While the circulation figure of a publication is an important factor, you also need to find out exactly who these readers are. If the readers are not members of your target market, you will be wasting your advertising money. To put it another way, if only a third of a publication's readers are potential customers of your business, it means that two-thirds of your advertisement cost will be wasted.

Most publications have their circulations verified independently by different national bodies, according to whether they are paid for or free publications. This data is available on-line and will also be given in the publication and in the media pack. The latter may give more details, in particular a breakdown as to just who is reading the publication. The more information you have, the better: if the information provided does not answer all your questions, phone and ask the publication for more details. Many smaller circulation publications are not independently audited to determine their circulation, so you are dependent on the information the publication itself supplies.

Readership, in contrast to circulation, is the estimated number of people who see each issue, so is likely to be several times the figure given for the circulation.

Many trade publications have what is called a controlled circulation. This means that the publication is supported by the advertising it carries and copies are sent out free (not on subscription). The circulation is restricted to those in the industry, possibly above a certain managerial level. A criticism leveled against both trade and consumer publications that are issued free is that, since people do not have to pay for them (and, particularly with free consumer publications, may not even wish to see them), their circulation figures cannot be compared directly with figures for paid-for publications. It is argued that someone who pays for a publication is more likely to read it than someone who has received one free. This is probably more true for those consumer publications that have little or no editorial.

Advertise only where you can monitor the results

Weigh the pros and cons associated with circulation figures. For example, if you have a fixed budget to advertise a niche consumer product, you may need to decide whether to advertise in a national weekly newspaper or a specialist monthly magazine. If the newspaper has a readership of one million, but your budget will only stretch to a series of very small ads, these may only be seen by one in 10 readers – about 100,000. Of these, only 10,000–20,000 may find your product relevant. The specialist magazine, on the other hand, may have relatively low advertising rates due to its lower readership of 50,000. You could afford a larger ad in the magazine, and your product may be relevant to more readers; also, the shelf life of the magazine is likely to be longer than that of the newspaper.

MONEY SAVER

Avoid pressure from salespeople to take out advertisements related to special features unless you are sure that these features match your target market and their buying habits. These features are often the subject of hard selling to small businesses, but may not be appropriate.

DEADLINES AND ADVERTISING SPACE

The media pack should also include the all-important copy date for each issue. This is the deadline by which all advertising material must be received. Ignore it at your peril for, if you have booked the space, you will usually be charged for it, even if your advertisement arrives too late for inclusion.

For placing display advertisements, costs are usually expressed in terms of a full page, half page, quarter page, and sometimes eighth and sixteenth page sizes, or in terms of the cost per single column inch (sci). This latter measurement is a space one column wide and one inch deep – obviously you are likely to need a number of inches for a single advertisement, and there may be a minimum size of ad specified. Where a publication is printed only partly in color, the display rates may be quoted as mono (black and white) with color charged extra.

Classified advertisements are usually expressed in terms of cost per word or cost per line (lineage). Sometimes you can take out a display (box) advertisement in the classified section, in which case it will usually be quoted in terms of cost per single column inch.

If you plan to advertise in a local newspaper, visit and speak to the advertising manager. He or she will also be able to advise which days are best for the advertisements and which part of the paper is the most suitable. They may also introduce you to one of their reporters with a view to their writing an article (see pp. 126–7).

LOCAL RADIO STATIONS

Radio stations will also send you a media pack containing relevant details, including any up-and-coming features. The size of the listening audience and their breakdown is the key information you need.

Costs of radio commercials are based on airtime, quoted in terms of cost for a 10-, 20-, or 30-second slot, but you need to add about 10 percent on top of this for production costs. Services that broadcast to major cities charge more than those broadcasting to small, rural communities. Try phoning the advertising manager for advice about the time of day or time of the week to air your commercial to coincide with the listening habits of as much of your target market as possible.

Booking the Advertisements

As soon as you know the desired timing of the advertisements you wish to place, contact the advertising department at the publications and make your booking.

For newspapers and magazines, assuming that a suitable publication is being used, the likelihood of an advertisement being seen and actually read depends on several factors:

- the position of the advertisement

MONEY SAVER

Turn pressure to advertise to your advantage. If you start to advertise in one publication, rivals soon pick this up and start pestering you to advertise in theirs. If you do wish to advertise with them, turn them down the first time they call, and try to negotiate better terms when they call back.

- the design of the advertisement
- the size of the advertisement
- the number of times the reader sees the advertisement
- the repetition of the advertisement.

The significance of position is covered below, and the design of the advertisement on pp. 90–97. Note that the likelihood of being seen and read is not proportional to the size of the advertisement; on the other hand, the cost is proportional, so a good rule of thumb is to use the smallest size necessary to convey your message comfortably.

With printed publications, in terms of the number of times the reader might see your advertisement, it depends on the publication. With daily newspapers it is probably only once, or perhaps twice, but with a specialist consumer monthly magazine the reader is likely to browse through it at least several

ADVERTISING AGENCIES

As your business becomes larger and your advertising budget grows accordingly to, say, over $50,000, you may consider appointing an advertising agency. Their functions can be all or part of the following:

- to carry out background market research
- to conceive advertising campaign themes
- to research which media to use
- to create the advertisements
- to place the advertisements, as cheaply as possible, for their client.

Advertising agencies often charge both their clients and the medium that is carrying the advertisement. They may charge a consumer publication 15 percent and a trade publication 10 percent of the advertisement cost and, in addition, they can make production and other charges to the client. If you plan to use an advertising agency, write a clear and well-defined brief as to your objectives, specify a definite not-to-exceed budget, and set aside time to discuss their eventual campaign plan and to check final artwork.

times. Repetition usually requires advertising in each issue, although some advertisers take more than one advertisement in the same issue.

ASPECTS TO CONSIDER

The details you will need to cover when booking space include:

- **PRICE** It is always worth trying to negotiate a discount. Giving a discount is very common, especially with smaller publications. One strategy is to request the same percentage discount they would have to offer an advertising agency (usually 10 percent). Another strategy, if advertising for the first time, is to ask if they will give a discount to encourage you to try advertising with them. If you are not supplying the advertisement on disk or as camera-ready artwork, ask if there is any charge for typesetting and laying out your advertisement. This should be a nominal figure, unless you want something elaborate.
- **PAYMENT TERMS** Establish what the terms are. A short period of credit (up to 30 days) may be allowed.
- **POSITION** With publications it is essential to discuss where the advertisement will be placed. The ideal place is usually a right-hand page (in the bottom right corner if your advertisement is only part of the page) and facing an article (facing matter, as this is called) rather than somebody else's full-page advertisement. It is usually better to be in the early part of a publication, unless you want your advertisement to be near some special feature that occurs later in the issue. Sometimes there is a small extra charge for specifying the position. If you are offered ROP, this means that the advertisement will be placed anywhere in the run of the paper.
- **ARTWORK** If the publication is doing the artwork, find out what they need and by what date. Ask if they charge for doing the artwork and request a proof of your advertisement. If you are supplying the artwork yourself, you will need to know the mechanical data, such as what size the advertisement should be, what resolution for any photos, and if the artwork is to be supplied as positive or negative film or on disk. It is most important that you provide the artwork to the exact specifications required by the publication.
- **DEADLINES** It is essential to know what the deadlines are. You will need to allow more time if the publication is doing the artwork. There are also usually different deadlines for color advertisements, mono advertisements, and classified.
- **VOUCHER COPY** Ask for a complimentary copy (often called a voucher copy) of the issue in which your advertisement appears.
- **BOOKING CONFIRMATION** It is probably prudent to confirm everything in a letter, fax, or email. Ensure that you specify the issue(s) in which you wish your advertisement to appear.

Be fussy about where an ad is placed in a publication

PRODUCING EFFECTIVE ADVERTISEMENTS

Having decided on the purpose of your advertisement and chosen when and where to advertise, you need to create an advertisement that has a strong impact and conveys your message clearly and simply. This chapter includes advertisements in publications, radio commercials, and websites; it also covers the importance of monitoring your results.

Successful advertisements are those that focus closely on the readers or listeners who are potential customers, rather than those that adopt a scattershot approach, hoping that anyone might respond. Even a highly targeted medium will be read or heard by many who are not potential customers, so you should always have a picture of your possible customers in your mind and aim to encourage them to respond to your advertisement. In the context of this book, advertising can be broadly categorized as aiming to create an image or to create a response.

IMAGE ADVERTISING

With image advertising, a business tries to associate its name, product, or service with a particular image. For example, a car manufacturer may show a certain car model being admired by the type of customer whom they believe will be the likely buyer of that model. The car will be photographed in a context appropriate to that person (or their aspirations), so a GT hatchback car might be shown competing with sports cars on a race circuit. This type of advertising is to help the business position itself in the appropriate part of the marketplace. It is therefore concerned with increasing (or reinforcing) the potential buyer's awareness of its brand, business name, product, or service, and the image the business wishes to project. Thus the individual advertisements may vary, but a strong image-linking theme will remain constant. Another aspect of image advertising is that it rarely requests any immediate response or action from

CASE STUDY: Advertising Using a Consistent Approach

HILLARY IMPORTED DECORATIVE floor and wall tiles direct from Mexico. Her principal customers were specialist tile retailers around the country, but she also sold direct to the public and local contractors from her business park, where she stored the tiles after unloading them from the shipping container. Her customer base was therefore diverse and geographically scattered, but she needed to let them all know when new designs arrived, and to keep reminding current and potential customers of her business. She took a small color advertisement in every issue of a specialized flooring trade magazine. Her advertisement was always in the same place and looked the same, except that she featured a different design of tile in each issue and she would occasionally advertise sales to move older inventory. Whenever a new shipment arrived from Mexico, she also took a larger advertisement in her local newspaper to announce an open day at her facility. This advertising backed up her direct mailings to existing customers.

CONVEYING AN IMAGE
An image advertisement aims to promote an image to which the customer aspires. Such advertisements often require few words, but build an image by use of recognizable typography, colors, and photographic style.

the reader, listener, or viewer, although an address, website address, or phone number is usually mentioned somewhere.

Such image advertising tends to be used largely by major multinational companies who are selling cars, airline travel, food, cosmetics, computers, confectionery, beverages, consumer electronics, and so on.

Few small businesses can indulge in image advertising because the required advertising spend (its budget) is relatively large, and the effectiveness of the advertisements can be judged only many months, or even years, later in terms of percentage changes in sales or market share, or by specially commissioned market research. As much of the advertising that we are exposed to in national newspapers, glossy magazines, and on TV, is of the image sort, many small businesses unwittingly mimic this in their own advertisements. They produce an image advertisement when, in fact, they need to create a response advertisement that will have a more immediate effect on sales. The various types of response advertisements possible are covered in depth in this chapter.

RESPONSE ADVERTISING

Response advertising's main objective is to get a prompt response from the person seeing or hearing the advertisement. If the advertisement does not produce this desired response, it has failed. Although image can still be projected in a response advertisement, and may even be required in part to achieve the desired response, it is always a secondary aspect. For instance, whereas a car manufacturer may run an image campaign at a national or regional level, the local car dealer who has to sell cars from his or her specific garage will tend to use response-type advertisements.

CHOOSING ILLUSTRATIONS

There are five distinct types of illustration that can be used both to enliven a display advertisement and to convey information about what is being offered.

■ **PHOTOGRAPH OF PRODUCT** The product is usually photographed in front of a simple studio backdrop in a straightforward way. This use of photographs is popular in trade publications, where the application or use of the product is understood by the reader.

■ **ILLUSTRATION OF PRODUCT** A computer graphic or illustration carries less conviction than a photograph, but may be necessary if the product is still at the design stage or difficult to photograph. Use a professional to generate the illustration.

■ **PHOTOGRAPH OF PRODUCT OR SERVICE IN CONTEXT** Showing the product in use or a service being undertaken can be very useful. The context photo is more demanding to produce than a simple product photo, since the context can have a marked bearing on the image portrayed by the advertisement. It is

Designing Display Advertisements

There are six parts to any good display advertisement that is aiming to elicit a response from potential customers:

- headline
- visuals (illustrations or photographs)
- body (selling) copy
- call for action
- name, address, and logo
- other details.

Use excellent-quality visuals – they have a far greater impact than words

ADVERTISING HEADLINE

A good headline is similar to one on the front page of a newspaper: it is designed to catch your attention. It should be punchy, but not so short that there is no clearly understandable message. The headline should capture the attention of that segment of the readership who is likely to become customers, and promise them some benefit. For example, for a business selling burglar alarms, the headline might read something like: "Worried About Burglaries?," or "Thieves Avoid These Homes!," or "Have You Had a Break-in?" These examples emphasize the point that the heading need not be short; in fact, ultrashort headings can be very restrictive. These examples also show two popular ways of writing a catchy headline:

- a question
- a challenging/puzzling statement.

There are other useful techniques that you can employ to catch a reader's attention and, better still, attract potential customers.

ideal for consumer advertisements, because it immediately gives a number of clues to the reader, such as the age, sex, lifestyle, and financial and social status of the likely user.

- **PHOTOGRAPH OF PRODUCT OR SERVICE IN UNUSUAL CONTEXT** With some ingenuity, you can make the product or service stand out by doing something unusual or slightly silly. For example, you might show off waterproof watches by photographing them in a washing machine being spun around with the clothes. Or you might illustrate the heat-retentive properties of the new thermal underwear you have designed by showing a picture of people wearing only these thermals while waiting for a bus in the winter (and standing beside others fully dressed, but looking cold).
- **ATTENTION GRABBER** A photograph or computer graphic could be used that does not show the product or service being advertised, but is a striking, unusual, or colorful image that is there simply to catch the reader's attention.

PHOTOGRAPH OF PRODUCTS
This photograph clearly shows a small range of products. The good quality of the photograph shows the sleek design of the flasks, and the fact that some of the flasks are open shows additional detail.

- **REFLECT CURRENT NEWS** Tie in the headline to a noncontroversial event that is being reported in the news.
- **INVOLVE THE READER** In the headline, include the reader. For example, "Working Mothers...," "Do You Need a Rest?," "Top Executives...," and so on. Note the use of flattery, and the use of plurals, too. The latter hints that others are buying or doing whatever your advertisement promises.
- **INCLUDE A WELL-KNOWN BRAND** A small business can increase its credibility and capture attention by incorporating a well-known and prestigious company or brand name in the headline, where that product or service is being advertised. Ask permission beforehand of the company concerned, since they will be sensitive about the use of their name. If they do agree to its use, however, it is possible that they may contribute toward the costs of your advertisement.
- **INCLUDE A CELEBRITY** Another way of making a catchy headline (and probably an eye-catching photograph, too) is to use a celebrity. For this you need the celebrity's specific permission, which should be secured in writing, and they will generally charge for this endorsement.
- **REFLECT OUR NEEDS AND DESIRES** A suitable headline can raise the profile of a need or desire, and even encourage us to think that a particular desire is in fact a need.
- **MISQUOTE A WELL-KNOWN PHRASE** You might misquote a well-known saying, a film or book title, or a line from a song, so that it

FACT FILE

A different and very effective form of display advertisement is one that looks and is written like other articles in a publication, but is in fact an advertisement. It will be labeled "Advertisement" or "Paid advertisement," usually at the top. Done properly, this is a very good way to get your message across.

alludes to your own products or services. This can be very effective, but be careful from a legal point of view – ask a lawyer for advice before running your advertisement.

In general, try to avoid overused words, such as "New," "Exciting," "Sale," "Discount," "Prices Slashed," and so on. Try to be more original. A common error for many beginners is to use the name of their business as the headline. This is only likely to work if the business name is descriptive of what is being offered; otherwise the name is unlikely to mean anything to a reader.

The headline, though it should be large, should not be too large in relation to the nearby articles or the other text in your own advertisement. If it is out of proportion, it is unlikely to be read. Also note that we read a mixture of upper and lower case letters more easily than upper case alone, but a small advertisement with a short headline may benefit from having its headline only in upper case. When you have drafted several versions of a headline, test it by asking yourself these questions:

- Why would a likely customer notice it?
- What benefit is offered or hinted at?
- Will people want to read on?

THE VISUALS

Display advertisements should, wherever possible, be illustrated with a photograph or computer graphic. Ideally, where there is sufficient space, you could include more than one illustration (see pp. 90–91).

- **PHOTOS** A wholesaler, retailer, or importer may be able to obtain suitable photographs of products from their suppliers. A manufacturer will need to ask a professional photographer to take photographs. Amateur photos usually look poor. A color photo that looks crisp and sharp when printed on glossy magazine paper will tend to lose its detail when reproduced in black and white on newsprint. This is important if it is the detail you are trying to show. Although the photo should be dominant, it need not be a plain rectangular shape.
- **GRAPHICS** Few small businesses will have anyone who can produce effective computer graphics, unless the business is itself a design business. Using outside help may prove expensive. To keep your costs down, do your research by studying other advertisements, and then produce a tightly drafted brief for the designer. Note that copying another graphic design may be a breach of copyright. Ensure that the design of your advertisement cannot be confused with that of a rival.

THE BODY (SELLING) COPY

The headline and visuals should have attracted those readers who are prospects, catching their attention, however fleetingly. The text, or body copy, aims to create sufficient interest for them to respond to your advertisement. Pointers for writing the body copy are as follows:

- **PUT YOURSELF IN THE READER'S PLACE** Although hundreds or thousands of people, may look at an advertisement, it should be written with an individual in mind. Put yourself in the shoes of the target reader and ask the sorts of questions they will be asking themselves. Specifically, try to overcome any sales barriers they may be erecting in their minds; these barriers can relate to any aspect of the product from price to quality.
- **TELL A STORY** The selling copy should impart some information. It should, if possible, be new to the reader, and not

simply state the obvious. The selling copy is often written in the present tense, rather than future, to give a sense of immediacy. As with a traditional story, it should have an introduction, a middle, and an ending. First, the advertisement must state just what is being sold in a way that is unambiguous. Then ask yourself if the reader will be seeking detailed information on prices, availability, performance, and comparisons with competitors. If so, provide it. If not, think about the focus of your advertisement – are you expecting to lure the reader away from a rival's product? What objections could the reader be raising? Involve readers by frequent use of the word "you," and by jargon or phraseology they can relate to.

- **SELL THE BENEFITS** A customer buys benefits, not features. Make a list of all the potential benefits of your product or service, and select the ones that are most likely to appeal to your reader.

SAMPLE DISPLAY ADVERTISEMENT

This eye-catching small ad focuses on particular items for sale. An incentive is offered to encourage a prompt response, and a 24-hour phone number is given.

Good-quality photograph is used both to attract attention and to show items for sale

Call for action by offering an incentive

10% OFF ORDERS PLACED BY MAY 31

Headline promises a benefit and may therefore catch the attention of more prospective customers than a specific heading such as "Patio Furniture"

Design is simple with no clutter to detract from the basic message

ENJOY THE OUTDOORS

Top brands of patio furniture in teak, cast iron, aluminum, etc. Prices from $19.95.

■ WIDE RANGE, ALL IN STOCK ■

Principal objective is to stimulate customers to request a brochure or visit the web site

For your free color brochure, call our 24-HOUR ORDERLINE

1-800 555 6789

or visit our website at www. ... .com

John Smith Garden Center

Rose Street, Any Town

Contact details are provided

- **PRODUCT DIFFERENTIATION** The unique selling proposition (USP) of the business – that unique factor that customers cannot obtain elsewhere – should be stressed. A sales slogan could also reflect this. If your business is operating in a competitive environment, your advertisement needs also to explain what differentiates your products or services from the competition.
- **BUILD CONFIDENCE** A small business, particularly one that is relatively new, has had little time to develop credibility in the eyes of its likely customers. Hence their confidence in your business's ability to deliver the promises made in the advertisement needs to be reinforced. This can be done by a variety of means, including the use of well-known, reputable brand names; a celebrity endorsing the product or service; or a statistic that reflects your popularity, such as impressive sales figures.

COMMON ERRORS WITH DISPLAY ADVERTISEMENTS

1. Assuming one large advertisement is all that is needed to get your message across.
2. Not having a clear idea as to the objective of the advertisement.
3. Using your business name for the headline of the advertisement.
4. Expecting a response from an image advertisement.
5. Stressing the features rather than the benefits of a product or service.
6. Not including people in your photographs.
7. Using amateur photographs or poor-quality graphics.
8. Omitting a clear call for action at the end of the advertisement.
9. Not changing your advertisement at each insertion in a publication.

In an industry context you could list well-known companies you already supply. Quite a sophisticated version of this approach is the true short story, which shows your business or product in an excellent light.

- **AVOID HYPE** In the majority of advertisements, you should avoid hype, since most readers are rather cynical about anything that is overplayed, even more so if your target readership is business buyers.
- **USE THE CORRECT NUMBER OF WORDS** In general, advertisers seem nervous about using too many words in an advertisement and tend to err on the short, almost cryptic, side. Equally, some writers of advertising copy seem to be attempting to win literary prizes by the lengths they write. There is an optimum depending on the context. People will often flick through magazines or skip through newspapers, stopping only to read articles and advertisements that catch their interest. Hence you should use lots of short, punchy sentences, short paragraphs, and paragraph headings that can encapsulate the message of the following paragraph in a few words. Look at other advertisements of similar size in your own industry sector to get a feel for what is obviously too short or too long. Count the number of words used in these advertisements to get a precise idea as to how many words you should aim at.
- **QUOTE PRICES** Whether to show prices or not is a frequent source of debate. There are probably only two situations when prices might not be mentioned in advertisements. The first is when you are selling top luxury goods or services to those consumers where price is not a first consideration. The second situation is when you are selling large capital equipment or a major service where the end price depends on too many variables to be able to quote a meaningful price in an advertisement. Otherwise, the balance is probably in favor of quoting your prices – after all, most of us want to know what a product or service is going to cost us before

we find out more about it. The omission of a price tends to create an impression that your product or service is likely to be expensive. Note that, where prices are shown, there must be no hidden extra costs; for example, if postage is always charged extra, this must be stated clearly. If you are reluctant to quote a price because your prices are uncompetitive, resolve that issue first (see pp. 30–39).

Use your logo in your advertisement – over time it will aid customer recognition

CALL FOR ACTION

In a response advertisement, the body copy must include a call for action. This point cannot be overstressed. Most people need a nudge to get them to act now rather than later (or never). Hence a call for action must involve a deadline after which the reader will have to pay a higher price, or the product may be scarce. Examples are: "Limited offer ends Saturday, June 3," or "Last 50 left in the city," or "Beat the Budget – buy before March 31," or "Prices rising on September 1, buy now and save $x." Note that what you say in your call for action must be true.

An alternative strategy is to link the call for action to another benefit, such as a discount or gift for all purchases made before a certain date, or meeting a well-known celebrity if you buy on a certain date. Another effective technique is a response coupon that the reader is encouraged to complete and return for more information. The coupon needs to be simple to complete, with enough space to write the name and address, and should also emphasize a deadline.

NAME, ADDRESS, AND LOGO

After getting the reader interested in what you are offering, you need to tell them how to get it. The name and address block in the advertisement does not need simply to copy your formal letterhead address. Will people contact you by phone, email, letter, fax, in person, or at a show? Give prominence in your advertisement to that which is most relevant to the reader. So, if most customers are likely to contact you by phone, the telephone number should be dominant. In contrast, if you are a retailer and people have no particular reason to phone, give prominence to where you are located. If people are likely to visit your premises, a small map indicating the nearest parking lot and, where relevant, public transportation, would be more useful. Alternatively, if there is a well-known landmark nearby, you might simply state something like "Find us opposite the station."

OTHER DETAILS

As in every aspect of business, it is the little details that count, and advertisements are no exception. Consider whether the following factors apply to you:

- **HOURS** If your business works unusual hours or is to be open during a holiday period, this fact should be mentioned so that potential business is not lost.
- **PHONE ORDERS** If you are able to take credit or debit card orders over the phone, this could be mentioned. The customer is more likely to respond if you let them know that you offer a convenient service. A space-saving practice is just to use the credit or debit card logos on your advertisement.
- **CREDIT FACILITIES** If the cost of your product or service is such that you need to offer credit facilities, you might mention this, but note the legal requirements referred to on p. 178.
- **CROWDING** Do not be tempted to fill every corner of your advertisement space. Allow some white space to remain, as this lets the important details stand out.
- **ACCURACY** Do be sure the spelling and your contact details are correct. Also ensure that all details, such as prices, are accurate, as an error in such information may constitute an offense.

These requirements may seem demanding, and producing effective display advertisements does require considerable effort and a lot of practice; however, such advertisements can be expensive for a small business, so are worth getting right. For a display advertisement to be effective does not require every detail to be picture perfect, but it helps if it is. With some practice, the winning criteria for your own business will begin to be more obvious.

Focus on differentiating your product or service from those of competitors

Designing Classified Advertisements

A classified advertisement is one that is listed in a publication according to the class of goods or services offered. It is therefore surrounded by other similar advertisements, mostly one column wide. These advertisements can be lineage (words only) or box, the latter being able to include some design input in the form of a small illustration and variable arrangements of words.

An important difference between display and classified advertisements is that with a display advertisement you are trying to catch the attention of a reader who is not necessarily in a buying mood. In contrast, those people who scan the classified columns are more likely to be actively seeking a particular service they require or they are just looking for a bargain. They are therefore ready to buy, and the advertisement needs to persuade them to buy from you rather than from someone else.

There are four parts to a good classified lineage advertisement:

- headline
- body (selling) copy
- call for action
- contact details.

Many of the criteria for designing a display advertisement (as covered above) need to be borne in mind for classifieds, but distilled down to their bare essentials to suit the smaller space available.

Most publications allow space for only a brief headline, which is in bold letters at the start of the advertisement. The headline is usually restricted to a couple of words in length so you need to be specific, mentioning precisely what is being offered.

As you are limited for space, the selling copy needs to emphasize the benefits. There will be minimal room for details. Use bullet points to get the information across, if appropriate. A call for action is as essential as for a display advertisement, and can use similar wording. Finally, to save space, you should only give the minimum (appropriate) business contact details, so in many cases a phone number will be sufficient.

With box classified advertisements, the width can be one or two columns and you can include a small and relevant illustration. On this scale, a computer graphic may be clearer than a photograph and can be eye-catching if done well. You could use good-quality computer clip art. One graphics technique that is not particularly recommended, but often used in such advertisements, is to reverse the text out of a black box so that the advertisement is mainly black, with white lettering. Our natural reaction is to notice light rather than dark, so we tend to avoid looking at such advertisements.

FACT FILE

A good technique is to use several small and different classified advertisements in the same issue of a publication rather than one long advertisement. If the publication lists classified advertisements alphabetically, choose a headline with a word starting with A or B.

Remember that all business classified advertisements must indicate clearly that they are in fact business advertisements. Using the business name in addition to a phone number or address usually covers this point.

WHEN TO USE CLASSIFIED ADVERTISEMENTS

Different advertisers use classified advertisements for different purposes. First, there are those businesses that need to advertise their services continually, such as plumbers, carpenters, tire repairers, and so on. They rely on prospective customers who might use their services from time to time, referring to the classified columns and contacting them as the need arises. Even if they attract repeat business, customers will often expect to find their number in the classifieds each time. Then there are small businesses that need to promote some special onetime event, such as an end-of-season sale. Finally, the classified columns are favorites of many businesses selling low-price bargains. When booking, check the different categories of classification first, and make sure you place your advertisement under the correct one.

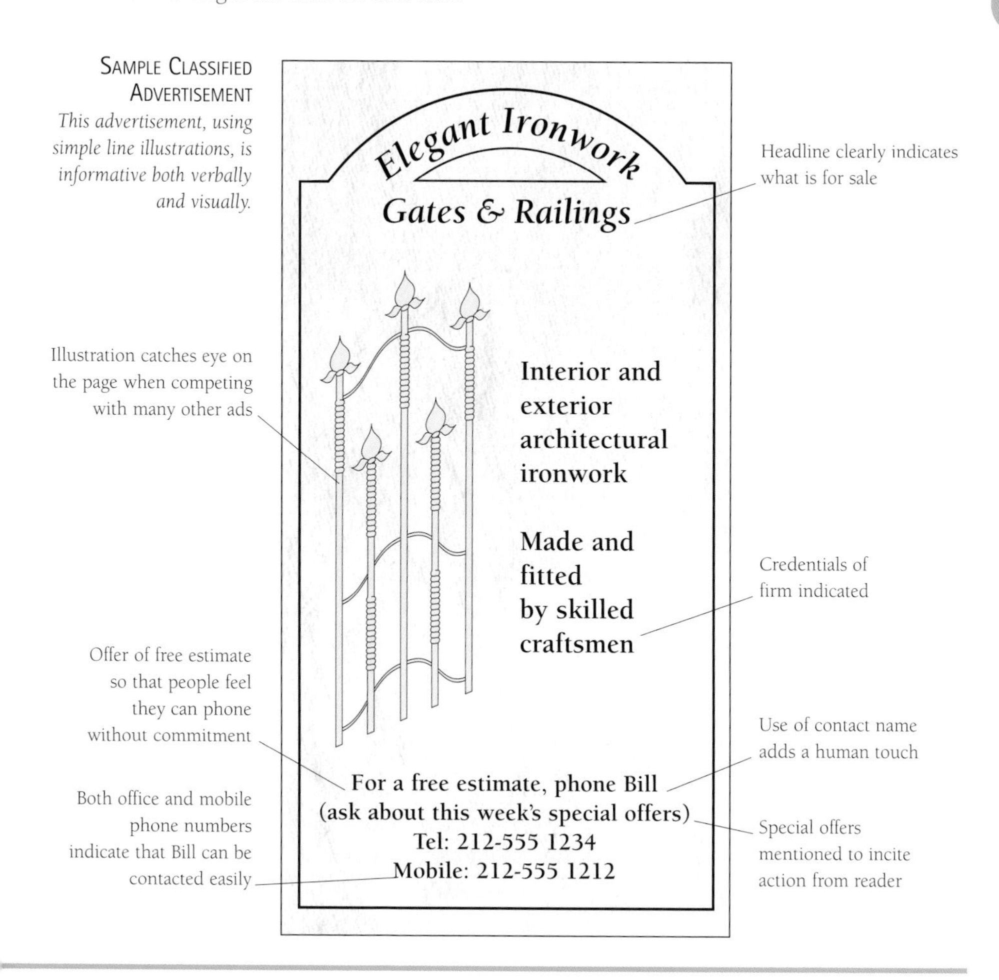

SAMPLE CLASSIFIED ADVERTISEMENT
This advertisement, using simple line illustrations, is informative both verbally and visually.

Designing Posters

A small business is more likely to find small posters aimed at the local market a more effective advertising method than creating large posters to place on billboards. The best use of posters is to advertise a specific event, such as a sale, or an opening, or a new launch of a product or service – readers tend to associate posters with an up-and-coming event. In most cases permission needs to be sought from the city council or local government before putting up posters in an area. Decide the sites you would like to use, then design the poster accordingly. If the people who are most likely to read the poster are passing on foot, you can create a slightly more detailed design. If your readers are likely to be passing in their cars, the text needs to be brief, understandable, and readable from a distance.

Producing a Radio Commercial

You do not have to be a big business to use commercial radio, and it can be an effective advertising medium for consumer and business-to-business products and services. In addition to listening to the radio at home, people listen while in their cars and in some workplaces too. Typically between one-third and a half of the adult population will listen regularly to a local commercial radio station.

USING POSTERS

Although this poster is an image advertisement for a large, international fashion company, it shows the effectiveness of making the message simple, clear, and easy to read from a passing car or when on foot.

RECORDING AN ADVERT

Here, two voiceover artists are recording a radio advertisement. When you record a radio commercial, a sound technician will be on hand to make the recording and may be able to offer advice.

Audience figures are therefore large. Individuals listen to the radio for a wide variety of reasons – for company, entertainment, background music, news, sports commentaries, and to obtain general information.

Sometimes the context is one where any advertisement has to draw the listener's attention from another activity they are doing, but some audiences, such as car drivers, are more captive. A key finding of audience research is that the vast majority of radio listening is habitual in that listeners will tune in at the same time every day and usually to the same station. To target specific listeners, such as businesspeople, the drive-to-work times are ideal, while many consumers who do not go out to work listen to morning programs.

LENGTH AND FREQUENCY OF COMMERCIALS

You pay for a commercial according to its length, but market research indicates that the typical length of a radio commercial makes little difference to its impact on the listener. So choose as short a slot as you require to deliver your message. Most radio advertising requires a lot of repetition to get the message across, so you should budget for at least a dozen slots per week for several weeks. To be really effective, your advertisement will ultimately require a higher level of exposure.

Use radio commercials to back up other promotions

PRODUCTION ISSUES

Before considering how your own commercial should sound, listen to other commercials and note what sounds good, what catches your attention, what irritates you, and who else is advertising on the station you have chosen.

Most local radio stations can offer a creative service to help you produce a commercial. This is important to ensure a professional advertisement that also complies with all relevant legalities.

A jingle, where a composer produces lyrics and music just for your advertisement, is expensive, but can be effective, making your advertisement more memorable. The radio station may have library music that you can use instead of commissioning your own.

A common mistake is to try to squeeze too many words into a radio advertisement. In a 30-second slot that finishes with a brief jingle, there is only time for about 100 words. Having a jingle at the beginning and end (known as a top and tail) can reduce the time available in the middle, so that there is only space for 30 to 50 words. Research shows that commercials with dialogue between two or more people achieve

Dos and Don'ts of Radio Commercials

✓ Do identify with your target listener's needs.

✓ Do use radio for immediacy and topicality.

✓ Do keep your advertising message simple.

✓ Do use humor and novelty in your advertisement.

✓ Do encourage the listener to visualize a scene involving your product or service.

✗ Don't have too many words in the script.

✗ Don't have a story that demands high concentration.

✗ Don't use excessive repetition of a word or phrase.

✗ Don't use strong or unintelligible accents.

✗ Don't use radio if you cannot afford a series of advertisements.

higher impact than a single voice. Aim to make the message memorable, and to include contact details that are also easy to remember. Ask for a demo commercial. This will cost extra but you can hear how the advertisement will sound before it goes on the air.

Designing a Website

A web site is becoming essential for businesses of all sizes. For many, a website is simply a way of advertising their presence in the marketplace, providing information about their goods and services, and giving another point of contact in addition to phone and fax. Some businesses sell via the internet as one of their distribution methods; others are set up solely to sell over the internet and have no other outlets for their products or services. Selling online is covered on pp. 46–7.

Typical tasks that are carried out by small businesses through their we sites, in addition to selling, include:

- Sending and receiving emails (both internally and externally).
- Sourcing inventory, raw materials, and consumables (the internet throws your buying net wider).
- Publishing online sales catalogs (which have the big advantage that they can be updated easily and quickly and can be used for publicizing special offers too).
- Providing technical support and backup (this reduces time-consuming phone calls from customers with problems, and provides customers with a more efficient service).
- Carrying out market research (there is a huge amount of information available online, much of it free).
- Checking out competitors (the amount of information available can be stunning and revealing).
- Exchanging order information with customers and suppliers (this reduces the amount of paperwork and provides trading partners with increased information about the other party, such as inventory levels and despatch details).

As exciting and potentially beneficial as the internet is, it is as important to determine exactly what you want to achieve via your website just as it is before embarking on any form of advertising. The internet is changing fast and maturing in the ways in which it is used. At present, the main growth area is in business-to-business trading and the slowest rate of growth is in businesses providing services in person to consumers. A service-based company might nevertheless use a website primarily to advertise and promote their business, rather than to sell their services online.

Creating a Good Website

If you have seen other business websites, you will know that the appearance, quality, and ease of use of different sites varies considerably. Some are straightforward to use, while others are far less so. See the box on pp. 102–03 for indications of useful features to include. As with the design of any advertisement, when thinking about how to structure your website, keep in mind your target market and their needs, plus your own e-commerce objectives.

Your opening home page should load quickly, have your business name clearly visible, and make a firm and direct statement as to who you are and what you do, so that the visitor knows at once if the site and its content is relevant to them. You want not only to attract the right visitors, but also to keep them interested enough to stay and browse your other pages. Ensure that your business is structured and your staff are trained and prepared to process new inquiries via your website, and to take care of the extra workload associated with the many emails (some of them junk ones) that are inevitable. Internet technology is characterized by speed and flexibility, at least in the minds of users, so you need to make sure that your response to business generated by your website is fast and efficient, rather than slow and frustrating.

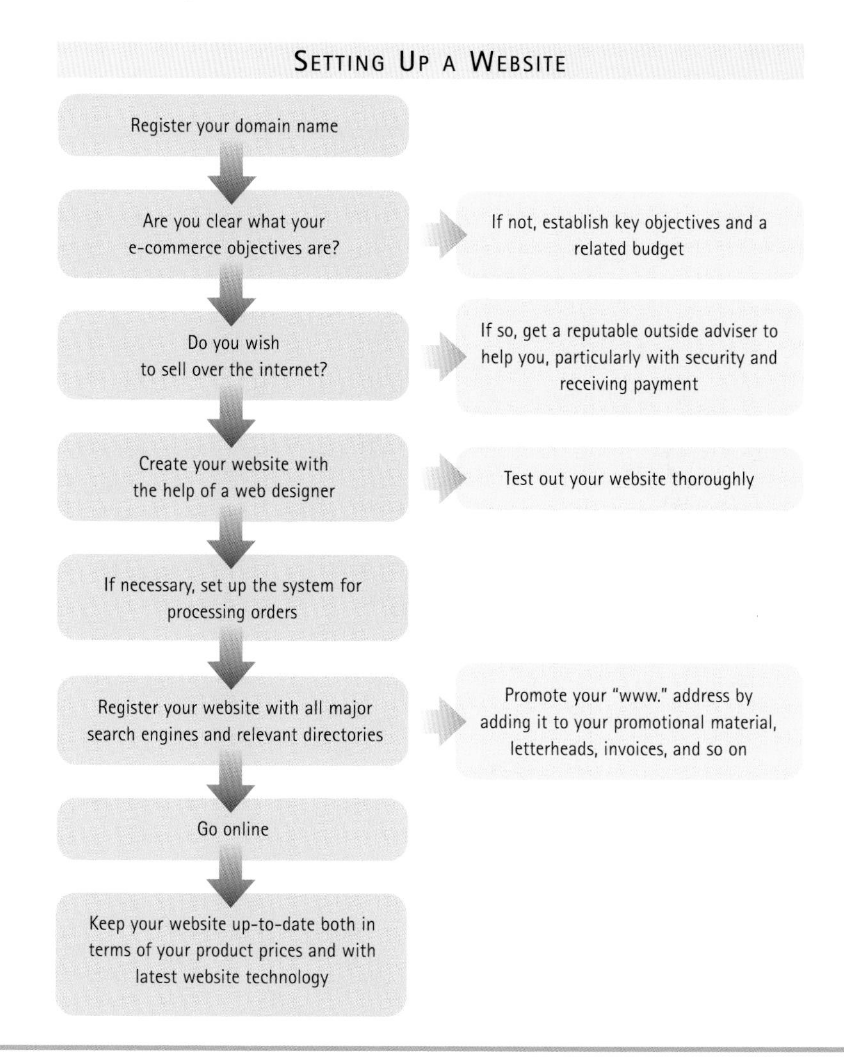

PROMOTING YOUR WEBSITE

Promotion of your website is as important as the creation of the website itself. Many small businesses go to a lot of trouble and expense to create a good website, but do not promote it adequately. They think, erroneously, that simply having the website is all you have to do for sales to roll in. Even with good promotion of your website it will take time, as with any business endeavor, for the amount of business to increase to the point where the whole exercise has been worthwhile.

Ensure that correct keywords are used on your website so that search engines can find you. Look at rival sites to see what keywords they use. Include common misspellings of your keywords as well. Have your new website registered with all major search engines – and

ELEMENTS OF AN EFFECTIVE WEBSITE

Make ease of use your top priority when creating a website. Here are a number of tips to make your website simple to use.

■ **NAVIGATION BUTTONS** Keep the buttons static (in a frame) or visible on the page rather than buried amid text. Do not make the page so long that the buttons can be scrolled away and left out of sight at the top. If necessary, repeat the buttons at the base of the page.

■ **EASY ACCESS** Make all information on your site easy to access – the user should not have to click their mouse more than three times to reach the information they need.

■ **SUBMENUS** Use submenus so that users can see where they can go next. So, while a site may be divided into a few broad areas, make clear which specific topics are covered within each area.

■ **MOVING WITHIN A SITE** Do not rely on users using the "Back" and "Forward" buttons on their browser. If they are a long way into a site, it can take numerous clicks to get back to an earlier point. Offer links to each page at every stage for ease of movement.

■ **SEARCHES** Providing a search facility is a good way for the user to access information fast. Make sure the database is written well and provides intelligent results rather than innumerable possibilities. Give users hints and tips about how to conduct a search.

■ **PRESENTING INFORMATION** Avoid having lots of dense text on a page. Users may become bored with scrolling down through such text and they may print it off to read later or jump to another site. Either break up the text into manageable chunks with clear headings, and perhaps the option for the user to go straight to a heading, or create more pages with good links back and forth. The object is to give users the choice as to whether or not they want to read the information.

■ **IMAGES** Avoid using too many images or flashing gimmicks on a page. These can take a long time to load and may not be worth the wait. Remember that users are busy people who don't want to waste their time, so try to make the experience as efficient as possible.

■ **ACCURACY** Keep your information up-to-date. This is particularly vital if you are selling on the net – users will be frustrated if the price is wrong or you are out of stock. Perhaps add a date when the site was last updated, to inspire confidence in the information.

■ **CONTACT DETAILS** Give users a choice of how to contact you and make it easy for them to find those details. Some may not wish to order online, so give phone and fax numbers. Give the options of paying by check or over the phone as well as online. Give direct email links so that users do not have to remember or write down your address.

■ **LINKS TO OTHER SITES** If you are including links to other sites, try to have them appear in another window. This means that, while the user visits that site, yours remains onscreen – otherwise you may lose your visitor altogether.

note that even the largest search engines each cover less than a quarter of the web. Contact organizations or associations who have their own websites and whose members might be interested in your products. Look for other complementary websites and suggest hypertext links between your sites. This is a time-consuming but potentially very worthwhile process. Once your site is up and running, promote it at every opportunity, giving your website address on all your correspondence, advertisements, leaflets, business cards, products, answering machine, and even the sides of your van.

UPDATING YOUR WEBSITE

After putting a great deal of thought, effort, and money into creating your new website, you need to keep it up to date to maintain its effectiveness.

LOOKING AT WEBSITE FEATURES

Examine a variety of websites set up by large and small businesses. Note features that you like and that make the site easier to use. Explore other pages apart from the home page to understand the site layout.

Name of business is a prominent feature of the web page

A "Search" feature is useful on large sites or those containing complex information

Navigation buttons make it easy for the user to find information and connect to other pages on the site

A "help" guide is useful where a site contains numerous pages, or to assist with an interactive process such as selling

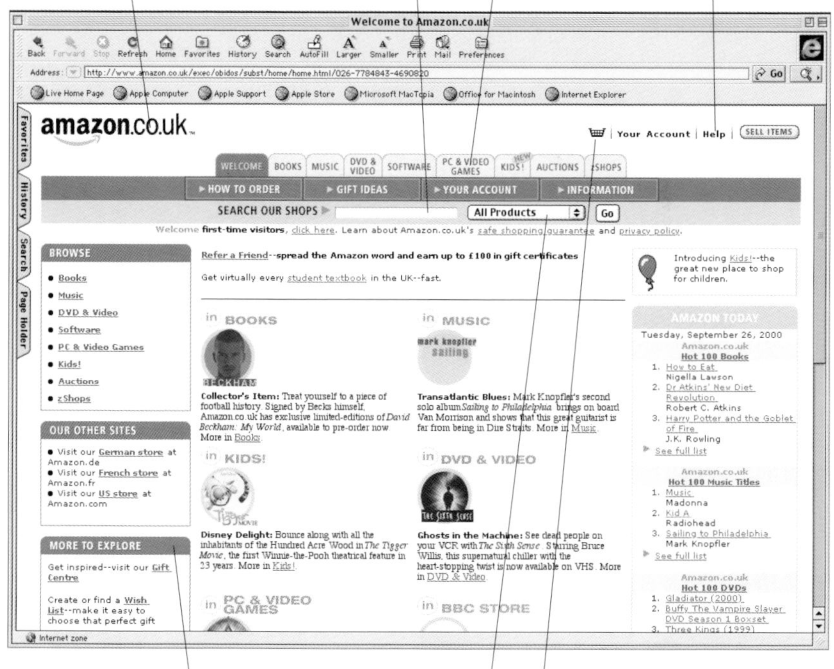

Users can choose whether to access more information

A submenu allows the user to narrow down searches

Shopping process is clearly indicated

INTERNET TERMINOLOGY

ACCESS PROVIDER A company that provides a connection to the internet. Also known as an internet service provider (ISP).

BROWSER A software program that allows your computer to search the internet.

DOMAIN NAME The individual part of your website address. Usually prefixed by "www." and followed by a suffix indicating the type of organization (".com" and ".co" for companies, ".gov" for government bodies, ".org" for noncommercial organizations, ".net" for access providers, and so on), followed sometimes by a country indicator.

DOWNLOAD To get a file from a host computer.

HTML (Hyper Text Markup Language) The universal software language used to create web pages.

HYPERTEXT LINK A "hotspot" or virtual button on which the user can click to go straight to another web site.

KEYWORD Topic or phrase entered into a search engine to find a relevant website.

META TAG Information about a web page that does not affect the visual display. The information may include who created the page, when it is updated, and which keywords represent the content.

PORTAL A website that specializes in leading users to related websites.

SEARCH ENGINE Websites that hold huge database indexes of web pages that can be accessed to find subjects on the world wide web. A search engine functions by searching its database using keywords entered by the user.

SPAMMING Attempting to gain a higher position on a search engine by manipulating or overusing keywords; also used to describe the sending of electronic junk mail or junk newsgroup postings.

THUMBNAIL A small version of an image that appears on screen to save space and download time. Clicking on the thumbnail downloads a full-sized image. Useful for online catalogs.

UPLOAD To send a file to a host computer.

Having out-of-date information on a website reflects badly on the business concerned. For some businesses, such as real estate agents, having out-of-date information makes the site useless. People will not visit a poor site twice. If you do not have the time or resources to update detailed information on your website, keep it simple; the site could act as an initial point of contact.

Monitor the major search engines to ensure they not only locate your site, but give it a high ranking when the right keywords are typed in. From time to time arrange to have your site checked over from a technological point of view to ensure that it remains compatible and easy to use with the latest browser software.

Monitoring Advertisement Response

Too few businesses (large or small) make enough of an attempt to monitor the results of their advertising campaigns. A small business cannot afford to waste money on ineffective advertising. By careful design of advertisements and close monitoring of results, the effectiveness of each advertisement or campaign can be measured, and future advertising fine-tuned.

Not all strategies work well for everyone everywhere. Find out those that work for you and those that do not. You might even discover that advertising does not prove to be effective for your business, and your budget is better spent on other promotional activity, such as public relations (see pp. 118–27). Depending on the circumstances, there are a number of ways to monitor your advertising (see the table opposite).

In practice your monitoring has to be done using some sort of routine. You could print or photocopy small cards that list the different ways a person might hear about you – through your various advertisements, mentions in the press, by word of mouth, or by other means – and check the appropriate box on a card, using one card per person. Depending upon your type of business, these cards could be held beside a phone, or by a cash register in a store, or kept in your briefcase at an exhibition.

What Should an Advertisement Earn?

It is sobering to calculate how many sales your advertisements need to generate simply to cover their cost. You do not simply need to make enough sales to cover the costs, you need to make enough profit. Do these calculations for your own business, with your accountant's help if necessary. For a small business, advertisements need to work, producing a response that more than covers their costs. If not, you will have spent valuable time planning and creating the advertisement, and will have made a loss – which few businesses can afford.

Choosing a Method of Monitoring

Method	What to Do	Points to Consider
Reply by Mail	If advertising in more than one publication, make small changes to the address so that you can tell from which advertisement the response emanates. If you are asking the reader to complete and return a coupon, add a different printed code to the coupon for each advertisement.	Highly effective. Suitable for any advertisement likely to get a postal response.
Reply by Phone	When potential customers call, ask how they heard about you.	Effective, although some callers cannot recall how they heard about you. Also, it may appear intrusive to question the caller.
Reply by Email	Add up the number of responses each time an advertisement appears.	Difficult to assess how sender heard about you – use a different email address on different advertisements to clarify where the sender saw your advertisement.
Website Counter	A counter on your website adds up how many visits the site has received.	Shows the number of visits, but does not reveal how visitors found your site or if people are visiting your site more than once.
Person-to-person	In a store or when selling business-to-business or on an exhibition stand, you can simply ask the customer where they heard about you.	Effective, although some people cannot recall how they heard about you.
Bring a Coupon	Where the reader is required to visit you (as in a store), include a coupon on the advertisement, which the reader has to bring to get some benefit, such as a gift or a discount.	Requires an incentive for customer to bring the coupon.

CREATING LEAFLETS AND BROCHURES

Leaflets, pamphlets, brochures, and catalogs are specialized forms of advertising, often produced by businesses to showcase or provide information about their products or services; these printed items can be a pivotal part of their marketing. To be successful, a leaflet or brochure needs to be produced with a precise objective and a target reader in mind. Although appearance is important, it should not take precedence over what the leaflet is intended to achieve for your business.

A leaflet is, strictly speaking, a single sheet of printed matter, whereas a pamphlet, brochure, or catalog consists of several sheets. In practice, these words are often used interchangeably. In this chapter, the word "leaflet" is used to cover all these items.

Why Produce a Leaflet?

The decision to produce a leaflet will stem from consideration of the many different ways of advertising open to you (see pp. 81–6). The next questions you need to answer are:

- What is the precise purpose of the leaflet I am intending to issue?
- Will the target reader respond to the leaflet?
- How will the leaflet be distributed?
- What is the budget for producing the leaflet?

DECIDING ON YOUR PURPOSE

Leaflets fall into two broad categories – those that introduce a new product or service to a likely customer, and those that turn an already interested customer into a buyer. An example of the first category would be a leaflet delivered through the mailbox. Since this leaflet is an attempt at a cold sale, it must be persuasive and brief. It also needs to be produced and distributed in large quantities, since the response rate to any cold-selling approach is low. This has implications in terms of the unit printing cost of the leaflet you are considering.

Create the least elaborate leaflet likely to achieve its objectives

An example of the leaflet intended to persuade an interested customer to buy is one given to someone who has requested more information about a product or service. The leaflet needs to provide sufficient details to enable the customer to make a purchasing decision.

What can a leaflet achieve that other forms of advertising and promotion cannot? The answer is that a leaflet will be looked at in isolation, without immediate competition for the reader's attention from other advertisements or articles in a publication. Leaflets also allow much more space for words and pictures than you can normally afford to purchase with an advertisement. To some extent, you can also control who receives leaflets. They are particularly useful in face-to-face selling situations to back up the sales pitch and allow the salesperson to leave product or service details with the potential buyer.

TARGET READERSHIP

Keep placing yourself in the shoes of the people who are likely to read the leaflet. Based on your market research and experience, you will have a good profile of your likely customers. Produce a leaflet that will catch their eye, relate to them and their needs, and encourage them to take the next step toward making a purchase. These considerations will influence the look and tone of the leaflet; for instance, a leaflet aimed at a buyer of electronic parts will focus on providing the relevant detailed technical information, whereas one aimed at the passing customer is likely to be less detailed but perhaps more eye-catching. The leaflet also needs to be readily available to likely buyers; this will affect your distribution decisions.

DISTRIBUTION

The distribution method you choose will have implications for the design of the leaflet. If, for example, it is being mailed, it is useful if the leaflet fits a standard sized envelope; if it is a loose insert in a magazine, it must suit the publication's own requirements. Distribution is discussed in more detail on pp. 114–15.

BUDGET

A leaflet can range from a cheap one-third 8½" x 11" size piece of thin paper right up to a full-color multipage heavyweight booklet. So what should you choose? The amount you need to spend will be dictated by several factors:

- the style of document necessary to compete effectively
- the size of document needed to accommodate the amount of information you need to impart
- the number of leaflets you need to print.

The overall cost should be in relation to the value of whatever you are selling and the likely sales the leaflet will generate. This is a complex mix. A useful starting point is to look at what your competitors are producing.

Deciding on the Look of Your Leaflet

Many decisions need to be made when designing and putting together a leaflet or a brochure, from the look of it to the amount of information contained within it. For examples of leaflet design, see pp. 110–11.

USING COLOR

An early decision is whether or not a leaflet needs to be in color. Full color is expensive, but is justified if the product or service you are offering needs color to show its features; for example, a wallpaper leaflet or a brochure of knitwear would not work effectively in

CASE STUDY: Producing a Targeted Leaflet

MICHAEL, WHO RAN a small electronics business, wanted to create a leaflet aimed at small hotels and guest houses to promote his new energy-saving switch. The switch prevented guests from running lights and air-conditioning in their rooms when they were out. The key factors to emphasize in the leaflet were the cost savings and likely payback time for the switches. As the hoteliers would not know Michael's company, the leaflet also had to convey credibility, so he added details of his technical qualifications, the number of years the business had been established, and the ISO standards the switches met. To further establish credibility, he mentioned the name of a prestigious hotel that had recently purchased several switches to test, and he included a captioned photo of the device in use there. He had a special offer of a ten percent discount for installations made before the summer tourist season. Distribution of the leaflet would be principally by direct mail, and he would also create a downloadable version on his website.

anything other than full color. Another reason for using full color may be to compete head-on with a rival's color brochure. A cheaper alternative to full color might be the use of two or even three colors. This can be quite effective, especially if part of the leaflet, such as large heading letters or a decorative band, is printed in a screened color that lightens the tone and gives the effect of another color. A limited use of color can look more sophisticated than bold colors. You might also consider using full color in only part of a leaflet, or you might try using colored paper – although that is quite tricky to do well.

Choosing the Size and Tone

The next decision to be made is the leaflet's dimensions and number of pages. These aspects are principally a function of the amount of information you need to convey, the intended method of distribution, and the size of your budget. Several standard sizes are: 8½" x 11", 8½" x 11" folded in two or three, 4¼" x 5½", and one-third 8½" x 11". Any of these sizes can be printed on one or both sides. Of course, they need not be exactly a standard size, but such standardization is usually economical. The size might also be constrained by the method of distribution.

Selecting the Paper

The thickness and quality of the paper used is an important factor, as the recipient will handle the leaflet, rather than simply looking at it. A thin or coarse paper feels cheap, while a stiff, smooth paper gives a feeling of quality. Paper weights are expressed in pounds; typically 65 lb. is a standard, medium weight paper for a leaflet, while 90 lb. is quite stiff. The finish to the paper can be matte or glossy.

A small, but not insignificant, aspect to watch is that some "white" papers are in fact quite yellow. A printer will usually show you a paper sample that is a blank sheet. It is very difficult to assess how such a paper will look and feel when it is printed. Ask if the printer has an example of that paper printed up, or find someone else's leaflet that uses a paper you like, and ask the printer to match it. Instead of (or in addition to) using colored ink, you might choose to print the leaflet on a colored, patterned, or textured paper. This requires some caution to do effectively. A bright red, blue, or yellow paper may look rather garish, even cheap, but a more subtle tone, such as light grey or a creamy paper, could give a more upmarket look in the right context. A fashion- or very consumer-orientated leaflet can afford to be more flamboyant than a trade-orientated leaflet.

Including the Right Information

The same rules apply as when designing display advertisements (see pp. 90–96), except that in a leaflet you have the space to say and show more as required. Remember to sell the benefits and to emphasize the unique selling

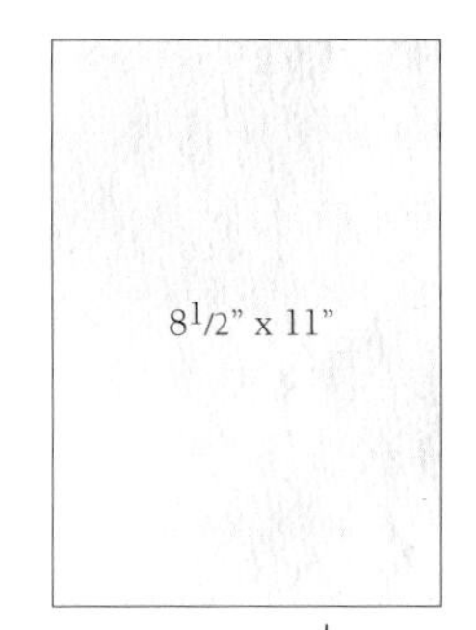

Paper Sizes

There is a huge choice of standard paper sizes. Choose one that suits the amount of space you will need to get your message across, and that is also convenient to distribute.

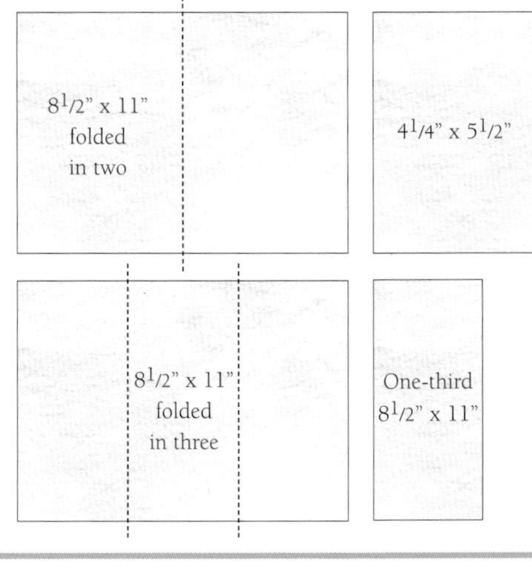

proposition of your business. Include a "call for action," as you want a reaction to your leaflet. The most fertile moment is when the person is actually reading the leaflet; aim to motivate them to take the next step there and then because, if they put the leaflet down, the chances are they will not pick it up again.

Keep in mind your target customers, who will be thinking "what's in this for me?" Avoid text that is too concerned about stating how wonderful your business or its products and services are. Another important point to watch is that, unlike an advertisement, which has a relatively short life, a leaflet is often required to last much longer. You may still want to be able to distribute a leaflet a year or more after it was printed. You therefore need to avoid incorporating details that are going to date the text quickly. Prices, in particular, are likely to change over a relatively short time, so many businesses print a separate price list to accompany their leaflet, usually in one color and on cheaper paper.

If some of your customers are located abroad and speak a different language, consider translating at least part of the leaflet into their language. This is obviously cheaper than printing two completely different leaflets.

COMMON ERRORS WHEN CREATING A LEAFLET OR BROCHURE

1. Being concerned with the looks, but forgetting the sales objectives.
2. Giving the printer poor artwork and expecting excellent results.
3. Forgetting to emphasize the unique selling proposition (USP) of your business.
4. Omitting (or hiding) prices if they are critical to the reader's decision-making.
5. Printing too many leaflets with details that date too quickly.
6. Giving insufficient thought to how the leaflet should best be distributed.
7. Using text on the leaflet that is too small to read easily.
8. Including poor-quality or inappropriate illustrations.
9. Allowing a fussy or complex design to distract from the key selling message.
10. Forgetting to monitor the response (as for any other type of advertisement).

TYPEFACES AND TYPESETTING

The different typefaces or fonts that you choose for the lettering can set the tone for a leaflet. Typefaces are usually available in bold, italic, and sometimes in outline forms, and can be printed in different sizes (the point size). Avoid typefaces that look dated and those that are very difficult to read. It is usually a good idea to use just one or two typefaces for a leaflet, since more can look muddled and distracting. Take time to experiment with different combinations to see which look best.

COMMON TYPEFACES

The choice of a typeface is subjective and related to image. The main decider is that it should be easy to read.

Times

A classic, elegant font that gives the impression of maturity

Times Bold

Bold type is good for picking out headings and key points

Times Italic

Large blocks of italics may be hard to read

Helvetica

A sans serif face is easy to read and looks modern

Helvetica Light

Helvetica Italic

A Poorly Designed Leaflet

This sample leaflet to promote patio furniture suffers from too much text that is hard to read. The design is muddled and distracting, likely to put off rather than attract the potential purchaser.

Company name is used as the headline; this is unlikely to mean much to customers and says little about the subject of the leaflet

As much text space is used for other items as for the furniture; this detracts from the focus of the leaflet, making it too general

Initial text about patio furniture is repetitive and does not include information on prices

A mixture of different typefaces is used; this can detract from the overall coherence of the leaflet's design

Text is very small and reversed out of a black background, making it hard to read in large blocks

Photograph is dominated by plants rather than the furniture and does not include people

Business name and phone number are stated, but the address is omitted – this is a mistake in a leaflet meant to persuade customers to visit the garden center

Call for action is omitted in favor of a caption that repeats the text above; caption is hard to read on dark background of the picture

Designing a Leaflet

For a leaflet to achieve maximum effect, its overall design needs to be eye-catching and appropriate to the target customer and to the product or service being featured. If you are inexperienced in design, a good way to start is to look at other people's leaflets (not only in your own industry) and build up your views about which designs you like best and why you feel that they work. Incorporate in your own leaflet those parts that you like and find most effective, but ensure that the different elements work together as a whole and look balanced. Try to avoid a layout that is either difficult for the customer to follow or hard to read. Long chunks of text can be included, but only if the text is all necessary to the reader; adding headings to direct the reader can help to make the text more accessible.

Consider the final look of the leaflet: if it is to be folded, or consists of more than one sheet, you will need to design a front and

A Better-Designed Leaflet

This sample leaflet to promote patio furniture in the spring attracts attention by offering a benefit. Information follows about the range of furniture available, prices, and contact details.

MAKE THE MOST OF SUMMER
WITH YOUR FAMILY & FRIENDS

PATIO FURNITURE – HUGE STOCK

We can now offer a complete choice of attractive, comfortable, and yet affordable patio furniture in pine, aluminum, or plastic. Elegantly designed and carefully made to be enjoyed and admired. Chairs from $19.95, tables from $49.95.

SPECIAL OFFER 20% DISCOUNT
If you bring this leaflet and buy at least one table and four chairs before May 31.

We also stock a full range of pots, plants, potting soils, tools, seed, hoses, fertilizers, gravel, seedling trays, sprays, garden sheds........

John Smith Garden Center
Rose Street, Any Town Tel: 555-6789
www. ... .com

FOR THE GREENEST OF GARDENS

Headline promises a benefit and may therefore catch the attention of more prospective customers than a specific heading such as "Patio Furniture"

Professional photograph is included, showing furniture clearly and in context, with people

Introductory comment clearly explains what is being offered

Main part elaborates on the offer. Enough information is given to arouse interest, and prices are given

Text is arranged in well-spaced blocks so that it is easy to read

Call for action by offering an incentive

Additional items in range are mentioned, but should only be included if there is space

Business name and contact details are clearly stated but not unnecessarily prominent

Business slogan is an optional extra

perhaps a back cover. Bear in mind, if you are producing a folded leaflet, that when borders or edges of solid black or dark colors are folded over, the white base paper usually shows through at the fold line, which can look a little unsightly.

Where a leaflet consists of several sheets, they may need to be stapled together. This is best done by the printer, who can carry out this procedure neatly and mechanically. As a final touch, the leaflet could be varnished or laminated by the printer to give a high-gloss finish. These finishes are quite expensive, but look good and resist finger marks, which are a particular problem if your leaflet has large, solid areas of black or other dark colors.

You may wish to use a professional graphic designer to help you with your leaflet. If so, prepare a detailed written brief that includes all the key details you require. Ask to see rough versions of several suggested designs before agreeing to the final layout.

Using Photographs

Photographs make a huge difference to a leaflet and often bring a product to life. A good photograph is in sharp focus, with the subject well positioned and large enough so that the viewer can see the details that are relevant. Photos should ideally indicate a sense of scale; having people in the scene is one way to achieve this. We tend to respond most to photos showing people, rather than inanimate objects, and a common error with amateur leaflets is that their illustrations lack people. However, people are not appropriate for every product; use your own judgment (and ask others' opinions) about what is most appealing.

If you are using photographs in your leaflets, be careful if you use pictures of your staff and/or your customers. Obtain their permission, ideally in writing, beforehand, and, since they are unlikely to be models, take great care to get the right feel to the finished shot. You are likely to need to take a large number of shots to achieve a happy, positive look – or the facial expression that is relevant in the context. If in any doubt, use models and a professional photographer, since a second-rate photo can completely spoil an otherwise excellent leaflet. Due to the issue of copyright, ask the photographer to sign a release form (and ask any models to do so, too); the photographer will usually have such forms available. This permits you to use the photographs for whatever purpose you have specified on the form.

If you are including a black-and-white image, the original can be in black and white or in color. In some leaflets black-and-white photos appear gray, flat, and gloomy. This can be for a number of technical reasons, such as the quality of paper used, or the way in which the artwork is prepared prior to printing; or it might simply reflect the quality of the initial photo. Ask to see a proof from the printer to check how a printed photograph looks.

For general photographs you can use photo libraries, where you pay a fee for using a professionally taken photograph. Although these photographs will not show your business or product, they can be useful scene-setters in a leaflet.

Using Illustrations

Illustrations can be useful to explain a process or to illustrate a feature that does not photograph clearly. Such illustrations can be a powerful element of your leaflet provided that they are done professionally. You can choose whether to have them computer-generated or created in more traditional media by an illustrator. As with photographs, request a proof from the printer to check the final clarity and quality.

Choosing a Photograph

This unusual photograph would make an interesting and effective contribution to a leaflet. Its rich colors and bold, graphic use of the subject – bars of soap – make for an appealing image.

Printing Leaflets

Printing costs and the quality of the end result vary enormously, so it is worth shopping around for the best deal and for exactly what you want.

FINDING A PRINTER

For a relatively simple one- or two-color leaflet, instant-print shops are worth approaching for a quote. Full-color (four-color) printing is more specialized and may require the services of a larger printer – see the Yellow Pages, or similar local business directories. For some simple black-and-white leaflets without images, such as price lists, a quick and cheap printing method is to run out copies as needed on a photocopier.

To assess a printer's capabilities, ask to see other leaflets they have printed recently. For an accurate quotation, supply the following details:

- dimensions of the leaflet you propose
- number of pages (if more than one)
- requirement for printing on one or both sides of the leaflet
- number of colors
- type of paper
- amount of typesetting required (if any)
- number of photos (if any)
- finishing required (folding, collating, stitching, varnishing, or laminating)
- quantity of leaflets needed.

ON THE PRESSES

For four-color leaflets, you will usually need to use a large professional printing firm for the best results. Unit costs go down as the numbers to be printed increase, but beware of printing too many leaflets that will date quickly.

Check how long it will take for the printers to do the job. Even if you are giving final artwork to the printer, or the leaflet is already laid out and on disk, ask for proofs from the printer and look at them very carefully since mistakes can slip through. Most people, especially when they are busy, read quickly, and the brain does not simply read what it sees but cleverly reads what it thinks it ought to see. Correct any mistakes you spot on a proof using unambiguous notes; it may be wise to request another proof.

MONEY SAVER

If you have suitable software and a printer, use your computer to produce small numbers of leaflets. This has the following advantages: you can customize the leaflets; they can be produced almost immediately; the cost is minimal; and you can update and reprint the leaflets easily.

Choosing a Method of Distribution

Distribution should not be an afterthought, but part of your initial decision to produce a leaflet. Just as with any other advertisement, the success or otherwise of your leaflet should be quantified. See the information on monitoring, pp. 104–5. Some of the different ways leaflets can be distributed are listed here in alphabetical order:

- **AD RESPONSE** A small ad invites the reader to write, phone, fax, or email for a leaflet. The leaflet is usually free. Requesting a leaflet or brochure allows the reader to obtain more information without feeling committed. Monitoring the response to the ad is also easy, as is any follow-up action.
- **CONSUMER SHOWS** These shows allow you the opportunity of distributing a large number of leaflets. Since not everyone is going to be a potential buyer, you might decide to restrict the availability of leaflets on your stand. One technique is to put copies of a small, free leaflet at the front of the stand, for anyone to pick up, and keep your more comprehensive (and expensive) brochure for those who show considerable interest and you think are likely buyers of your product.
- **DIRECT MAIL** Sending out a leaflet by direct mail (see pp. 53–4) is an obvious and effective way of using a leaflet.
- **INSERTS** Leaflets can be enclosed as inserts in a newspaper, magazine, or supplement. Sometimes they are loose and sometimes they are bound in. The practice is particularly common with trade magazines. The cost normally depends on the weight of the leaflet and the quantity you would like distributed. There are usually size or weight restrictions. This is a very cheap way of distributing a leaflet (much cheaper than sending out individually) and can be effective if the publication's readership matches your own market.
- **MAILBOXES** Delivering leaflets direct through mailboxes is another way to distribute leaflets for many consumer-orientated products or services.
- **NORMAL MAILING** This no-cost method of distributing a leaflet involves enclosing it in the same envelope as your normal correspondence (where appropriate), especially your invoices and statements. It makes most sense if the combined weight of the leaflet and other correspondence qualifies for the minimum postage price. In the right context, mailing can be a very effective method of targeted distribution; for the most success, ensure that the person who is likely to open the letter is a decision-maker appropriate to your business.
- **PROMINENT PLACES** There may be places where your target customers congregate and are possibly seeking information. For

example, a hotel lobby (or guest house, bed and breakfast, or tourist information center) is a good place for leaflets aimed at tourists; a travel agent for travelers; and a sports center for sports enthusiasts. Some of these outlets will allow you to leave your leaflets at no charge, while others may charge commission or some other legitimate payment for providing the space. In most cases there will be restrictions on the size of the leaflet (one-third 8½" x 11" size is common), and you must visit regularly to restock the supply of leaflets.

Spread your leaflets about – people do not like to disturb leaflets in neat piles

- **RETAIL COUNTERS** A popular method of displaying leaflets and offering them for distribution in shops is in a point-of-sale dispenser on the counter by the cash register. The different leaflets can give details of special offers, new ranges, and so on. Some of these leaflets may be produced by the retailer, some by their suppliers.
- **STREET** When appropriate to your business, consider handing out leaflets to passers-by in the street. The response rate to this method of distribution is usually very low. Inquire first with the local town council to find out if there are any bylaws against doing this.
- **TRADE SHOWS** If you have a stand at one of these shows, a leaflet is particularly useful because some buyers, depending on the particular show, make their purchasing decisions afterward. Be careful that you (or your staff) are not inadvertently handing out your leaflet to a competitor; most visitors to trade shows wear identity badges, so check just who is walking onto your stand, and be particularly wary if they are not wearing a badge. Before handing them a leaflet, ask who they represent. Note that most trade and consumer show organizers expressly forbid anyone to hand out leaflets except from their own stand.
- **WEBSITE** If you have a website (see pp. 100–04), you could have a downloadable leaflet and order form.

PROMOTION and sales

The interrelated techniques of promotion and sales can be enjoyable and rewarding to learn and to employ. Promotion is the art of stimulating interest in what your business has to offer; selling is the process of clinching a deal – turning a potential customer into an actual customer, and then encouraging repeat business.

WORKING WITH THE MEDIA

Any business, and in particular a small or newish business, has to shout to be heard amid the thousands of other businesses. Too few small businesses make use of the virtually free publicity they can achieve by working closely with the media. An enterprising business can therefore get one step ahead by making full use of this excellent means of promotion. Working with the media (often referred to as PR, or public relations) will take up valuable time but, done well, it will represent one of the best marketing activities you can undertake.

Making the most out of a relationship with the media demands from you a basic understanding of their needs. The media in this context refers to local newspapers and radio, regional and national newspapers, consumer magazines, trade press, and television; their readership or audiences obviously vary in size and makeup, but cover all possible combinations of likely customers, and will certainly include members of your target market.

These different publications and broadcast media consume news at a prodigious rate. They have a continuing requirement for new stories, especially good stories. Every business generates (or can contrive) at least several worthwhile stories every year. In general terms, the elements that combine to make a good story include:

- relevance to a publication's readership or a radio/TV station's audience
- human interest (this is always important to the media)
- connections with other news stories, past or present
- relevant timing (particularly for radio and television stations)
- entertainment value (unusual or humorous items are particularly popular)
- opportunities for good photos or video footage.

CASE STUDY: Trying a Variety of Approaches

MEGAN AND MARIE were both trained fashion designers. They produced an initial sample collection of exclusive nightwear that they wanted to sell to the fashion industry. Although they had limited funds, they knew they had to promote their designs vigorously in a very competitive market dominated by known brands. They decided to put what time and money they could into a concerted PR campaign to cover both trade and consumer publications. They photographed their garments, modeled by fashion students, and sent press releases to many publications, but, disappointingly, their efforts resulted in little editorial coverage. Looking for something extra to catch the eye of the press, they asked a celebrity to model their garments and had some stunning photography done. This time some of the more influential fashion editors mentioned their nightwear and used some of the photos they had supplied and this helped to kick-start their sales.

TALKING TO LOCAL RADIO
Local radio reporters may wish to cover a story relating to topical local issues. Even if you are asked to comment in person on short notice, prepare the points you wish to get across carefully.

Considering Different Media

With such a variety of media available, it is important to select those appropriate to your business – media whose readership or audience includes as closely as possible your target market. The process of deciding which media to approach is similar to that required when selecting which media to use for advertising (see pp. 81–4). However, not every advertising medium carries editorial content, so with PR activity you can afford to cast your net a little wider. The main ways of communicating your potential story to the media are by press releases, press events, and giving interviews, all of which are covered on pp. 121–7. If you are not familiar with any of the publications or other forums you are considering, buy a copy or listen to or watch the broadcasts to see what subjects are covered, the style of reporting, and the use of images.

LOCAL NEWSPAPERS AND RADIO

The inclusion of human interest in a local story is vital. Telling local media that you have just installed a new machine in the local city hall is probably a nonstory; if, however, the installation of the new machine is likely to lead to the recruitment of new staff in an area with high unemployment, that would be more interesting to the paper or radio show. If a new operator of the machine had to go abroad to receive special training, that would make an even better story.

Although the setting up of a new business, launching a new project, taking on more staff, or changing premises may get some news coverage, the key to making the most of the story is to look for a connection with wider events. This could be historical; for instance, if your project was located in a port town and was related, however slightly, to the marine industry, and it is the anniversary of some major nautical event (or if one of your staff is related to a nautical family who have lived in the town for years), you might be able to make something of the links.

An entirely different connection is where you can link your own story with some other more major story that the local media are running. For example, if a major continuing story has been the closing of a large local company, and one of the laid-off workers sets up a business employing several others from the same company, there is an obvious connection to be exploited.

Aim to get editorial coverage for your business – readers trust editorial more than ads

With radio, timing is particularly important; one of the features of radio items is that they appear fresh and relevant, and are reported as soon as they happen. If your story has a wider appeal, there is a chance that it might be picked up by national radio.

As for photographs to accompany a story, local papers will frequently use their own photographers, but there has to be something interesting for them to capture (see the information on photographs on pp. 123–4).

FACT FILE

When dealing with some local papers or trade publications, you may be told that if you do not advertise with them it is unlikely you will get a mention editorially. If you are confronted with such an attitude, consider contacting another publication. Although magazines or newspapers may ask if you would like to advertise, this should not be a precondition for editorial.

NATIONAL/REGIONAL NEWSPAPERS

Since these publications tend to report matters of regional, national, and international interest and importance, for a story to be suitable it would need to be of interest to such an audience. Obviously you may have a story that is of interest to a regional paper but of less interest to a national one. Again, any connection with a major news story that the paper is already running greatly increases the chances of inclusion. Since the readership of these publications can be huge (even regional newspapers can have readerships in excess of a quarter of a million people), just a mention of your business or product can give your promotion quite a boost.

CONSUMER MAGAZINES

Generally, consumer magazines focus more on special interests than news stories and have considerably fewer items in an issue than any newspaper. Individual stories tend to be longer features. Such magazines tend to make greater use of color and, in contrast to newspapers, those people submitting press releases tend to supply a greater proportion of the photographs.

Within their specialist areas, consumer magazines have large readerships and considerable authority, and an editorial mention by them can be very beneficial (provided, of course, their remarks are positive). These magazines are usually working on their feature articles several months ahead of the publication date. A request to their advertising department will usually secure a features list, which outlines all the major up-and-coming articles. Should one of these features relate to your own business, that may be a useful connection. You may then consider submitting a press release in ample time. Particularly if your product is design- or fashion-orientated, consider approaching the magazine for inclusion in their news pages, where they list new products, latest crazes, innovative gadgets, and so on.

It is worthwhile making the effort to meet and speak to some of the editorial staff, since this could pay dividends in the future. If a particular magazine closely follows your own target market, you may also at some stage consider advertising in it as well.

SPECIALIST TRADE PRESS

Trade magazines and newspapers tend to be distributed free or under subscription to a particular trade, and rarely appear on the magazine racks of a newsstand. Almost every trade has these publications and they act as useful disseminators of relevant information.

Many trade buyers base their purchasing decisions on, or are influenced by, what they read in the trade press, so if you have trade customers, a positive editorial mention is very useful. Most trade publications have news sections that thrive on a diet of press releases. Whereas general consumer magazines are read essentially for pleasure, the reader of a trade publication has more serious motives. Thus a story that might be completely inappropriate for a consumer publication may be ideal for the relevant trade magazine or newspaper – such as news of appointments, changes of business address, reports on trade shows, and launches of new products. One important point to remember is that, in some sectors, a product may be unveiled to the industry many months before it is launched to consumers. In that case the product will require two press releases – one for the trade press and a second one several months later for the consumer press.

TELEVISION

Television is an astonishingly pervasive, persuasive medium. Although many small businesses may think TV is too big to be interested in them, this is not necessarily the case. A regional news program or a series on a specialist topic relevant to your business could be very interested in hearing from you. In addition to the normal story requirements outlined on pp. 122–3, it is important to understand that TV is, first and foremost, a visual medium. A story is unlikely to be shown unless it has a strong visual content. With the increasing deregulation of television, and the increase in the number of channels, opportunities for businesses to obtain exposure should increase. Send your press release to a specific program, addressed to the editor.

Writing Press Releases

A press release is an announcement of an event, or a news story sent to the media, usually with the object of gaining publicity. A typical press release package may consist of one, two, or even three parts:

- the typed press release itself
- photograph(s)
- sample(s).

DOS AND DON'TS OF PRESS RELEASES

✓ Do put a date on your press release.

✓ Do explain what the press release is all about in the first sentence.

✓ Do put the key facts first.

✓ Do caption any photographs.

✓ Do provide a contact name.

✓ Do make your business name and address and other contact details clear.

✗ Don't write long press releases.

✗ Don't write boring press releases.

✗ Don't forget to double space the text.

✗ Don't send press releases to inappropriate publications.

✗ Don't send a press release too late for inclusion.

WRITING A BASIC PRESS RELEASE

A press release should be typed, ideally on a letterhead, and clearly entitled "Press Release." Ensure that it is double spaced, since the extra spacing makes it easier to read quickly and allows the journalist to add comments or make changes.

A good descriptive headline is essential, to allow the first recipient to know if the press release is relevant to their department (news, sport, business, features, travel, finance, and so on). Do not try to emulate a catchy newspaper headline style – leave that part to them. The main body of the press release has three parts:

- **INTRODUCTION** This sets the scene and should consist of one short paragraph that encapsulates the whole story.
- **MAIN TEXT** The story is then covered in more detail, with certain aspects tailored or

PRESS RELEASE

Keep your press release short and to the point, but ensure that it includes all the information a journalist will need to write an article.

Headed notepaper is used, with contact details

Since press release ties in with a specific event, it indicates the earliest date for publication

Subject of press release is clearly indicated in heading

Start with the newsworthy event, then put it into context

Quotations and comments are included from relevant people

Indicates that photographs are included

Direct contact details

SPEEDY RALLY CONVERSIONS
8 Main Street, Old Town

PRESS RELEASE
NOT FOR PUBLICATION OR BROADCAST BEFORE MAY 2ND

LAUNCH OF NEW RALLY CAR BUSINESS

At a short ceremony in the downtown today, Bobby Millar, the rally driver, launched a new rally car preparation business called Speedy Rally Conversions.

SRC, located at 8 Main Street, will take high-performance road cars and prepare them to full rally standards. This will entail completely stripping down the original vehicle, strengthening the body shell, and adding a protective roll cage, then carefully installing the new, highly tuned engine, transmission, and running gear.

Jim Smith, the proprietor of the new business and a former amateur rally driver, said: "At present many rally drivers have difficulty in finding the right expertise in this part of the country. I hope SRC will meet their needs."

Bobby Millar, who now lives in the town, said: "I need my rally cars to be prepared to the highest standards and I am confident that SRC has the very people to do this for me in the future."

PHOTOGRAPH attached

FOR MORE INFORMATION:
Contact: Jim Smith
Tel: 765-4321

emphasized to suit the particular publication. Provide quotes from relevant people; if there are useful statistics, include these to help give authority to the article. In terms of the text, do not use superlatives or make extravagant claims (such as "the world's cheapest...") unless they are true. Put the most important points first because, if space in a publication is tight (it usually is), most editors delete from the bottom up. Avoid jargon unless the press release is for a technical or trade publication, and spell out any abbreviations the first time you use them. Finally, ensure that your press release does not read like an advertisement – it should read like a news story. Remember that publications often rewrite the information in their own words, probably abbreviating it greatly in the process.
- **CONCLUSION** A concluding sentence is useful; for example, you could state where and when the items discussed in the news story are available.

One page should suffice for your press release, two only if it is a major story. If you are using two pages, type the word "MORE" at the foot of the first page and "###" at the end of the text on the second page. Include a contact name, phone number, and email address, so that a journalist can get more information; if there is a photo included, add a statement to that effect.

ADDING AN EMBARGO

If you do not want premature publicity, you can use an embargo note on the top of the press release. This is a polite request to the recipient not to print anything on the story until the date (and sometimes a time, too) shown on the press release. Only use an embargo if it is essential.

Note that if you are launching something on a Tuesday, and you send your press release to a Sunday newspaper, the paper may use the story the Sunday before the event, because by the following Sunday it will not be news any more. If you are not including an embargo date, add the date when you send out the press release at the top.

MONEY SAVER

Consider sending out photographs only on request, to save the cost of making duplicates of a print. If you choose to do this, add a comment at the foot of your press release stating that black-and-white/color prints are available.

FACT FILE

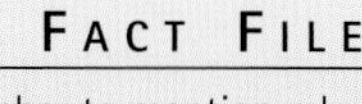

Remember to mention relevant staff in your press releases. This can add a human dimension to your story and may boost staff morale. Before you send the press release, ask the relevant staff if they are happy for their names to appear – some may have personal reasons for not wanting to be mentioned.

SENDING PHOTOGRAPHS

If you propose to enclose any photographs, you need to consider a number of aspects. For copyright reasons, obtain permission to use a photograph from the photographer and any models in the shot (see p. 112). If the publication is printed mainly in black and white, send black-and-white prints or transparencies; if most of its photos are in color, send color prints or transparencies.

Ensure that each photograph or transparency is captioned, preferably by typing the caption on a piece of paper or self-adhesive label, and sticking it to the rear of the photo or the edge of the transparency. The caption should include your business name and address in case the photos accidentally become separated from your press release. Whenever photos are sent by mail, ensure that they are in cardboard-backed envelopes and marked "Photos – Please Do Not Bend." Attach the photos to the press release by a paper clip.

Generally, publications do not return photos, but if the photos you are sending are rare, valuable, or you just want them back, include a note requesting their return. You might also enclose a stamped self-addressed envelope.

SENDING SAMPLES

Certain businesses may be able to send a sample or samples of their products with the press release. This can be very effective, provided the sample is quite small, of relatively low value, and helps the recipient to understand the product. If you are sending a sample that has not been requested, it is not really acceptable to ask for it back, as this is a nuisance for the recipient.

Package samples carefully and label them clearly with the name and contact details of your business

Judging the Timing of Press Releases

Although the media's own deadlines are paramount (because if your story arrives late it cannot be used) there are other aspects of timing that need to be considered to get the most impact from your story:

- **THICK AND THIN ISSUES** Publications tend to have some thicker and some thinner issues. For example, some daily newspapers are thinner on Mondays, while business publications tend to be thinner in the summer months. Obviously, the chances of getting some exposure are higher when the publication is hungrier for news, although its readership may be fewer than normal.
- **CRISES** If there is a major regional or national crisis or disaster the day after you mailed out your press release, your story is unlikely to be used because there will not be enough space in the publication. This is one problem you cannot plan for.
- **TIME OF DAY** Check deadlines carefully – even the time of day by which your press release needs to arrive is important if you are trying to catch a specific radio or television program (such as local news), or weekly newspapers, evening papers, and so on.
- **BEFORE OR AFTER** Should you send out a press release before or after an event? It obviously depends on the circumstances but, if in doubt, send out one before and a second (different) one afterward, thereby providing two opportunities for the media to use the story.
- **FOLLOW UP** If the publication you are dealing with is a local newspaper or a specialist publication and you have had some contact with the editorial staff, you might try phoning them a few days after you send the press release. This is to check that they received it, to ask if they want any other information, and to inquire if they are likely to use the story. This approach may be regarded as slightly pushy, so you may be rebuffed. It is unlikely that you will achieve much by contacting a more major publication.

Ensuring Your Press Release Is Used

As you gain experience in dealing with the media, you might like to try a variety of different tactics to give your business an edge over similar small businesses.

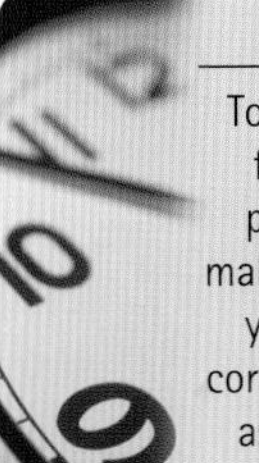

TIME SAVER

To ensure that you meet deadlines for submitting press releases to publications, radio, or television, make a list of all the media to whom you send information, with their corresponding deadlines. Use this list as a reference every time you are planning a new release.

CREATING A STORY

When you do not have any particular story, but want to encourage some media attention, a little ingenuity (a gimmick, even) is required. Although this is an artificial device, it is as useful for the media as it is for you and can provide them with a lighthearted, amusing, or unusual news item. Such items are often visual in their essential content and require thought, planning, and probably some expenditure. Typical items that may gain attention are attempts to break records, stunts, and appearances by celebrities.

EXCLUSIVE STORIES

The media operate in a very competitive environment, and the opportunity of running an exclusive story, provided it is of sufficient quality and interest for their readers or audience, can be attractive. If your story is of that quality, try offering it to the best publication (from your point of view) first. Explain that you will not offer it to anyone else if they use it – this may increase its chances of it being used. The risk with this strategy is that the publication may accept the story but not use it when you expect them to. There is also a risk that a rival publication may not regard you so favorably in the future.

DEADLINES

To complete a story for publication, journalists have to do background research, conduct interviews, and juggle items on several topics at the same time, all within the constraints of pressing deadlines. Presenting your story in a professional manner helps them and significantly increases the chances of your item being published or broadcast.

COMPILING A MAILING LIST

Since you may be sending out regular press releases, at least several times a year, to a number of publications, it will save time in the long run to produce a mailing list. Your main source of information about relevant publications, other than your own knowledge, will be your local library. Look for the various directories that list publications; they will normally give names of editorial staff. A librarian will be able to point you in the right direction.

You are aiming to have a list of all relevant publications, with the names of editors responsible for appropriate features or news. If you are unable to discover the editor's name, address your correspondence simply to "The Editor." You can use a version of your mailing list to record which items you have sent to which publication, and to note when stories were used, building up a picture of publications that are open to your stories and others that may need more persuasion.

USING PR PEOPLE

Big companies know the value to be derived from working with the media. As a small company you can gain benefits from emulating their example.

Many large businesses employ part-time freelance or full-time PR staff whose job is to feed the right media with the right stories at the right time and then gently cajole them into using at least some of the stories. As your business grows, you may consider contracting out your work with the media to a professional PR person rather than trying to do it all yourself. Up to that point, the experience of doing it yourself will enable you to brief a new PR person about your requirements and, equally, to understand what can and cannot be achieved by PR alone.

QUANTITY OR QUALITY?

Some individuals seem to work on the quantity rather than quality principle and send out huge volumes of any press release to anyone and everyone. This is a complete waste of effort. Different types of publications have different needs (a simple example is the trade magazine publishing a story that a consumer magazine would never consider newsworthy). Also, a press release that has had excessively wide exposure becomes a little worn and of less value (particularly with national newspapers, who are always vying for something new and different). Put your efforts into targeting your press releases carefully, just as with any marketing mailshot.

NO GUARANTEES

Even if you submit a well-written and highly relevant story to the right publication in a professional manner and (very importantly) on time, there is no guarantee that the publication will use the story. This can be for any number of good reasons – lack of space is probably the most likely. Try not to be disappointed, but keep on submitting other press releases as appropriate. Assuming that the press release has been sent to a number of media, at least one may use the story.

If you have established some rapport with the editorial team, there is no harm in asking at some later stage why the story was not used – this may provide some useful feedback.

Another aspect relating to press releases that you need to bear in mind is that, although you may wish your item to be published or broadcast on a specific day or week, it may appear at any time, and possibly a long time after it is of much use to you.

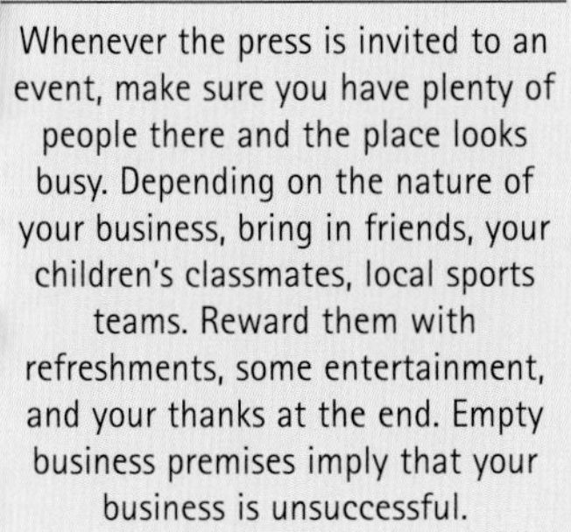

FACT FILE

Whenever the press is invited to an event, make sure you have plenty of people there and the place looks busy. Depending on the nature of your business, bring in friends, your children's classmates, local sports teams. Reward them with refreshments, some entertainment, and your thanks at the end. Empty business premises imply that your business is unsuccessful.

Organizing Press Events

It is unlikely that a small business can command enough attention to justify a press conference but, on a smaller scale, you can hold press days. A press day is when members of the press are invited to your premises or showroom and perhaps given some refreshments while being told all about your company and its business. To make the press day attractive, you probably need to invite a celebrity or VIP. For this type of occasion, you might give each journalist a press pack containing a press release, photo(s), and general company information. The pack may also include current leaflets or brochures, a price list (if you want to make that public), and possibly background notes (even photos) of the partners or directors and key staff. To make it look professional, present the press pack in a folder. Remember to send copies of these press packs to any publication or local radio reporter who did not manage to attend.

If you have something specific (and transient) to photograph, almost certainly involving a celebrity or politician, you could organize a photo opportunity. This could be in isolation or as part of a larger event, such as a press day. The normal practice is to invite the media editor; they will decide whether or not to send a photographer.

Dealing with Press Interviews

Whereas a trade journal may use your press release as the basis of any item they publish about your business, and will generally cover the main points you make, a consumer publication or local radio station often prefers to put their own angle on a story. They may therefore ask to interview you to provide them with more detail. Ask the journalist exactly what the topic of their story is – often your business will be a small part of a story making a wider point. Be aware that the journalist is after a good, interesting story and that promoting your business or even showing it in a good light are not at the top of their list of priorities. Many will ask straightforward questions simply designed to elicit more information from you. Aim to be honest and open in your replies, and to build up a friendly working relationship with them. Others may try to lead you down paths you do not wish to tread; journalists are very skilled at getting information out of people and may have no reservations in what they ask you, however embarrassing or sensitive the issue.

Just as positive press comments can benefit your business, criticism can also damage your business, possibly significantly. Readers (and listeners or viewers) seem to recall negative aspects more easily than positive ones, so that even a minor complaint or criticism can assume importance. You may even be quoted out of context or possibly misquoted, which can be upsetting. Should an article appear that is factually incorrect and, as a result, potentially damaging, contact your lawyer without delay.

THE INTERVIEW

Whether an interview is face to face or over the phone, you have little time for preparation or to consider your reply. If you are on the phone and feel uncomfortable with the direction of questioning, say that you will phone back with a statement. You could also restate what you want to say, confirming that you have said all you would like to on a topic. If you feel you are getting out of your depth, make some excuse and politely withdraw or put down the phone.

Monitoring Your Coverage

Carrying out PR work takes time and money. It should therefore be monitored, just like any other promotional work. Although it may seem to be a major benefit simply having your name in print, try to assess what tangible results it has brought your business. First monitor which publications actually print your story and, where relevant, which broadcast media use the story. This is more difficult than appears at first sight. If you are regularly asking new customers where they heard about your business, they often cannot remember. You may need to visit the library and look through past issues of publications to which you sent press releases to see if they did in fact use the story. Take a photocopy of the article for your records.

Once you have established which media used your press release, try to quantify the response it has brought your business. This may be little more than a good guess, but it will give you some idea of what your PR effort is doing for you. If a publication has used your story, they are more likely to report a later story that follows up on the first, so you can target your future efforts accordingly.

DOS AND DON'TS OF HANDLING A PRESS INTERVIEW

✓ Do give the journalist your own details and the story, in writing.

✓ Do be guarded as to what you say to journalists.

✓ Do try to avoid questions on controversial or political issues.

✓ Do remember that any interview may be severely edited.

✓ Do bring the interview to a polite end if you do not like the questions.

✗ Don't give "off-the-record" comments.

✗ Don't make critical remarks about your competitors.

✗ Don't forget that a journalist may be pursuing their own (less than flattering) story line.

✗ Don't provide an opportunity for a photographer to catch you unprepared.

✗ Don't lose your patience or temper.

PROMOTING SALES

Promotion is a proactive technique, aimed at stimulating sales. There are almost as many ways to promote sales as there are business ideas. Although often cheaper than conventional advertising, promotion still costs in terms of money and time. Promotion techniques depend on the circumstances. For example, promotional work will be needed when a new product or service is launched, especially if it is innovative; a different approach might be required to counter a competitor's activities; and a different approach again to increase market share.

You need to direct your promotion at the part of the distribution chain where you feel the key buying decisions for your products are made. A manufacturer who supplies retailers, for example, should perhaps focus their promotional efforts on the intermediaries (the wholesalers and retailers) rather than on the consumer – although some promotion aimed directly at the consumer is also likely to stimulate sales. Make promotion part of your overall marketing plan along with advertising, PR work, and your sales efforts.

> Collect good promotional ideas from other businesses to give you inspiration

Different Promotional Techniques

Promotional work can be enormously successful in generating business, but in recent decades consumers have been subjected to a flood of promotional gimmicks, so really effective promotion is becoming more and more difficult, especially on a small budget. Business buyers are not quite so saturated as the general public, but are perhaps more cynical.

Businesses use any number of promotional techniques, alone or in combination. When deciding which promotional technique to try, choose one that interests you, since your enthusiasm will help to move it along. Plan out what you wish to achieve with your promotion, and target all your efforts toward your goal. The most important aim is to appeal to your potential customers. It is a good idea to start with one promotion, and add others only if you have the time and energy to do so. In addition to the variety of techniques covered in alphabetical order below, many businesses use the more involved methods of making presentations and discounting goods; these two techniques are covered on pp. 132–7.

BUSINESS LUNCHES

Arranging to see an important customer over a meal can be a useful promotional activity for both service-based businesses and manufacturers. However, although the concept of a business meeting over a meal seems an attractive one at first sight, all too many seem to go on for too long, with too much time spent on unproductive chat, nobody taking any notes, and few real decisions being made. Meals for several people also tend to be expensive.

Bear these points in mind, and if you wish to arrange a business lunch ensure that it has a clear focus and be sure in your mind about the desired outcome. Check that the outcome will justify the expense.

CASE STUDY: Combining Promotional Techniques

DAVE AND MATT were planning to set up a guided tours business. There were rivals offering city tours, but these all used coaches. Dave and Matt planned to offer a cycle-based tour of the central city area: the bikes gave better access to the attractions; they would not be held up in traffic jams; and parking would not be a problem. Research showed their main market to be visitors staying overnight or longer, so they decided to do a presentation to bed-and-breakfast, guest-house, and hotel proprietors, encouraging them to recommend their tours. This approach was backed up by leaflets in the relevant establishments and their new website. They chose the annual tourist convention and put on repeated presentations during the show to familiarize the local tourist industry with their tours. The presentations raised their profile dramatically. They allowed the hotels and guest houses to book tours on commission, hoping that this would lead to a flow of customers.

COMPETITIONS OR RAFFLES

A raffle or competition is likely to be an effective means of promotion to attract people to your exhibition stand or into your store. These are specialized techniques of use mainly to manufacturers and retailers.

Either offer raffle tickets to customers, or distribute competition entry forms to be filled in and returned. The prizes being offered are your products – note that the prize has to be suitably attractive (in practice, this usually means expensive) for it to act as an incentive for people to enter. On a minor level, at a trade show you could invite people to put their business cards into a hat and the one drawn out wins a bottle of champagne. This is a simple technique to build a mailing list. Get the ball rolling by putting in a number of cards you may have already collected. In addition to providing a mailing list, or data about your likely customers, competitions and raffles can bring more customers onto your premises, where they may make more purchases. Note that, where consumers are concerned, there may be legal constraints when running competitions.

COUPONS, GIFT CERTIFICATES, AND LOYALTY CARDS

Coupons are limited-lifespan offers of money off an item – the customer presents the printed coupon to the store or other business and receives a cheaper price as a result. Gift certificates are sold as gift items. Loyalty cards provide rewards for buying at a certain store, often in the form of points that can be exchanged for goods.

These three promotional methods are calculated to generate repeat business and so are suitable for outlets such as grocery stores or tire retailers who have regular customers. They tend to work best with national chains and when accompanied by hefty supporting advertising budgets, and are therefore less likely to be relevant to smaller businesses. Loyalty cards can be used to build up a profile of the buying habits of a customer, which helps you to target promotions more individually; this requires a fairly sophisticated method of recording purchases over time.

FASHION SHOWS

A fashion show is an appropriate forum for displaying all apparel and accessories. The show can be held in-store or at any suitable venue. To be effective, a fashion show needs to attract a

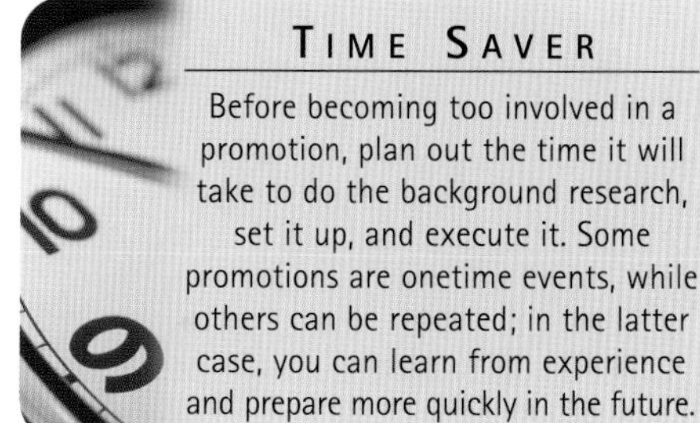

TIME SAVER

Before becoming too involved in a promotion, plan out the time it will take to do the background research, set it up, and execute it. Some promotions are onetime events, while others can be repeated; in the latter case, you can learn from experience and prepare more quickly in the future.

Comparing Different Promotional Ideas

Promotion	Relative Cost	Relative Time
Business Lunches	Low	Low
Competitions/Raffles	Highly variable	Low–medium
Coupons/Gift Certificates/ Loyalty Cards	Highly variable	Medium–high
Fashion Shows	Medium (when shared)	Medium (when shared)
Free Gifts	Highly variable	Low
Free Trials	Low	Low
In-store Demonstrations	Low	Low–medium
Joint Ventures	Highly variable	Medium
Mailshots	Low–medium	Medium
Newsletters	Medium–high	High
Open Days	Medium–high	Medium–high
Samples	Low	Low
Videos and CDs	Medium–high	High

large enough audience of potential buyers (businesses or consumers). Shows are usually held at the start of the fashion season or at peak buying times.

Putting on such a show demands time and organization. You need to arrange experienced models, proper sound and lighting, a catwalk, stage props, professional choreography, rehearsals, ticket sales (or ticket distribution, if free), and good promotion of the event itself. To make a bigger and more attractive show, several firms often team up; that works well, assuming they are not in competition with one another. Although your objective is to sell, the audience needs to be entertained rather than just to be shown an endless parade of garments. Use a master of ceremonies to describe the garments and accessories as they are modelled. Place a sales leaflet on each seat before the guests arrive. A video of the event (or of a rehearsal) can be used later to promote sales in your own showroom or shop.

Free Gifts

Used widely to promote sales, especially with industry buyers, free gifts differ from samples in that they are not necessarily examples of your own products. Free gifts are usually distributed at some special event, such as a trade show or launch ceremony. Such gifts can be effective but need to be chosen carefully with the following guidelines in mind:

- Choose an item that will be used frequently by potential buyers, and not be put straight in the garbage.
- Ensure that the item carries your business name and, space permitting, a selling message and contact information, just like any other advertisement.
- A gift should, wherever possible, have a connection with your business's product or service, however slight.
- A gift should be durable, with a lifetime of at least several months.

Note that there are tax implications with business gifts; consult an accountant.

FREE TRIALS

One way of promoting and demonstrating a product is to offer a potential customer a free trial. This promotional technique is appropriate for quite a range of products, particularly high-value, durable items, such as cars and business machines, and low-value, repeat-purchase items, such as foods, toiletries, and other consumable goods.

Since providing something for free will cost you money, it is vital to ensure that the uptake of the free trial will be by someone who is highly likely to buy. This requires very precise targeting to ensure that the person needs the item and can afford it. You or your salespeople may need to ask some direct questions before making the offer.

IN-STORE DEMONSTRATIONS

If you are offering a consumer service or product, the opportunity of doing a demonstration in a large store should not be missed. There has to be something in it for the store, too – they may be selling your product in one department. If the product is new, an in-store demo can give you valuable market feedback. Make the demonstration as enthusiastic as possible – for inspiration, visit any street market to see how experienced traders get the attention of passers-by. Ensure that the demonstrator knows your product thoroughly, so that they can explain or demonstrate all its features in response to questions. Hiring a celebrity to help may make the demonstration more attractive; make the most of this by publicizing the event with small advertisements and a press release.

JOINT VENTURES

Joining up with other businesses can be beneficial for all concerned. You may arrange to distribute each others' leaflets or refer customers to one another if the businesses are complementary. For example, a retailer selling wedding dresses may team up with another operating limousines for hire. In some cases, a small business can ride on the back of a larger noncompetitor if an arrangement can be found that benefits both parties.

MAILSHOTS

Probably one of the most common promotional techniques is the simple mailshot. A mailshot can be used for selling to both consumer and business customers. It may consist of a personalized letter or a letter introducing an enclosed brochure or sample. Usually the most effective method is the carefully thought-out letter, where the address and salutation are personalized and the content is specific to the recipient (see pp. 53–5).

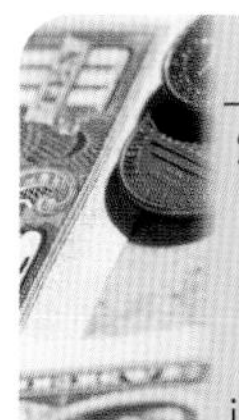

MONEY SAVER

Spend as little money as possible on your promotional effort to achieve your objective. As with advertising, the response to any promotion in terms of increased sales and profits is not proportional or even related to the amount you spend on the promotion.

NEWSLETTERS

A sophisticated promotional tool, the newsletter is best used if you have a wide range of products or services to write about and your customers are so diverse that communicating by other means is difficult. Your newsletter loses credibility if it reads like one long advertisement; instead, ensure that it covers other people and other businesses (possibly your customers). Include interesting feature articles and appropriate news, with the occasional reference to your own products or services.

The frequency of the newsletter will be ruled by cost and, to a lesser degree, by the amount of time-sensitive information you wish to convey – such as special offers for a limited period, new products, or new services. Quarterly is a good starting point, since a less frequent newsletter starts to lose continuity. Distribution is usually by mail; you could save money by sending it out with another, regular item of mail, such as a statement.

Arrange presentation lighting so that it is not too dark, allowing people to write notes

OPEN DAYS

If you have an office, workshop, or craft studio that is attractive and interesting, you might consider holding an open day. The day can be for invited guests (selected customers and buyers) or made more widely accessible to the general public. Make certain that the event is well publicized beforehand, there is plenty to see and do on the day, refreshments are available, staff are fully briefed as to how they should handle visitors, and security is arranged (to prevent theft). It takes a lot of organization to make an open day successful. Have alternative programs for both good and bad weather if necessary, and check that your insurance covers you for having visitors on the premises. If you plan to make sales at the open day, this should not be too dominant a part of the day – the main objective is to offer your customers an enjoyable experience for free.

SAMPLES

Providing samples can be effective where the recipient of the free sample is a decision maker with the potential to place repeat orders, or an opinion leader, such as a trade publication's editor, who would not place an order themselves, but who can influence others who may. Include with your sample a cover letter with a description of the product and its benefits, including prices. Follow up with a phone call a week or so later.

VIDEOS AND CDs

If you need to convey a complex visual message or demonstrate something working, a videotape or short video clips on a CD-ROM may be good methods to consider. The latter could have an interactive aspect and a FAQ (Frequently Asked Questions) section, too. Avoid showing an obviously amateur video or one that runs for too long. Several minutes is ideal; anything over 10 or 15 minutes is probably too long for most sales situations. Neither a video nor a CD-ROM is cheap to produce. Videos and CD-ROMs can be sent out to those who respond to an advertisement, either for free or for a nominal charge that could be deducted from a customer's first order. Alternatively, they could be sent free to a carefully selected mailing list.

Giving Presentations

Holding a presentation can be very profitable indeed if you are addressing the right people – potential buyers – and you can speak convincingly or arrange for a suitable professional speaker. At a presentation you can obtain the undivided attention of your audience and give them your sales pitch. These events are an ideal promotional method for many different businesses in the manufacturing and service sectors, and with industry buyers or consumers.

PREPARING FOR A PRESENTATION

To justify the organizational effort and expense involved, you need to ensure your presentation is to the highest standard. The first point to consider is the venue. Find one, perhaps a room in a major hotel, of the right size in a convenient location for your audience. If you are selling to trade buyers, you may be able to set up the talk through a trade association or chamber of commerce. You may even be able to tag on to some other event, such as a trade exhibition; this should reduce your costs.

Consider the logistics of your presentation at an early stage to ensure that you can use the sound or video equipment you want to, and can control lighting or screen windows as needed. Check whether or not you will need a microphone. In an empty room a voice will be

PREPARATION CHECKLIST

Step	Action
Find and book a suitable venue	Check its size, the number of seats, facilities for visual aids, and lighting
Arrange for one or more speakers	Specify time, place, and dress
Brief the speaker(s) on what to speak about and the length of the speech	Produce a script or detailed notes
Prepare visual aids	Work these into the speech at appropriate moments
Issue invitations in good time	Mention refreshments, and provide directions with details of parking and transportation
Organize refreshments	Arrange who will serve them and clear up afterward
Organize for staff to welcome guests and provide assistance with audio-visual equipment as necessary	Make up name tags for staff
Have final rehearsal at the venue	Make changes as required
Design a display table or stall	Arrange who will look after the display at the start and finish of the presentation

easily carried to the back, but in a room full of people the sound is absorbed, and the audience creates background noise too.

Decide who is to speak. You could give the presentation yourself or ask an expert in a certain field or a professional speaker – ideally a combination of both. If you need to make a choice, select your speaker for their speaking abilities more than their in-depth knowledge – they will need to entertain the audience as well as impart information, and can be briefed about the latter. Consider using more than one speaker, if your budget and the occasion allows, to give variety and provide interest for the audience. Decide on the details of the content and length of the speech and, if necessary, brief the speaker(s).

Work out the visuals, annotating the script as to where the visuals should change. Visual aids (such as slides, an overhead projector, video, computer visuals, and a flip chart) hold the audience's attention, but only if they run smoothly. Combinations of visual aids are effective, but include only as many as are useful and can be comfortably handled. Include photos, illustrations, and graphs, and ensure they complement the speech rather than simply repeat the same content.

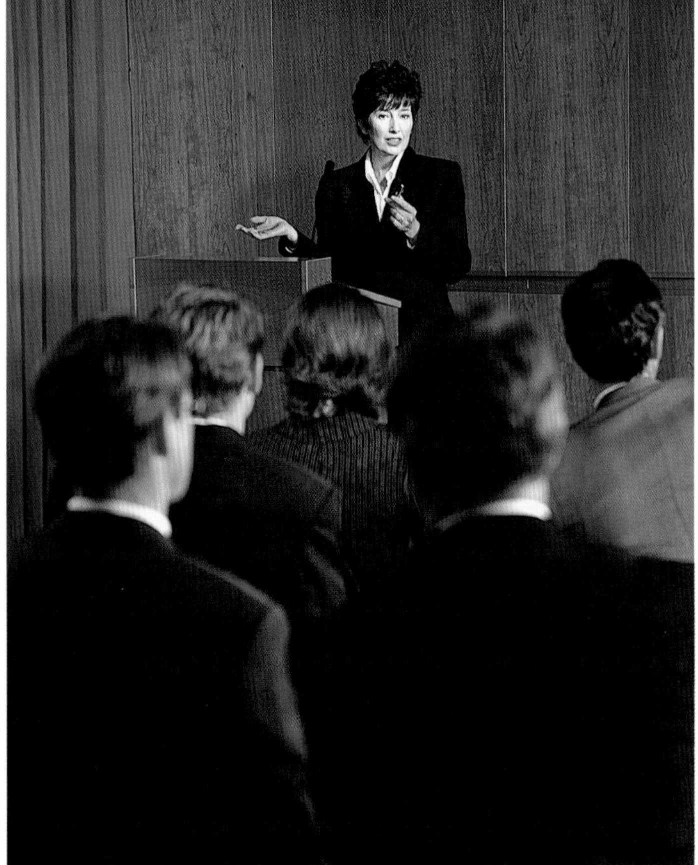
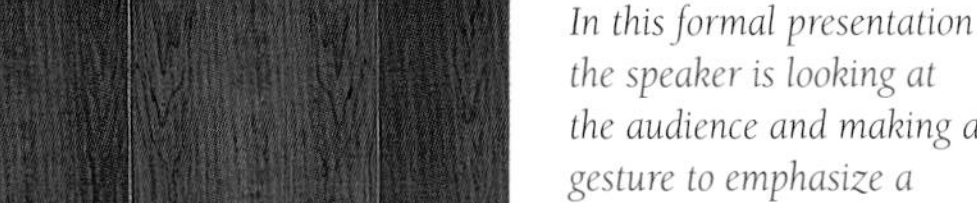

PRESENTING

In this formal presentation the speaker is looking at the audience and making a gesture to emphasize a point. Although she is using a lectern, a hand-held microphone gives her some freedom to move about.

Compile a list of your likely buyers (or use your existing mailing list, if you have one) and send out invitations (with RSVP) in plenty of time. If you wish to provide refreshments – which often act as a good incentive – consider who will provide them, serve them, and clean up afterward. Budget permitting, hiring outside caterers may be the answer. Think about the timing – it is usually best to serve refreshments after a talk.

Arrange for your staff or helpers to welcome the guests and make sure that the event runs smoothly. They may also need to run any display stand you have at the venue, giving information, photos, or samples of your products or services. Whether or not to sell goods at a presentation depends on the circumstances. For example, with a presentation selling direct to the public, the audience would expect to be able to buy on the spot. At a presentation to other businesses, the audience is unlikely to expect to buy there and then – imparting information is the main aim. If in any doubt, do not sell on the day.

Allow time after each speaker for the audience to ask questions

Hold a full rehearsal at the venue long enough in advance so that you can make changes should they be necessary.

TIPS FOR SPEAKING

The talk should be written out in whatever form is most useful (as notes on cards or as a script, for example), rehearsed on colleagues, and refined as necessary. If you are giving the speech yourself, and are not a very experienced speaker, it may be best to have a full script to fall back on. A good basic structure is the chronological one, starting with the background of the business (or the particular product or service), how it came about, and then coming up to the present day, explaining what the business can offer, and selling the benefits. In the context of a sales presentation, each talk should be five to 15 minutes long.

If you have hired a professional speaker, they will know how to hold an audience. If you are speaking yourself, use your rehearsals to perfect your technique. Remember not to speak too quickly, and to pause now and then, look up, and make eye contact. Ideally, try to look at the audience in every direction at some point – you are communicating with each person as an individual, not just with an anonymous assembled throng. Try smiling, too. Speak as if you are addressing someone at the rear of the room. Avoid distracting movements, but pause and make gestures to emphasize key points in the speech.

THE PRESENTATION

Arrive in plenty of time to sort out the inevitable last-minute hitches. Being at the venue early may also help to calm the nerves. Have a checklist to ensure that everything is as planned.

Try to start the presentation on time, even if people are still slipping into the room or have not yet arrived. Depending on the audience and the occasion, the presentation can either be very formal or more relaxed. One way to relax the event is for the speaker to remove their jacket at the start of the talk and to stand immediately in front of the audience, rather than behind a lectern or desk.

To keep the speaker from overrunning their time, arrange a system, such as a signal from a colleague, when the speaker should be coming to a close. Then invite questions. Members of the audience are often reluctant to ask the first question. To avoid an embarrassing silence, talk to a couple of friends in the audience beforehand and prime them to start the ball rolling. Often the acoustics mean that the audience cannot hear a question from another member of the audience. To counteract this, the speaker should repeat a question before answering it. If you run out of time, offer people the opportunity to approach the speaker(s) at the very end to ask any further questions.

Discounting and Sales

Discounting can be a sensitive issue. Usually the reasons for discounting are to encourage sales or early payment. Discounts may be permanent for certain categories of customer, or the discounts may be temporary and available to all customers, in which case they are more usually called a sale, especially in a retail context. Permanent discounts include those openly quoted for special-category buyers, such as senior citizens or students. There are also commercially confidential discounts that are offered to industry buyers.

There are legal constraints on how you indicate the price of discounted or sale goods (see pp. 178–80). Note that continuous or regular discounting or sales teach your customers bad habits. If you always have a sale at a certain time of the year, they may delay their purchasing until then. A more insidious aspect is that regular discounting reduces the perceived correct market price for your product or service, so your normal prices begin to appear expensive.

Give significant discounts to ensure your sale succeeds

Using Temporary Discounts

The circumstances under which temporary discounting can be used vary widely. They include the following:

- **Launching a New Product or Service** You might offer a "come and try it" discount to encourage early sales.
- **Disposing of Old Inventory** This allows space for new inventory, helps cash flow, and may catch some customers before the inventory is too obsolete to be sold at all.
- **Selling Perishable Inventory** You may be able to discount old inventory as it approaches the end of its shelf life.
- **Matching or Undercutting a Competitor** This needs to be done with extreme caution, since it diminishes your precious margins and may trigger a price war (see p. 173).
- **Getting Early Payment** When dealing with business customers who expect credit, a small discount (such as one to 2.5 percent) can be offered if payment is made within a specified period (such as seven to 30 days).
- **Increasing Sales** You may discount simply to increase sales in order to remedy a cash flow problem.
- **Loss Leaders** A loss leader is a product that is sold at a loss by the retailer to entice customers to buy other products. This strategy is commonly used by large supermarkets. Its advantage is that it encourages new customers to come into your store; its disadvantage is obviously the financial loss incurred on each sale of a loss leader.

Clinching a Deal

It is a very common (and successful) tactic to close a sale by offering a discount to a potential customer who is wavering. This is normally done on the basis of "x percent off if you decide here and now." Such discounts can range from five to 15 percent, but may sometimes go further (although this may make a buyer wonder how big a markup the supplier is adding on in the first place to afford such generous discounts). In an industry context, to keep your credibility and to maintain your prices for the future, you need to think of some reason for the discount. This might be an introductory offer to a new buyer, a special promotion on a new product, or a discount for all orders taken during a trade show.

If you have calculated your prices correctly (see pp. 30–37), any discount means reduced profit, so discounts should be given judiciously and for a specific purpose. If you have to discount heavily on a continual basis, it is a clear indicator that something is wrong with

CLEARING OLD INVENTORY

A classic department store sale is designed to clear old or discontinued inventory before the new season's inventory arrives. Clever prepublicity can draw people in for a few "star" bargains; they are then likely to buy other items.

your pricing policy. For example, if intense competition or lack of demand is forcing your prices down, your normal prices may be too high for the market.

HOLDING A SALE

Sales are a specialized form of discounting and were traditionally held to clear old inventory before new inventory arrived. It is still common to have sales in the fashion industry where the previous season's inventory is sold off to make space for the new season's inventory. In the wider retail industry, sales have become a promotional tool and take place frequently, mainly to increase volume sales or market share, or to improve poor sales figures. Their usefulness in generating sales in the consumer market has reduced due to excessive use and some abuse. For example, it has been known for retailers to promote a sale with advertisements claiming that everything in the store is in the sale; in fact, most items may be hardly discounted at all, perhaps by less than one percent.

When selling to industry buyers, sales can still be very effective particularly if they are genuine – perhaps for end-of-line or old model equipment, or display-soiled inventory.

ENCOURAGING BULK BUYING

By offering a discount for buying more than a certain number of a product, you may encourage customers to order a larger quantity than they might do otherwise. This often takes the form of the "three-for-the-price-of-two," "buy ten, get one free," or "x percent extra free in this packet" types of promotion. Used widely by supermarket chains on food and some toiletry lines, it has lost some of its edge. A more sophisticated version is the type of promotion that promises a (desirable) gift if you buy so many.

SELLING TECHNIQUES

Making a sale is the end result of all your marketing initiatives. The selling process involves numerous techniques that can be learned, from a general understanding of how selling works to how to deal with specific selling situations. These techniques apply not only to salespeople, but to everyone who works in your business, especially if they have any contact with customers. The skill of negotiating is an essential component of many sales, and is covered in detail on pp. 157–9. Finally, providing customer service will encourage customers to return, and it builds the reputation of your business.

Professional salespeople refer to all those who might become buyers – the total likely market – as target customers. Those target customers who are prospective buyers are called prospects, and prospects who become buyers are in turn called customers. Customers who are big spenders are often referred to as key accounts.

Stress benefits to arouse interest in potential customers

WHY DO PEOPLE BUY ANYTHING?

People as individuals (or acting for the companies or organizations that employ them) make purchasing decisions for only two reasons: to meet an essential need or to meet a nonessential need (a desire). For individuals, essential needs include basic food, shelter, and clothing, while for businesses they include inventory or raw materials. For meeting an essential need, a purchasing decision has to be made, and the only variables are who to buy from and what quantity to buy. In practice there might also be an element of choice. Since the customer is obliged to make a purchasing decision, the selling technique is principally concerned with encouraging them to buy from your business rather than from another.

By contrast, with nonessential purchases, the potential customer need not buy at all, so the sales effort needs first to attract their interest before attempting to make a sale. Hence, catering for nonessential purchases involves a distinct two-stage selling process. One particular type of nonessential purchasing is when a customer buys on impulse. This is exploited especially in the retail sector, with store layouts and point-of-sale items placed near the cash register.

SELL THE BENEFITS

There is an old saying that "customers buy benefits, not features." What this means is best illustrated by an example. Electronic contactless ignition may be a feature of most new cars, but the purchaser is unlikely to be interested in that feature in itself. They will be much more interested in the benefits this brings, such as easy starting, keeping in tune longer, and so on. In fact, many drivers will not even know (or care about) contactless ignition; all they will know is that their car starts and runs reliably.

A common fault with both service and manufacturing businesses is that they become focused on the technical details and innovative improvements at the development stage of their project, and they may forget that, at the selling stage, the customer is only interested in what benefit those improvements may bring them. However, it is those unique features of your business that give you a competitive edge, so your selling technique can outline the benefits while explaining that they are down to your unique features.

CONSUMER BUYERS

There are significant differences between consumers (the general public) and industry buyers. Once a consumer's basic needs are met, much more complex reasons for buying items come into play.

Thus, purchasing decisions can have more to do with portraying social or financial status than with the intrinsic usefulness of what is bought. Purchasing decisions may also relate to hobbies, sports, or pastimes, or they can reflect an instinct to follow the herd, or conversely to express a sense of individuality. These wide-ranging and complex desires are the result of our upbringing and experiences, but are continually shaped and reshaped by the media and the influence of friends and family. They play a crucial role in terms of nonessential purchasing behavior.

Make buyers feel important when you are selling to them – they are

Price also plays a significant part in consumer purchasing decisions. The cash available to meet a consumer's purchasing wishes is often limited, or requires credit facilities. Consumers also tend to show great concern about relatively small sums of money, sometimes choosing a particular product or service almost solely because of its price.

INDUSTRY BUYERS

The needs of industry buyers are different from those of consumers, and the same person may make decisions on a totally different basis when buying for themselves rather than when they are buying for business purposes.

First and foremost, the industry buyer's primary concern is that whatever they buy must do its job, be delivered or done on time, and give them minimal problems. The quality of the product or service is usually of more importance to them than the price. That is not to say that price is irrelevant, but simply that it often has a lower priority than other factors, provided that it is within the budget allocated.

In comparison with an individual consumer, the buying power of even a small business is considerable, but credit terms will normally be requested, and there is always the risk of a business then defaulting on payment. Other characteristics of selling to certain business buyers are that you may become involved in negotiation or competitive tendering.

FINDING CUSTOMERS

All your marketing efforts are directed at finding, and then selling to, customers. Your various marketing initiatives, including advertisements and other sales promotions, are intended to bring you customers by indirect means. You can also find customers, both other

CASE STUDY: Making Improvements at a Trade Show

BARBARA AND LLOYD had not been in business together for long when they decided to book a stand at a major printing trade exhibition to sell their imported printers. The show itself was very busy, but by the end of the first day they had taken no orders. This was worrying, so that evening they reviewed the day, concluding that their signs were confusing and did not make it clear what they were selling. They also felt that their stand seemed deserted in contrast to others at the show, which was very off-putting. That evening they phoned as many friends as they could and asked them to come to the stand in shifts. This created a more industrious and approachable atmosphere, and led to a marked improvement on the next two days of the show.

businesses and the general public, by more direct means. For example, if you are a service business, you can look for potential customers in listings in trade directories, and then contact them directly and approach them to arrange a sales meeting later.

In some cases, potential customers will find you as a result of a recommendation from another satisfied customer, and they are very likely to become buyers.

COMMUNICATING FOR SALES

METHOD	CHARACTERISTICS
EMAIL	■ Great for short questions and answers, and for acknowledgments ■ Quick to produce, fast to send, and usually elicits a response without delay
LETTER OR FAX	■ More formal than writing an email, so takes more time to compose ■ The recipient may take days, weeks, or longer to reply, so you are left not knowing their reaction to the contents of your correspondence
PHONE CALL	■ A very flexible means of communication for a wide variety of circumstances ■ Limited by not always being able to reach the person you want to talk to, and it is not possible to see reactions
MEETING FACE-TO-FACE	■ Ideal for making a major sale or resolving a difficult problem ■ The best way of showing and explaining your products or services ■ You can see each others' reactions

Improving Communication Skills

Selling involves communicating with other people. Good communication skills are an essential part of an excellent sales technique. Communications cover both written and verbal transactions, and in a sales context include meetings, phone calls, written sales proposals, faxes, and emails. All communications, written or spoken, should be made with the following aims in mind.

- **ACCURACY** Particularly with product claims, prices, and terms.
- **BREVITY** Keep it brief and to the point.
- **CLARITY** Do not confuse the other party.

Communicating is a two-way process, and there are times when listening is perhaps even more important than talking. There are several

EXAMPLES OF BODY LANGUAGE

Five examples of body language are shown here. Body language is not a fixed set of gestures, but needs to be viewed together with what a person is saying.

very good reasons for learning to be an attentive listener.

- You need to discover what the prospect's needs are, and the best way to do this is to listen to what they have to say. You may then have to ask questions to clarify points.
- Whenever you try to sell to someone, they will often erect a defensive barrier. By listening you can work out the best approach to overcome their defenses.
- People generally like to talk, so your prospect will think the better of you if they do most of the talking.

Selling should never be an "us and them" situation, but rather it should be seen as a joint arrangement between you, the seller, and your customer, the buyer. Both parties need each other, and making a sale should form the start of a long-term business relationship, based on mutual trust and respect.

BODY LANGUAGE

Whether you are speaking or listening, your body is giving subconscious signals that express what you are thinking – these signals are known as body language. Even if you do not know how to interpret body language, you may notice that you feel uneasy or sceptical when an individual is speaking – this could be because their body language is contradicting what they are saying.

When selling, it is useful to learn an awareness of other people's body language so that you can see whether their interest or lack of interest is genuine. You can use signals from them to prompt you to use a different technique. Note that not all signals mean the same in every context. Crossed legs are often cited as an example of "closed" body language, but for many people this is simply a comfortable way of sitting. Look at the whole picture when interpreting signals.

This works both ways – learn to be aware of your own body language too. If, for example, you are making an effort to listen, but are in fact fidgeting and doodling, the buyer will realize that your efforts are not genuine.

ENTHUSIASM IS INFECTIOUS

All successful salespeople are enthusiasts, or at least they are able to appear to be enthusiastic. They will be enthusiastic about what they have to sell, their company, and the customer's business. There is no quicker way to kill off a potential buyer's interest than to show a lack of interest. In some contexts, such as retailing or at an exhibition, it may require some effort to maintain this enthusiasm over a long day.

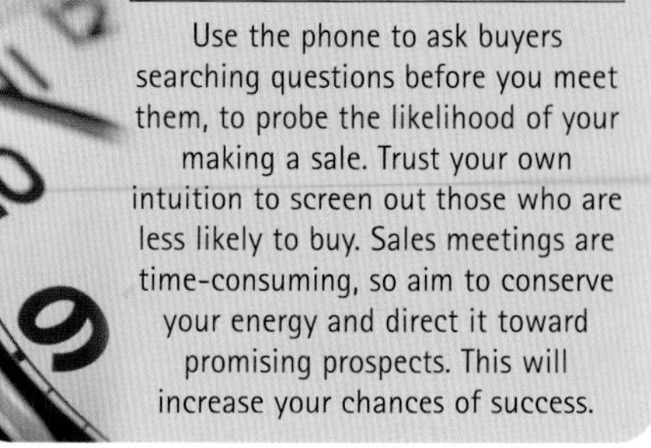

TIME SAVER

Use the phone to ask buyers searching questions before you meet them, to probe the likelihood of your making a sale. Trust your own intuition to screen out those who are less likely to buy. Sales meetings are time-consuming, so aim to conserve your energy and direct it toward promising prospects. This will increase your chances of success.

Selling Face-to-face

For a small business, with a limited number of staff, you should only visit likely prospects. A little research beforehand will reduce the number of wasted visits. The most successful type of face-to-face selling is at a prearranged meeting. Calling without an appointment is known as cold calling. Not surprisingly, most salespeople do not like cold calling. It is hard work, takes a lot of time, has a low success rate, and you can be confronted with some pretty rude people. If cold calling is essential, you should at least first "soften up the target" with an advance mailshot and/or advertising.

GETTING AN APPOINTMENT

To get an appointment with a prospective customer, first find out the name of the person who has the buying authority. You can usually do this by phoning the business concerned, explaining that you wish to write to the buyer, and asking for the buyer's name. Occasionally, you will be put directly through to the buyer even though this is not what you asked for, so be prepared for this possibility. Once you have the buyer's name, write a letter enclosing relevant sales information. In the letter, state that you will phone to discuss the contents in about a week's time (if you ask the buyer to call you, you will rarely get a response).

When telephoning the buyer to make an appointment, be positive and friendly, but not pushy. Some buyers will be eager to see you; others will refuse directly; others may simply avoid you. Try a few times, and if you are not successful, try another business, and make a note to approach the original buyer again in a few months to see if their needs have changed.

PREPARING FOR A MEETING

To ensure as successful an outcome as possible, prepare yourself carefully before you set out. Your sales material is a key element in face-to-face selling. It may consist of your business card, samples, price list, brochures, customer record card, order form, calculator, and possibly a laptop computer if you need to produce an estimate or quotation. A pen and notepad are required, too. Ensure you know your sales material backward and forward – it is not good enough to have to search through a brochure every time a question is asked. Some of this information may be held on a laptop; this can be useful, provided you can find the information quickly and you have the facility to print out any material the prospective customer might request.

If you do not have a good brochure, and it is not possible to carry samples due to their size, a very effective sales tool is a photo album or loose-leaf folder with clear pockets. Each pocket can contain an $8^{1/2}$" x 11" piece of blank paper onto which photos are afixed, accompanied by a typed description. The photos can illustrate your premises and staff (to give more credibility to your operation), your products, and, where possible, the product (or service) in use by other customers. The album can also contain letters of recommendation (testimonials), certificates of technical competence, newspaper cuttings, membership of trade association certificates, and so on. Of course you need not show every page to every customer. This information could also be held on your laptop.

Before you set out, read all the information you have regarding the prospective customer you are about to meet, and look at any records of previous contact with them. If you have not met the prospect before, they will assess you and your business in a matter of moments on the basis of your appearance and dress. Stylishness, neatness, and a style of clothing appropriate to the situation is called for – in most businesses, a fairly conservative style of dress is the norm.

Whether you are traveling by public transportation or by car, plan your route carefully, allowing for plenty of time to reach your destination. If you are on public transportation, check how you will reach the prospect's office from the train or subway station.

Handling the Sales Meeting

Give yourself a few moments before the meeting to compose yourself, catch your breath if you have been hurrying, and focus on the meeting. If you are nervous, run over what you know about the customer and remind yourself that you have an excellent product or service to sell. If you are going to be late for an appointment, phone and let them know.

On meeting the "prospect," give a firm handshake and hand over your business card if you have not met before. If you are not sure of the prospect's full name and job title, ask for their business card. Normal business etiquette usually requires an exchange of pleasantries before getting down to business. It is useful to have something sensible and noncontentious to talk about for a few minutes, such as the weather or your journey.

Then you will need to start the meeting in earnest. It is worthwhile having an idea of what you are going to say, in the form of a short pre-planned speech that explains very quickly what you have to offer and promises some exciting benefits for the buyer. You have only a minute or two to catch the prospect's interest. If the buyer shows an inclination to talk first, listen

MEETING THE PROSPECT

First impressions are vital in a sales context. Approach the buyer confidently, make eye contact, and shake their hand. Exchange business cards if you have not met them before.

carefully. The most important goal of the first phase of the selling meeting is for you to understand exactly what the buyer is looking for. You should then be able to tailor the next part of your presentation to their needs, explaining how your product or service can meet their requirements. A common mistake is to launch into a long sales pitch only to discover that what you are trying to sell does not meet the buyer's needs.

Encourage the prospect to handle any samples you have

Once you know what the buyer wants, and they have shown some interest, you can move on to showing your catalog or samples. If possible, try to demonstrate your product, since this can be both appealing and persuasive. As the meeting develops, try asking more open questions to show your interest in the prospect (and their company, if applicable), and help you to learn more too. You may find out about other possible opportunities that can be investigated or developed later.

If the prospect raises objections, it can be a sign that they are seriously considering your product or service. Listen to the objections carefully. It may help you to note down what is said, so that you can overcome any questions and objections one at a time without missing any.

This often marks the start of the negotiation phase of the selling meeting. For more guidelines on how to negotiate, see pp. 157–9.

HARD SELL VERSUS SOFT SELL

Salespeople fall into two camps – some do a hard sell, while others prefer to adopt a soft-sell approach.

Characteristics of the hard-sell brigade tend to include fast talking, elaborate and possibly exaggerated claims, continual reference to other buyers (so the buyer feels they are missing out), and insistence upon ordering now. In general, a buyer feels under considerable pressure with such a salesperson and resents it. This is not a sales method to use if further sales are hoped for. Although none of us likes to be on the receiving end of a hard sell (and in fact some people totally reject it), there is no doubt it can be very successful in certain situations, such as when dealing with relatively unsophisticated buyers.

By contrast, the soft-sell approach is more of a two-way process, with the prospect talking and asking questions, which are then dealt with. There is less of a feeling of being under pressure to buy and to buy now, and the whole buying experience is intended to be pleasant. In most situations, this is the approach to use.

TECHNIQUES FOR CLOSING THE SALE

There are a number of techniques to use to close a sale. Learn to sense when a prospect is ready to buy, and then choose the most appropriate technique.

- **FOLLOWING THE CUSTOMER'S LEAD** The customer may start to ask detailed questions, talk about methods of payment, or inquire about delivery. Then you can close the sale by, for instance, taking out your order book (very visibly) and asking something like "So, how many do you want in your first order?" or "On what date would you like your first order delivered?"
- **BYPASSING THE YES/NO DECISION** Jump from the negotiation stage to asking if the customer would like a particular option, concluding by writing out an order in the usual way.
- **ENLISTING OTHERS** If the customer is unsure whether or not to buy because they need the opinion of a colleague or boss, ask the other person to join your discussions, or arrange to come back and see them all. Try

CLOSING THE SALE

Whatever techniques you use to clinch a deal, ensure that you take leave of the customer in a friendly manner – making a sale is ideally the start of a long and mutually beneficial relationship with the customer.

not to let them decide in your absence.

- **MAINTAINING CONTACT** If the customer says they need to think it over before deciding, leave something like your personal catalog (marked "only copy"), or some samples, which you arrange to collect the next day (or the day after – do not leave too much time or the prospect's interest may wane). This allows you to see the customer face-to-face again, giving you a second opportunity to close the sale. It is much more difficult for the customer to turn you down in person than over the phone.
- **CHECKING OBJECTIONS** Very often you can detect that a customer is interested but wavering. The key to closing the sale is to find out what is causing them to be uncertain, so ask some questions. Only when you know what the customer is unsure about can you overcome the objections and close the sale.
- **DISCOUNTS** The customer often wants to buy but is unsure if they can afford it. If this is the only sticking point, you should be able to close the sale by having already prepared several different payment options, or by offering a straightforward incentive discount, provided they decide there and then, or perhaps within a limited period.

- **LAST-MINUTE CONCESSIONS** Before you close the sale, an experienced buyer may suddenly try to force a concession, such as a discount, or early delivery, or throwing in something extra (such as free installation). When faced with such requests, try to get something in return. So, if a discount was requested, you might agree provided the usual credit period was set aside and the bill was paid in full immediately (see also pp. 157–9).
- **PROMPTING A DECISION** Sometimes you may feel that you are having a successful sales meeting, but you have not detected any buying signals and the meeting is beginning to drag. In such a situation you have to remember the purpose of the meeting is for you to sell something. Ask a direct question, such as "I've shown you our complete range and it seems the x or y will suit your needs, so which would you like to order?"

Once the buyer has agreed to the purchase, ask them to sign a copy of the order form, and leave them a duplicate copy of the order, which should always include the agreed upon price, terms, and timescales. If your business is such that you need to go away and prepare a written quotation, do so promptly (see p. 34).

If no sale is made, but there is a possibility of a sale in the future, ensure that you keep the door open. Do this by leaving your card, any relevant brochure, and, where appropriate, make a tentative appointment for the future, even if this is simply a request to call the prospect in a month or so.

TIME SAVER

After any successful sale, take a few moments to look back at how the discussions went and try to analyze why the sale was successful. This will help you to define which techniques work for you, so that you can hone your skills for future sales.

Sales Techniques for Retailing

Small retail shops fall into two categories: convenience shops (such as a newsstand, corner shop, or drugstore), and specialized shops (such as a boutique or gift shop). In a convenience shop, the customer tends to make most of their purchasing decisions before entering, while in a specialized shop the customer tends to make their decisions after entering. That statement is a simplification, but it does help to emphasize the differences between the two categories of shops and how the selling technique needs to differ.

CONVENIENCE SHOPS

In the case of a convenience shop, there is little active selling needed, since you are primarily responding to the customer's requests. Selling can still play a part, however, since you can persuade the customer to make additional purchases. For instance, a customer may enter a newsstand asking for their regular automotive magazine, and the sales clerk might draw the customer's attention to a new, onetime auto publication, thereby encouraging an extra sale.

SPECIALIZED SHOPS

In specialized shops, where more active selling is required, there are numerous ways in which to encourage sales. First, always acknowledge the presence of a customer very soon after they enter the shop, by a nod, smile, and possibly a brief greeting, even if you are already dealing with another customer. This makes the new customer feel more at home on unfamiliar territory (especially if they have not visited the shop before), and it also tends to "hold" them until you are free.

Let the customer browse for a few moments and then approach them. The ideal moment is when they stop to examine or touch something. Do not say, "Can I help you?," as you will probably receive the universal reply, "No, I'm just looking!," which stops your sales pitch at once. Instead, choose a question more related to the situation. For instance, if a woman is looking at blouses, you might ask, "Is the blouse to match a particular skirt?," "What colour are you looking for?," or "Is it to be worn in the evening?" You might also ask in some shops if the customer is looking for a present.

The key point with these questions is that they allow you to start a conversation, which has several advantages:

- stopping the customer from taking a quick look around the shop and then leaving
- allowing you to find out what the customer needs
- allowing you to offer your products to match those needs
- giving the customer a helpful and friendly impression.

Where practical, encourage the shopper to touch and handle the goods. This helps to create a bond between the customer and the article for sale. Watch an experienced retailer at work – they soon hand the goods over to the customer to hold.

Do not be too pushy – it can lose you sales

A retailer in a specialized shop will often be regarded by the shopper as an expert and they will ask advice, so you do need to know your subject. Just like the salesperson conducting a face-to-face meeting, you need to know all the inventory and options so that if a customer picks up one item but expresses a preference for a slightly different version, you immediately know what you have in stock, including suitable alternatives. Opinions should be voiced, whenever possible, after you know your customer's views.

A key element of any retailing is the add-on sale, such as shoe polish when you buy a pair of shoes, wrapping paper when you are buying a gift, and so on. Once a customer is in a buying mood, they are open to be shown and sold additional items, especially if the items are related to the first purchase. These add-on sales often command higher margins than the main items, so are particularly worthwhile.

If you do not have a particular item in stock, do not lose the sale. Instead, suggest that the customer places an order secured by a deposit, and then obtain the required goods. Make sure you have the customer's name and phone number so you can phone them when the goods arrive.

In a small specialized shop, it is unsettling for a customer to be alone with an assistant who is doing nothing. The customer will feel watched. The assistant should therefore appear to be busy, but not ignoring the customer, so they still know when to approach them. It may even require the assistant to make up work, such as unpacking and repacking a box.

Background music can be useful, too, to avoid the silence of an empty shop – but whether or not you wish to use music will depend on the type of shop and the image you wish to put across. As with all selling, you need to be aware of when a customer is ready to buy; some of the general face-to-face selling techniques covered above are appropriate.

RETAILING TIPS

1. Keep your main shop door open whenever possible.
2. Divert passers-by into the shop by having goods outside.
3. Remember that your window is your best advertisement.
4. Keep your inventory levels up, and discount slow-moving lines before they become dead inventory.
5. Train your sales clerks in how to sell effectively.
6. Let customers feel that you enjoy helping them.

RETAIL SELLING TECHNIQUES

These selling techniques are ideal for a specialized shop. They are intended to encourage purchases while making shopping a pleasant experience for the buyer. They can be adapted to whatever products are being sold.

1 OPENING THE SALE
The salesperson greets the customer with a friendly "Hello" as she enters the store.

2 GIVING THE CUSTOMER SPACE
The customer browses alone through the inventory for a while.

3 MAKING AN APPROACH
The salesperson asks "Are you looking for anything specific?" in a friendly manner.

4 LOOKING AT ITEMS
The customer selects an item and considers it, inviting the salesperson's opinion.

Customer feels fabric

Salesperson makes suggestion

5 EXAMINING OPTIONS
The salesperson offers a top in a different style to give the customer a choice to try on.

6 Trying it on
The salesperson shows the customer to a mirror in a good light to look at the top.

7 Additional Sale
The salesperson offers another item to go with the first, to make an extra sale.

8 Furthering the Sale
The salesperson helps the customer into the jacket, to improve the chances of a sale.

9 Finishing Touch
The salesperson wraps each item in tissue carefully and without hurrying.

10 Handing Over the Purchases
The salesperson gives the customer the packaged items.

11 Mailing List
The customer agrees to be added to the boutique's mailing list.

DRESSING THE SHOP WINDOW

A crucial factor in selling from a specialized shop is your shop window. This is the magnet that draws people in (very often on impulse). It should be bright (lit up with lights) and attractive, and articles on display should be clearly priced. Change the window regularly, ideally once a week, to coincide with the typical pattern of many people of shopping weekly. They will then see a new window display each time they pass. Clean the outside of the window at least daily to remove any fingerprints. If your shop window is on a busy street or thoroughfare, put a timer on your shop window lights so that they remain on into the evening after the shop is closed.

Dressing a window really well is an art that can make a big improvement to sales. If you are planning to do this yourself, you will probably require some props, usually to create verticality in your design. Give the display a theme, such as a subject or a common color. Experiment to get a pleasing balance of shape, props, colors, and range of products. If you prefer, you can employ a freelance window dresser.

SHOP LAYOUT AND DISPLAYS

The shop layout is important to assist your selling and should be discussed with professional designers. In particular, thought should be given to:

- **CIRCULATION** How are people to enter, move around, see all your displays, approach the cash register, and then leave the shop? There should be a natural route that takes them around all, or most of, the shop. Avoid cul-de-sacs in your layout.
- **DISPLAY** Are items displayed at their best? The scan of most people's eyes is very limited, and anything above eye height will

be seen only if standing away from the display. Can people reach items easily? The more expensive items should not be close to the door for security reasons, and because they may give an initial impression of the shop being expensive. Move inventory around every so often so that regulars see different items. Always give prominence to best-selling lines.

- **SIGNAGE** Although a retailer may know the inventory very well, finding specific items can be confusing for a new customer who has just entered the shop. Try to group similar products together and use signs as needed.
- **SECURITY** Shoplifting is a major problem for retailers; the layout of the shop can either make it easier or more difficult for shoplifters. Ensure that the layout does not have any blind spots – staff should be able to see every part of the shop, perhaps with the aid of security mirrors. Inventory near the doorway is particularly vulnerable, as are small, high-value items.
- **POINT-OF-SALE** At the cash register point-of-sale displays can be used to good effect for selling low-price, small, impulse-purchase, popular goods.
- **SALES MATERIAL** Use any showcards, posters, leaflets, or stickers provided by the suppliers of your inventory. These are all helpful in brightening up a shop, and, more importantly, show off the products to their best. They may also reflect a national advertising campaign that customers have noticed elsewhere.

Smile when phoning – it can be heard in your voice

WINDOW DISPLAYS
Many chains and department stores have large budgets for window displays. If you want to learn about how to create effective displays in your shop, visit a few major stores to gain ideas and see how professionals tackle this aspect of retailing.

Selling by Telephone

To use the telephone effectively for selling requires skill and practice. Selling by phone, or telesales, is of particular use to the small business with limited numbers of staff, or where the proprietors have to do the sales work themselves in addition to running the rest of the business. The main uses of the phone in this context are:

- cold-calling prospects
- as a follow-up to a sales letter, mailshot, or quotation, either to make an appointment or to secure a sale
- responding to someone contacting your business wanting more information or to place an order.

Selling by phone enables you to contact prospects from your own desk, to make use of travel time by phoning customers from your mobile phone, to contact a large number of people in a relatively short time, and, with some perseverance, you can often get through to the decision maker. On the other hand, you cannot show your product or other sales material to the customer or see their facial reactions, and you do not have agreements or decisions in writing. If you are planning to make unsolicited telephone calls to consumers at home, there are various legal restrictions (see pp. 180–81).

Handling the Phone Conversation

As with any sales work, preparation is essential. Research who you are calling so that you have their name and any relevant details at hand. This is where a customer record (on a card or on a computer database) becomes invaluable. Pause a moment before you lift the phone, to compose yourself and to think through what you are trying to achieve with the call.

Since there is no visual contact, it is important in your opening statement to identify yourself and your business and to mention the purpose of the call. You have a very brief opportunity to catch the listener's interest and, if you fail, the call is wasted. Use a prewritten and rehearsed opening statement, but do not recite it in a parrot-like fashion. Speak clearly so that the customer can readily understand what you are saying. It is also useful to have your fact-finding questions and sales message written down as a prompt.

What makes someone listen? You need to be offering them something that is relevant to them, interesting, and possibly new. To build your sale, involve the listener. Ask questions that relate to the potential customer's needs. Listen to their answers and be careful to meet any objections they voice. Keep a brief record of what is said in all your calls. To save time, with a little practice, this record keeping can be done while you are still on the phone. To remind you which customers you need to call back, if you are using cards, place their customer record cards on their ends so that they stand up.

STARTING A CALL

As you start a sales call, say your opening statement, making sure that you sound fresh and enthusiastic. Smile as you are speaking, as it makes your voice sound warmer.

Hints for Telephone Sales Conversations

1. Keep your product or sales information in front of you as it will help you to remember details, to describe things, and to sell the benefits.
2. Remember the prospect will be thinking "What's in this for me?" and, as you have interrupted what they were doing, they may be impatient to get back to it.
3. Close the sale or, where appropriate, arrange an appointment to visit the prospect.
4. As there is nothing in writing, always summarize verbally what has been agreed, and later confirm it in writing if necessary (by letter, fax, or e-mail).
5. Bear rebuffs bravely – do not be rude or become angry.
6. At the end of the conversation, pause and then put your phone down after the other person.

LISTENING TO THE CUSTOMER
As the call continues, make notes as you listen to what the customer needs, so that you can ensure you tailor your sale accordingly. You can keep the notes for future calls.

Participating in Exhibitions and Shows

Exhibitions and consumer shows tend to be open to the public, whereas trade shows are not. In this chapter, the words "exhibition" and "show" are used interchangeably. For non-retail businesses, shows provide regional, national, or even international exposure, and contacts that are vital and might otherwise be very difficult to make. They also provide both direct and indirect selling opportunities.

Exhibiting requires a great deal of preparation, an adequate budget, and hard work before, during, and afterward to make the most of the opportunity. Because it can take up a great deal of time and can also be quite an expensive exercise, the decision to participate should not be made hastily. Many new exhibitors are disappointed with the results of their initial showings. This is mainly due to inexperience and unrealistically high expectations, but it might also be that their product or service is not of sufficient interest to potential buyers.

DECIDING WHERE TO EXHIBIT

You may already be familiar with the various shows relevant to your own industry. If in doubt, look at the trade publications and ask your industry association or other people in the trade. Even a very small business can consider participating in a major show but, before deciding to do so, make yourself familiar with the show by going to it at least once as a visitor.

Contact the organizers for details of stand availability, costs, and details of who has visited the previous shows. The better national shows are very well organized in this respect and can provide very specific visitor data. The best shows have their stand space booked many months in advance, with some exhibitors booking the next show (which may be one or even two years away) while attending the current one. This makes it difficult for the first-time exhibitor to break in, but it does mean that, once you have made a decision to participate in a show, you should immediately apply for stand space.

WHAT WILL IT COST?

Costs for stands are usually quoted in terms of dollars per square foot, but only certain standard sizes will usually be available. Choose the smallest stand space necessary to display your products – having a larger stand does not generate more passing traffic. Note that essentials, such as lighting and electric sockets, are often quoted as extra costs and can be disproportionately expensive.

When working out the cost of participating in any show, you also need to remember the real cost should include accommodation (if the show is not local), travel, transport of exhibits, printing extra brochures, staff overtime, and so on. There may be other costs, too, such as the cost of building your own display, insurance,

PREPARING FOR AN EXHIBITION OR SHOW

Read the rules and regulations supplied by the organizers

Finalize the design of the stand

Decide who is going to run the stand

Organize a shift system with usually more than one person on the stand for most periods

Arrange accommodation close to the show. Decide on transportation between the accommodation and show site as necessary

Obtain entry and, if needed, parking passes for yourself and your staff from the organizers

Decide what literature is required in terms of handouts (brochures, price lists, etc.) and, possibly, free samples

If sales material needs printing, allow sufficient time for this

Decide what preshow promotion you need to do to ensure that the maximum number of people visit your stand

For trade shows this is best done by editorial and advertising in the relevant trade press. Send your potential customers a printed invitation to visit the show

For consumer shows, try to get as much publicity as possible in the relevant consumer press. You may choose to advertise as well

Be sure you will have an entry in the official show catalog, so that visitors can find your stand

If you expect to make sales, ensure that you have the facilities to handle cash, checks, or credit card transactions safely

and promotion. There is also the less quantifiable cost of being away from your normal workplace and normal sales activity for a period of days, perhaps as long as a week.

WHAT CAN BE ACHIEVED?

For a trade show, an initial objective is usually to take orders during the show. Other objectives include receiving feedback and meeting potential customers. These new customers can be visited after the show, if necessary. This follow-up activity can be critical. A new exhibitor may also use the show to find agents by putting up a small sign in the stand to that effect. A trade show also lets you see existing customers, some of whom you may not have seen for some time.

A small business cannot afford to attend a show simply to raise the flag. Typically the first appearance at a trade show will not produce dramatic results – industry buyers tend to be conservative and stick to familiar suppliers. By the second and third appearance, you should be able to justify the costs of attending by the amount of business you are doing both at the show and immediately afterward as you follow up the contacts made.

For a consumer show, what you can achieve depends on what you are selling. If you are selling relatively expensive products or services (such as cars, boats, RVs, or sunrooms), you may take some orders at the show, but the main business is likely to come afterward from following up the inquiries. By contrast, if you are selling a relatively cheap item, you would be more likely to calculate the success of the show simply by the number of sales made then and there. This is then akin to retailing, and the sales techniques of retailing apply (see pp. 146–51).

An important long-term benefit of participating in any type of show is that it gives exposure to your name and what your business does. So even if a person does not buy anything now, the next time they see your business name, it will help that important reinforcement that overcomes buyer resistance.

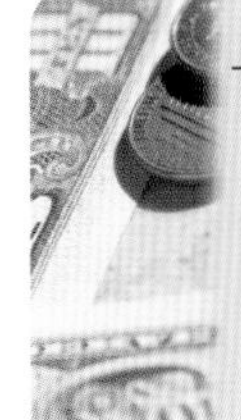

MONEY SAVER

Make sure that you obtain the right location for your stand at an exhibition or show; if you do not, it may not be worth exhibiting there at all. Avoid deadends and dark corners, as well as different floors or satellite areas away from the main show space.

EXHIBITION OR SHOW PREPARATION

A brief plan of action should be drawn up and discussed with your partners, directors, and staff (especially those on the sales side) well in advance of the show, as suggested in the chart opposite. Most importantly, agree on your objectives and allocate responsibilities.

STAND DESIGN

Exhibition space is usually offered as either a bare site or a basic stand (also called a shell stand), comprising carpet, walls, and a name board. Exhibition stands need to look sophisticated, and an amateur-looking stand will be obvious among those that have been professionally done, so a basic or shell stand is usually a worthwhile investment.

Decide how the stand is to be designed and whether it requires props to be built and other visual aids made (such as poster-size photos). A surprising number of stands do not indicate clearly to a passer-by exactly what they are selling. If you are designing a stand for the first time, either get professional advice or set aside time to look at other stands at previous exhibitions to see what works and what does not. The design must catch a passer-by's attention and encourage them onto the stand.

TRAINING STAFF

Selling from a stand is a unique experience that requires training, as with any other aspect of business. Simply knowing your business and trying hard may not be good enough. Selling at an exhibition combines aspects of retailing with

TRADE FAIR
This stand at a book fair is busy, with plenty of products to pick up and handle, as well as eye-catching photographs and promotional literature.

those of face-to-face selling in that you have to attract customers in as for a shop, but then are more likely to engage in negotiation as in face-to-face selling. The environment is highly unusual, with the bright lights, music (or just noise), flashy displays, lavish hospitality, general excitement, and hype all giving a sense of unreality. It is very tiring to run a stand for several days; allow plenty of time for breaks, and organize overlaps between staff shifts.

THE EXHIBITION

At the start, you need to overcome the resistance people may feel about walking on to a small stand. (The same problem faces small boutiques.) The resistance is greatest when there is only one person on the stand and they either seem to be guarding it (by standing at the front like a sentry) or they are sitting in the middle passing the time reading. Resistance is also created by a stand that has a layout that makes someone feel they are going to be trapped.

Try to look welcoming. Do not appear so occupied in talking to each other that to venture onto the stand feels like an intrusion, but try to seem busy (even if it is made-up work). Keeping to the sides of the stand is better than staying in the middle, but you may not have much choice on a small stand. With a tiny stand, it is not possible to have more than one person running it, so the only thing you can do is to stand outside the stand (far enough away so that you do not seem to be hovering over it).

When someone comes onto the stand, there should be plenty of things for them to see and touch. Leave them for a few moments until they stop at something. Then approach and ask a question relevant to the object, photo, or whatever item they are looking at. Some trade shows provide each visitor and exhibitor with a prominent name tag. This is helpful as you can see who you are dealing with; otherwise, ask when you first encounter someone, since they may be a competitor checking you out.

If the person is genuinely interested in your products or services, the sales discussion should then proceed along the lines of a face-to-face sale (see pp. 142–6). When you hand out a brochure or leaflet, ask for the name and address or business card of the prospect so that you can follow it up later.

During the show you and your staff need to pace yourselves, especially if the show lasts for several days. Take time out to rest, eat, and sit down whenever you can. Avoid alcohol and do not become dehydrated. Each evening, hold a review of how the day went and make whatever changes are necessary for the following day.

Security

Do not forget about security. Your stand is vulnerable to industry competitors, so guard customer lists and completed order forms and avoid leaving new designs of products unattended. Theft is also a problem at many shows, either during the show or overnight, and especially during the vulnerable setting-up and taking-down stages.

Ensure that your stand looks busy so that it attracts people

After the Show

Dismantle the stand after the last visitor has left. Resist the temptation to do this earlier, since you can sometimes make a good contact in the closing minutes of a show. Pack up exhibits and display boards, since you will certainly need them again. Once you are back in your office, make it a priority to follow up all the contacts you made at the show.

Negotiating Skills

Your business may be the type where you fix your prices and you do not expect a customer to question them. Retailing, and running a restaurant or a guest house, are examples of such businesses – although in these businesses you will almost certainly have to negotiate with your suppliers. In many types of business, it is routine to negotiate a price with each customer. Negotiation is an important part of the face-to-face selling process, and also comes into play when you are selling by phone.

As always, preparation is essential. In particular you need to know either the bottom selling price below which you are simply not prepared to go, or the top buying price you are willing to pay, and you must stick to that.

Negotiating as a Seller

Your ability to negotiate comes into play once the customer is interested. The skill is not to lose the order, but equally not to give too much away. At this stage you have one important factor in your favor – the buyer obviously wants what you have to offer. Your position is weakened if you have a competitor offering a similar product or service at a better price, but do not be panicked into giving away unnecessary concessions.

Once you have a fixed bottom price in mind, all you need to remember is, first, to keep calm and not let on how eager you are to get the order and, second, every time the would-be buyer asks for a concession, ask for something in return. When the prospect starts to show a definite interest and is at the stage of wanting more information, including what the cost will be, introduce your starting price. It should flow naturally in the conversation, but if not, create the right moment by saying something like: "I know you will want to know the cost, so..." and perhaps taking out your price list at the same time.

The buyer is likely to say that your price is too high. You might defend the price by explaining the high quality of the product or service, or making clear its benefits once more. The buyer may then harden their position by stating what they are prepared to pay. Your starting price should have allowed for a little discounting, and an experienced buyer will presume this. Take your time before replying since your reactions will be carefully assessed. Again, defend your price, but offer a reduced price as an introductory offer (or some other plan that does not create a precedent) and ask for the customer to pay sooner or buy a greater quantity – you are granting a discount but asking for something in return. Another alternative is to negotiate on non-money issues, so you could maintain your price, but offer a better guarantee, or add more features.

The best deals are where both buyer and seller feel they have done well – a "win–win" situation. This is not only fair on both parties but is good business, for the buyer is more likely to come back to you, will act as your ambassador, and neither party will have driven such a hard bargain as to jeopardize the other's business. In all your negotiations, avoid confrontation. As a small business, it is unlikely to achieve anything.

Be wary of a buyer if the top price they are prepared to pay is much lower than your stated price. If their price is below the minimum you have in mind, this is not a good sign. Ask again what exactly the buyer requires, to help you form a better idea of their needs, and maybe why their offer bid is so low. Also, watch out for the "Why don't we just split the difference" offer, which, at first glance, may sound fair. Work out if the final figure is still above your bottom price.

Finally, sometimes it is better to lose the sale altogether than to enter into a working relationship with a difficult customer or to get into a deal that makes you no money. Experience has also shown that customers who are difficult to deal with are frequently poor payers, too – so be warned, and if you are unhappy, or have a bad feeling about the deal, trust your instincts and just walk away.

NEGOTIATING AS A BUYER

The first rule is not to show too much interest in what is being sold. Do not appear to be enthusiastic or excited. Show a slight interest in

CARING FOR CUSTOMERS

Customers remember places where the service has been excellent, both during and after a sale. In a shop, you might be able to order goods that are not in stock. Clothing shops sometimes offer alterations as an additional service. Such care can make the difference between making and losing a sale.

something you do not actually want and only move to what really interests you as almost an aside. You might also mention other suppliers you have already visited or are about to visit. If you are dealing with a business customer, some background on that business might also help your negotiations. For instance, if you know that business is going through a difficult patch you may be able to get a better price if you offer quick payment, as that will help their cash flow.

TIME SAVER

Use customer feedback as a simple and direct way of keeping abreast of changes in the market, and to enable you to update your products or services so that they more closely match the needs and desires of your customers.

Caring for Your Customers

Selling does not end when you receive payment. For many customers, the difference between two companies is in the aftercare they receive. Customer care is about developing a long-term relationship with a customer. It is seeing beyond a single sale, to the customer becoming a regular buyer. As in all relationships, there may be ups and downs. If you make a mistake, make sure you rectify it promptly, and, as importantly, apologize to the appropriate person. Occasionally you might be confronted with a customer who, for whatever reason, is angry and possibly unreasonable. Make a contingency plan for such an event – a key aspect of which is that you should stay calm.

What this means in practice is that your business should be customer-focused, and that whenever you consider a new marketing strategy or develop a new product or service you should put yourself in your customers' shoes and ask yourself how they might react. The concept of caring for customers is not simply a matter of looking after them – the whole focus of your business should put customers at the very center of things.

Becoming a Customer-Orientated Business

There are a number of practical changes you can make to ensure that your business focuses on its customers.

- Create a database of your customers and keep it up-to-date.
- Standardize how your phones are answered and what level of sales information is given over the phone.
- Decide between you and your staff who is responsible for different areas in terms of dealing with customers.
- Brief all your staff who come into contact with customers as to how they should behave.
- Develop plans for dealing with your key accounts and difficult customers.
- Write to customers regularly to keep them informed of new products and services and of changes in personnel that might affect them.

Asking for Customer Feedback

One major advantage of having a customer-orientated business is that you are more likely to receive feedback from customers. By keeping lines of communication open with customers – via emails, meetings, mail, and phone calls – you increase the chances of hearing their comments, views, and suggestions. Complaints can be very instructive, and you need an efficient procedure for such situations. View them as a chance to learn about your customers' needs. You can request feedback directly by providing a form or registration card if appropriate. You might also phone a customer to ask for their reaction to work that has just been done or goods that have just been received. Indirect feedback may come from customers simply contacting you.

17
17
ZÓN

STAYING on track

The ultimate challenge, and the proof of the success of your marketing strategy, is staying in business. Keeping on top of your sales data – the figures that tell you how your business is doing – is essential, as is being aware of trends, threats, and opportunities that may affect your business, and being prepared to take the appropriate action.

ANALYZING YOUR SALES DATA

Gathering detailed sales data is a key task of running a business and a part of your ongoing market research. Analyzing that data provides one of the most powerful tools you have to find out just how well your business is doing, and how your marketing strategy is paying off. You can also pinpoint areas where you could do better. Graphical or tabular representations of sales data allow you to get a feel for specific aspects of the business and make it easier to discuss trends and results with others. As with all aspects of marketing, do not look at your results in isolation, but as a part of an overall picture.

Your business record keeping should be as simple as possible, yet provide enough raw information to be analyzed usefully. Every business will have its own priorities in terms of what information is required, and these priorities need to be reviewed regularly to ensure that you are always recording the most useful sorts of information. Typical categories of information to analyze are:

- **SALES FIGURES** You will know your weekly or monthly sales figures, but have you studied them in detail? What are the proportional sales of each part or section of your business, and how do these figures compare with those from the previous months or years? Are there any trends you can spot?
- **CUSTOMERS** Who exactly are your customers? If your customers are the general public, it could be illuminating to know details of their age ranges/sex/income groups. What are their preferences? Who are your main (biggest) spenders? Are your actual customers the same as the customers you have in mind when you think about marketing strategy?
- **PRODUCT/SERVICE** What are your best sellers? Are sales of each individual item

CASE STUDY: Looking at Profitability

MAKING LUXURY hand-made chocolates had been a speciality of Mario's family business for several generations, but he felt that the market was changing and he was keen to know just where to direct his sales efforts. The business currently sold chocolates in bulk, but at a high discount, to one supermarket chain, and they also supplied an increasing number of gift shops and had irregular but large overseas orders, too. More recently they had begun to sell their chocolates online from their web site. The online sales were at full value, but each order took a lot of time to despatch, and they had problems with chocolates being damaged in transit. Mario had the problem of comparing sales made at quite different price levels and some at irregular intervals. Mario realized that the only way to compare the sales from each sector was to look at the profit contribution that each sector provided. Slightly to his surprise, he discovered that the sales to gift shops were his key sales; he decided to give that sector priority.

rising, stable, or falling? How profitable is each product or service?

- **SALES STAFF** How do individual performances of staff compare?

Provided your record-keeping method is suitable, an analysis can be done in a few hours. It is not simply an academic exercise – if you do not learn something useful, think about what you ought to be analyzing. The sort of questions you should be asking yourself are: "What do my customers want from me?," "Am I giving them what they want?," "What more could I do?," and "What does each aspect of my business earn in relation to its cost in time, labor, and capital investment?"

Every business is different and has its own requirements; there are no general rules to follow when analyzing data. The text below covers four examples of different businesses and how they collect and analyze data; between them, these examples will have relevance to virtually every small business.

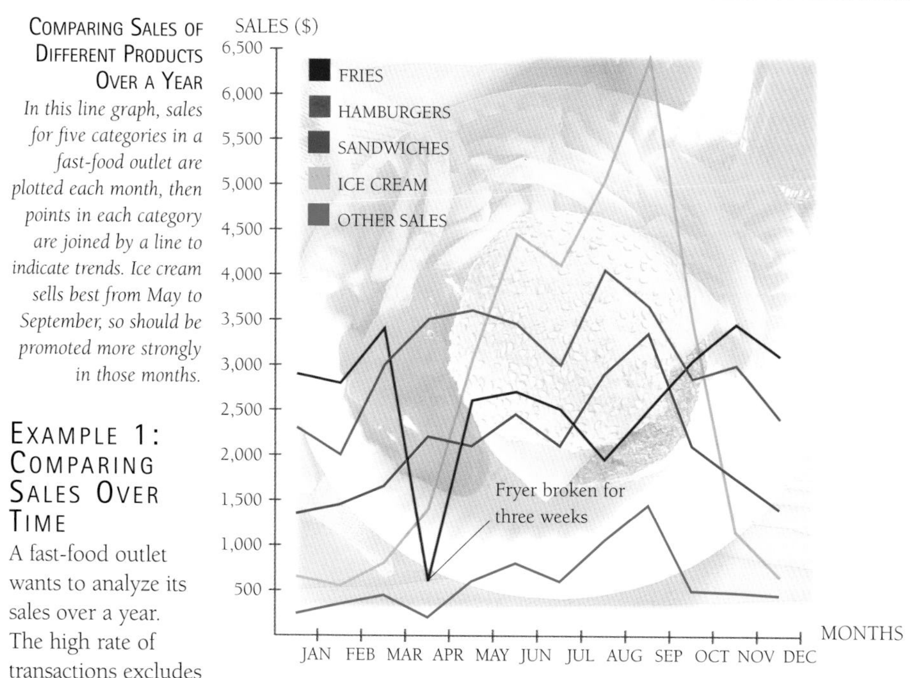

COMPARING SALES OF DIFFERENT PRODUCTS OVER A YEAR
In this line graph, sales for five categories in a fast-food outlet are plotted each month, then points in each category are joined by a line to indicate trends. Ice cream sells best from May to September, so should be promoted more strongly in those months.

EXAMPLE 1: COMPARING SALES OVER TIME

A fast-food outlet wants to analyze its sales over a year. The high rate of transactions excludes the possibility of any manual recording, and inventory data would be difficult to interpret on its own, so a multidepartment cash register would be the typical way of recording sales. The sales could then be represented by a line graph, as shown here. Unusual occurrences should be noted. This type of sales-versus-time graph is a very popular method for analyzing sales information, since it can show trends. In some cases, it may be more relevant to have the vertical column representing numbers of customers or numbers of units sold, depending on the business concerned. The information provided by showing sales made (or customers or units sold) over time could indicate which product lines should be dropped seasonally or altogether, and which others could be promoted more at certain times of the year.

EXAMPLE 2: LOOKING AT SALES AS A PROPORTION OF TOTAL INVENTORY

A small shop selling a range of women's fashions (including skirts, blouses, knitwear, hosiery, and accessories) wants to analyze the types of products that are selling the best. This information is vital so that the limited purchasing budget is spent as wisely as possible, on the best-selling and potentially most profitable lines. The information required to make the analysis could come from one of three sources:

- a multidepartment cash register
- manual recording of sales
- regular inventory counts.

Information collected by any of these means could be analyzed in a variety of ways. The retailer may wish to examine the price bands that are selling best for each category of product. In the table illustrated below, the value of skirts sold over a given period is analyzed. The table clearly shows that the shop should concentrate on skirts retailing at up to $60 (representing 80 percent of all sales, by value). A variation on this method is to analyze sales within a category based on sizes, or colors, or styles. The information gained by analyzing sales in this way can be used to help refine inventory ordering. The easiest way to purchase new inventory is simply to replace what is sold, but by finding out what is selling more you can weight your orders in the right direction. Note, however, that inventory purchasing is a complex process and should not be based on past sales data alone – what is fashionable or popular one season may not be the next.

Predict sales by superimposing forecasts on historical sales data

An alternative way to analyze information in a retail context is by breaking it down into categories and totaling the sales in each. For a fair comparison, sales should be given in relation to the amount of inventory held (as you cannot directly compare sales of two product categories if there is a lot of inventory of one but little of the other). Ideally the information should be presented graphically, since it is easier to understand; one example, of a bar chart, is shown opposite. A practical complication arises if inventory is

COMPARING SALES IN DIFFERENT PRICE BANDS

Using the raw data of total stock of skirts in each price band, and skirts sold, this table shows the percentage of each price band sold. To calculate the percentage of total skirt sales contributed by each price category, multiply the price in the middle of each price band (e.g. $38 in the $31–45 price band) by the total sales of skirts in that band. Add the sales for all the bands to give total sales, then work out the percentage each band represents.

PRICE BAND	TOTAL INVENTORY (of skirts)	SALES (of skirts)	SALES (as a % of inventory)	SALES (as approx % of total skirt value)
UNDER $15	10	7	70%	4%
$16–$30	21	17	81%	14%
$31–$45	32	24	75%	32%
$46–$60	28	16	57%	30%
$61–$75	15	6	40%	15%
OVER $75	8	2	25%	5%

arriving on a continual basis so that the inventory level is always fluctuating. To overcome this problem, you could take the initial inventory value (for each category), then add all the inventory (of that category) that arrived during the period to make the total inventory figure. It would be illuminating to repeat the exercise at regular intervals and compare the different graphs over time. In this example, accessories, followed by hosiery, sell particularly well in relation to the proportion of inventory held. Although accessories represent the least sales in terms of total value, the margins on them are normally higher than those for other categories; the profit contribution of each category should also be considered.

The same information could be represented another way, as two pie charts, to illustrate what proportion of overall shop sales each category contributes. Over time, this technique could also be used to show whether a certain category was growing or declining in overall importance. A shop might choose to drop a category of lesser importance and specialize in another.

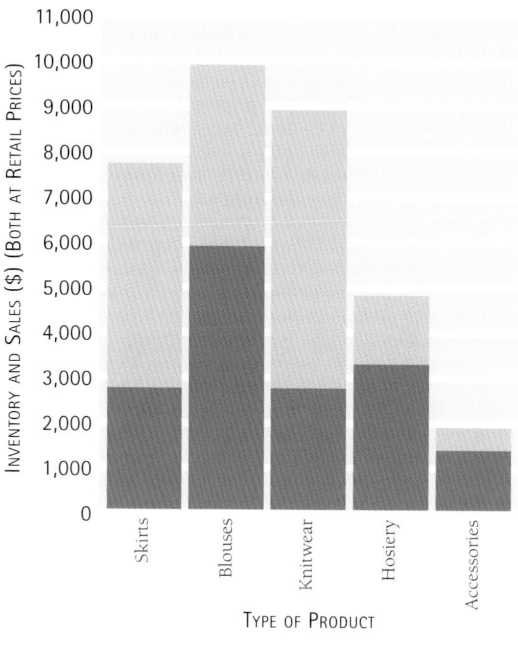

PLOTTING WHICH PRODUCTS SELL BEST
In this bar chart, the lighter bars represent the total inventory held of a type of product, while the darker bars represent the total sales of each type of product for the period concerned (which could be a month, a quarter, or a fashion season).

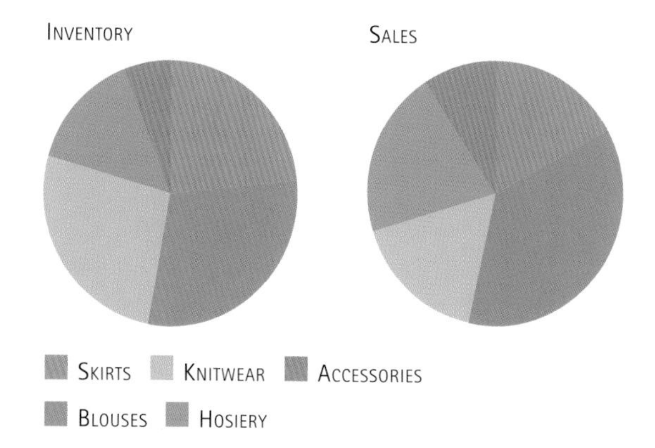

ANALYZING PROPORTIONS OF SALES
These pie charts use the same information as the bar chart above, but focus on the contribution each category makes as a proportion of the whole. By comparing the two charts, it is possible to see how well each category performs. Blouses and hosiery, for example, sell more proportionately than their inventory levels in the shop.

EXAMPLE 3: COMPARING SALES BY AREA

A business that uses agents around the country may want to compare sales in each territory. The information would be readily available from the invoiced sales or commission payments being made to the agents and this could then be represented in a graph as shown. This method does assume that their territories are of equal value in terms of potential customers and hence sales. If this is not the case, to make the comparison fair a factor would need to be added (such as saying that one territory equals two-thirds of another); this factor can only be a best guess.

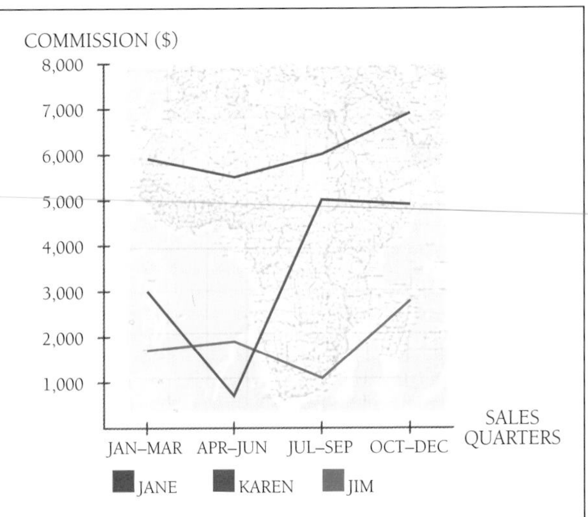

COMPARING SALES FIGURES ACHIEVED BY AGENTS

This line graph compares the performance of three sales agents in three territories. Jane is shown to make consistently high sales, while the other two have more erratic success.

EXAMPLE 4: COMPARING SALES TO VARIOUS CUSTOMERS

A small company providing a printing service to other businesses wants to analyze how its customers contribute to sales figures. They look through their sales invoices for the past two years to produce a table, shown here. This information (which could also be represented graphically) helps to indicate which markets are worth pursuing so that sales efforts are focused on the most promising areas, rather than dissipated on less fruitful ones. This method would work equally well for manufacturers.

COMPARING SALES TO DIFFERENT CUSTOMERS

This table shows a period of two years, with data from each year side by side. As well as showing that unit sales fell by 19 percent in Year 2, it is also possible to see whether certain customers are buying more or less over the year. The business might also consider the consequences of losing their major customer.

CUSTOMER	SALES PERIOD (JAN–DEC, YR 1)		SALES PERIOD (JAN–DEC, YR 2)	
	SALES (UNITS)	SALES (% OF TOTAL)	SALES (UNITS)	SALES (% OF TOTAL)
ABC CO.	510	66%	404	65%
LOCAL GOVT	26	3%	33	5%
JOHN SMITH INC.	84	11%	75	12%
EXPORT	126	16%	105	17%
OTHERS	28	4%	8	1%
TOTALS	774	100%	625 (-19%)	100%

Deciding What Action to Take

The results of your analysis should indicate how your business is doing overall, and how each constituent part is performing. Other than your annual report, there is no better assessment of just what is happening. The analysis can have a number of outcomes, depending on what you find. In particular, you might consider promoting some parts of your business more strongly, or you might drop other parts. The data should not be taken in isolation: analysis of industry trends and observation of competitors will also play an important part in your decision-making.

In a retail context, you may also wish to know the profit contribution of various categories of inventory.. The profit contribution is a function of the margin and the sales of a category. This information, along with an analysis of the sales data, might show a category with high sales and high profitability. This category could then be more vigorously promoted by being placed in a more prominent location, or by ordering more inventory.

Another relevant calculation used in retailing is the annual sales made per unit of floorspace – this can be worked out by dividing your annual sales by the selling area of your shop. You need to know the norms in your sector in order to assess how you are performing in relation to others.

Analyze your sales weekly in a retail context, or at least monthly in other businesses

In a business that employs salespeople, it might be useful to analyze the number of sales being made by each person, and the number of meetings they arrange. You could deduce whether too much time is spent selling easier products to established customers, rather than generating new business, or vice versa.

The key factor in all sales data analysis is to look at long-term trends. Some trends are short-lived, others are cyclical – these are useful to let you know what lines to promote immediately. However, the long-term trends, which can only be revealed through careful and comparative analysis over time, will show you the rising stars of tomorrow, and those that are in decline, enabling you to plan and modify your marketing strategy on a sound basis.

TIME SAVER

Experiment with using computer software for analyzing your sales data and creating line graphs and bar or pie charts. Many spreadsheet programs will create such charts and graphs at the touch of a button, enabling you to assimilate the information easily and quickly.

DEALING WITH CHANGES AND COMPETITION

In every business, you may confidently plan what sales you expect as part of your marketing plan and your overall business strategy, but the market may react very differently. Instead of the expected sales, you might experience anything from falling sales to rapid growth, or competitors may pose more of a problem than anticipated. Each situation brings its own special problems and requires its own solutions. As a business, you need to be flexible and ready to react, whatever may happen.

As you analyze your sales data (see pp. 162–7), you should be able to form a picture of trends in sales figures over time. If the trend is undesirable, you need to take action as soon as you can to remedy the situation. If a competitor is adversely affecting your sales trends, you need to defend yourself against them.

Managing Falling Sales

Even successful businesses go through patches of falling sales. To detect this potentially serious situation early, you need to do regular cash flow forecasts – predictions of the cash flowing into and out of the business. Once you have diagnosed falling sales, move fast – the business will be growing weaker and, as time goes on, fewer options will be available to you. The first step is to reduce overhead to a level that can be supported by your sales. Overhead is the fixed costs of your business, such as power, staff wages, and expenses to do with your premises. If you can reduce your overhead sufficiently, this will buy you time.

The next step is to consider how you can increase your sales. It is important not to overreact and institute panic measures. To direct your efforts in the most effective way, look carefully at each step of the marketing and selling process:

CASE STUDY: Looking for the Causes of Falling Sales

AFTER JANE AND HENRY had been in business for a year, the sales at their downtown bistro suddenly slowed and then began to fall. This was not what was expected or planned, so the two partners were alarmed. Their first year had been good, but so hectic, demanding very long hours, that there had been no spare time to analyze their sales. Now they looked back through their records and started speaking to some of their regulars as well as other customers whom they had not seen before. What they discovered was that many of their customers were from the large financial-services headquarters in the adjacent street. This organization had recently changed its working times to match overseas stock markets. Many of the staff were now coming out when the bistro was closed. The solution for Jane and Henry was obvious, and with new opening hours sales were restored. Their research also highlighted a few other areas that they were able to improve on.

- **SEEKING CUSTOMERS** Is your advertising and promotion producing enough response? If not, look into the reasons why. Ensure that your efforts are reaching your target customers. Ask any new customers exactly how they heard of you. Refine your marketing strategy accordingly.
- **STIMULATING CUSTOMER INTEREST** Is your product or service still right for the market? Do customers realize exactly what you are selling? Try to look at your product or service objectively and seek the opinions of others. Compare your methods with those of your competitors. Look at market conditions and see if they have changed since you did your original market research.
- **SATISFYING CUSTOMER NEEDS** Why are potential customers not buying? Look again at what is likely to attract your target customers in terms of your pricing policy and the image you are trying to project. It may be possible to ask your customers whether there are any improvements or adaptations they would like to see.
- **SELLING** Are your sales techniques satisfactory? Consider whether you or any staff need some training or refresher courses to improve sales skills.

DOS AND DON'TS OF FALLING SALES

✓ Do make a break-even forecast to see what the critical sales level is.

✓ Do react to a rising overdraft, keeping the bank informed of your intentions.

✓ Do put all capital expense plans on hold until the sales figures start to rise again.

✗ Don't allow cyclical or seasonal changes to mask falling sales.

✗ Don't fall behind with paying off your creditors.

✗ Don't overreact to the situation – think before you act.

Improving Stagnant Sales

Also known as zero growth, this is where the level of sales is such that all overhead is met and the proprietors or working directors take out some remuneration, but the business is static and shows no sign of growth. This type of business is sometimes called "the living dead," and it certainly is not very healthy. By being static, a business can be vulnerable. First, its lack of growth suggests that it is not probing new markets or trying out new products or services, and in a changing marketplace could find itself unexpectedly obsolete. Second, the business may be producing insufficient profits to create reserves for future contingencies. The pursuit of growth in itself need not be an objective, but the lack of growth may be a symptom of underlying problems, such as a declining market or being tied to just a handful of large customers.

Examine all the evidence before you decide what action to take to remedy a situation

The normal route out of having stagnant sales is to continue with the current business relatively unchanged (as it is, after all, viable), but to make management time, staff, and cash available for diversification. You may be able to introduce a new product or service, or adapt your existing one – do thorough market research first to ensure that any changes will take the business in the right direction.

The major stumbling block that prevents a business in this predicament from taking any action is usually the owner's complacency or resistance to change. If you become aware that this is the case, you could try bringing in fresh talent to the business even if only for a short period. For example, you could take on a summer vacation college student, or a consultant could look at different options.

Making the Most of Controlled Growth

Most businesses try to achieve controlled growth; the challenge is deciding exactly how to grow. If your marketing strategies have been successful, and your business is growing, you need to underpin this success with a sound business structure. Traditionally, taking on more and more staff – first junior staff, then managers to supervise the junior staff – has been the usual way to expand. This can bring its own problems, since precious management time is spent recruiting, training, and supervising the new staff. A number of the following alternatives might be considered.

OUTSOURCING

Rather than taking on staff, you might be able to use contract workers. These are self-employed individuals you contract to do an aspect of your work for you. Contract workers are a flexible option, and save on overhead. Alternatively, you might decide to subcontract part of your business to another company.

BRINGING IN NEW PARTNERS OR DIRECTORS

As a business grows, management time and ability will be in short supply (and capital probably will be, too). If so, consider inviting someone you know and trust (in a business sense) to be a partner or director in your business. Before making any decisions, interview them thoroughly, and ensure that their business ethics are sound and their personal finances and health are in good shape. The prospective partner or director needs to consider the onerous liabilities they are taking on and will therefore, at some point, need to scrutinize the business financial statements and ask pointed and maybe difficult questions. Taking on a new partner or director is a complex process with long-lasting effects – ensure that you seek legal and tax advice first.

> **MONEY SAVER**
>
> Seek legal and financial advice and, if necessary, undertake market research, before radically changing the purpose or structure of your business. Making such major changes can be akin to starting a new business altogether – by taking advice you can continue on your profitable path.

FRANCHISING

Business format franchising is an interesting option for many service businesses to consider if they have a local customer base and their business format can be replicated in other areas across the country. Franchising is a popular method for dealing with rapid growth, but to offer franchises professionally takes a great deal of time, effort, and expenditure (see pp. 55–7).

> *Consider existing customers when making changes – you are unlikely to be able to afford to lose them*

EXPANDING BY ACQUISITION

Even a small company can expand greatly, and quickly, by buying another business to give it increased market share, more control of its outlets, greater buying power, or perhaps access to a greater production capacity. Seek legal advice before following this route.

LICENSING DEALS

Rather than handling entering new markets yourself, you might license existing companies to do so for you, while you enjoy the royalties that can be gained. Licensing can be a particularly useful method for expanding into overseas markets. Seek good tax advice at all stages in the process to ensure that the proposed structure of the business is such that future tax liabilities are minimized.

Managing Rapid Growth

In many ways, rapid growth is the dream of most entrepreneurs, and is the ultimate result of successful sales and marketing, but it is not without challenges. As your turnover rises steeply, one of the first problems is that your cash requirements increase in tandem. This is due to the need for increased inventory, or having to take on more staff, or perhaps to fund more customers buying on credit. In addition, your business may need more equipment, vehicles, and possibly larger premises. The extra cash is normally found by increasing your overdraft, and banks are usually quite amenable to providing more financing because the business is obviously doing well, provided the proper financial controls are in place. Such controls include having an accountant actively involved with the business, having formal bookkeeping procedures in place, having up-to-date fincancial statements readily available, and producing regular cash flow forecasts. The business also has to demonstrate, through its bank account, that it can manage its finances.

An increase in sales may not be sustained in the longer term, however, and if sales drop you may find you have taken on too many new commitments. Be cautious before making big decisions based on your rapid growth rate. A drop in sales may occur because your success has attracted imitators (see p. 175), who are taking some of your market share.

After a period of rapid growth, the real Achilles heel is likely to be inadequate management procedures. These procedures might have been adequate at one time, but have perhaps not been upgraded or rethought to meet the new demands for controlling cash, staff, stock, credit, and so on. The consolation of such a weakness is that changing management procedures is one of the easier aspects to put right, if necessary by bringing in outside management advice.

Coping with Competitors

If a market is large enough to sustain more than one business, the appearance of a second one can produce healthy competition. On the other hand, if the market in an area cannot support a new competitor, a difficult struggle will ensue. The situation may be worse if there are a number of firms chasing too little business.

Competition is almost inevitable for every business, and your marketing strategy should take account of this (see pp. 68–73). It is when the existing competitors change or new competitors arrive that you may need to take additional action. Competitors come in all shapes and sizes; some of the hardest to identify are indirect competitors. For example, if you operate several minibuses, you might think your only competitors are other minibuses, but the competition in fact includes buses and taxis. There are various strategies for

COMMON ERRORS WHEN DEALING WITH THE COMPETITION

1. Under- or overestimating the reactions of your competitors.
2. Thinking that, because you have a strong business, competitors are not relevant.
3. Underestimating the wiliness of some competitors.
4. Trying to avoid meeting competitors at public events.
5. Not using the built-in agility of your small business.
6. Thinking that a large competitor is not vulnerable.
7. Forgetting that competitors make good takeover bidders or targets.
8. Not exploiting the weaknesses of your competitors.

coping with competitors, but the choice of strategy depends on whether you assess a competitor as benign or hostile.

Benign Competitors

A benign competitor could be described as one that keeps mainly to their own territory or shares the same customers as yourself, and either keeps a stable market share or, if it is expanding, then at least it is not expanding at your expense. Characteristically such a business is well established, does not attempt to steal your ideas or customers, and, most importantly, does not perceive you as a threat, so there is a state of peaceful coexistence. You may be happy with this situation and, if the competitor is much more powerful than you are, you might even be glad of it. However, this cosy situation may not go on forever, so monitor the activities of your competitor to detect any change in the status quo. Potential danger signs are when such a competitor:

- has a change of senior management
- moves into larger premises
- takes over another business (or is taken over)
- starts to recruit more sales staff
- raises capital (on the stock market, for example)
- launches a product or service similar to yours.

In each of these cases, find out more. If the

A Strategy for Managing Competitors

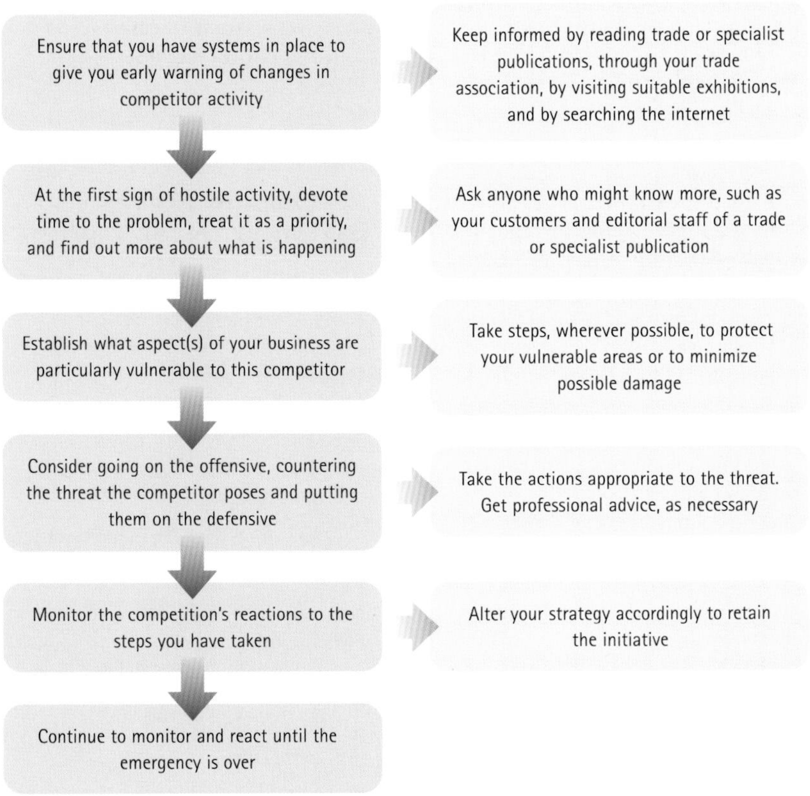

Ensure that you have systems in place to give you early warning of changes in competitor activity	Keep informed by reading trade or specialist publications, through your trade association, by visiting suitable exhibitions, and by searching the internet
At the first sign of hostile activity, devote time to the problem, treat it as a priority, and find out more about what is happening	Ask anyone who might know more, such as your customers and editorial staff of a trade or specialist publication
Establish what aspect(s) of your business are particularly vulnerable to this competitor	Take steps, wherever possible, to protect your vulnerable areas or to minimize possible damage
Consider going on the offensive, countering the threat the competitor poses and putting them on the defensive	Take the actions appropriate to the threat. Get professional advice, as necessary
Monitor the competition's reactions to the steps you have taken	Alter your strategy accordingly to retain the initiative
Continue to monitor and react until the emergency is over	

new senior managers are marketing- or sales-orientated, for example, this might indicate a change in the status quo. If the competitor does launch a product or service similar to yours, they can no longer be considered benign.

HOSTILE COMPETITORS

In contrast to a benign competitor, a hostile one poses an active threat (or perhaps multiple threats) to your business as they are pursuing your customers to gain market share at your expense. The degree of hostility can range from what outsiders might class as healthy competition (it never feels quite so healthy when it involves you) to positively aggressive. In the latter category your competitor attempts to make you either go out of business or at least move out of that market sector entirely, and is prepared to go to considerable lengths, and expense, to accomplish that objective.

Elaborate plans will be devised by particularly aggressive competitors, and some of their tactics may be unethical, possibly even illegal. Typical aggressive tactics include:

- engaging you in a price war
- spreading disinformation about your business
- stealing your customers
- poaching your key staff
- interfering with your sources of supply or your distribution channels
- taking legal action against you.

Your first action must be to learn as much as possible about them (see pp. 21–2). Next, counter the threats that they pose, as follows:

- **PRICE WAR** Like any war, a price war is costly for all sides. If it develops into a war of attrition, it can spell the end for the smaller business with its limited resources, or might even lead to the demise of both businesses. The biggest threat comes when your competitor is a branch of a larger company. In that case, they can drop their prices against you locally and keep them low almost indefinitely (until you go bust) since the profits from their other branches can finance them. In general, price wars are to be avoided at all costs, but if a competitor's actions unavoidably draw you into such a conflict, it is important to have a feel for the situation and to take what action you can.

  So how should you respond if a competitor drops its prices? Importantly, it is not always necessary for you to drop prices in order to compete. The factors that are relevant are: the price sensitivity of your commodity (for example, food items are price-sensitive); the frequency with which a customer uses you or your competitor (are customers usually passersby and always changing, or do the same customers keep returning?); convenience; special features (if you have features that your competitor does not, this may save you having to drop your prices). Rather than dropping your prices, focus attention on the features that make you different from your competitors. If you do feel you need to drop your prices, one strategy is to drop them to the same level or just above that of your competitor so as to discourage them from dropping their prices further.

Take legal advice before referring to competitors in any advertising or sales literature

- **DISINFORMATION** The spreading of incorrect information about your business amounts essentially to a propaganda campaign, which can be very effective and so needs to be countered. The information that is spread about you will be misleading and spread verbally without witnesses, so there is unlikely to be recourse through the legal system. Your competitor may be talking to mutual customers or the media. Some mud inevitably sticks. Propaganda can be fought by a counterpropaganda campaign. This can be defensive, trying to set the record straight, or it might attack the competition to put them on the defensive (although first seek legal advice on this). You might consider attacking, for instance, if you have reliable evidence that their product or service is inferior to or more costly than yours – but think how they are likely to react to your attack. Perhaps the best way of beating any propaganda is to win the hearts and minds of your customers – woo them, keep them informed, and look after them. One advantage you have is that most customers do not like to hear one supplier speaking badly of another.

- **STEALING CUSTOMERS** A competitor who is dropping its prices and spreading propaganda is obviously trying to steal your customers, but even more direct action may be used. For example, if your business depends on a relatively small number of customers (as is often the case in a business-to-business situation), the competitor may visit each of your main customers and offer various inducements to encourage them to change supplier. You need to face up to such direct action by ensuring that you make contact with your buyers. First, this may give you more detailed information about what your competitor is doing, saying, or promising, so that you can counter specifics. Second, it demonstrates that you care about the business you get from that customer. Finally, it keeps your business name at the forefront of your customers' minds.
- **POACHING STAFF** If you have key staff who are critical to your smooth operation, losing them could present two main threats. First, they may take sensitive inside knowledge of your operation to your competitor. A little thought will indicate confidential subjects that should never be discussed with employees (and any relevant files should be locked away); if necessary, aspects of sensitive subjects may be revealed only on a need-to-know basis. Second, a member of staff may have skills that are difficult to replace quickly. This usually occurs in a small business, where one employee becomes the best at doing a particular skilled activity. The solution is for every key operator to have a trained, nominated deputy who could fill the breach if the key staff member departs suddenly (or is simply ill or injured).

  In a more positive vein, staff poaching can be combated by generating a team spirit, looking after your staff, and rewarding them (verbally, then financially, and by increased responsibility), so that the incentive for them to move to another firm will be reduced.
- **INTERFERENCE** Another popular tactic used by hostile competitors is to interfere with your sources of supply. This is normally possible only if there are a limited number of such suppliers and if the competitor purchases considerably larger quantities than you do. Interfering with your supplies can be a serious problem and will require you to take action. Visit your suppliers to make personal contact with them to try to restore your supply. In some cases your only choice is to try to locate alternative suppliers quickly, even if they are abroad. Another, more subtle, approach is to find an ally whom the supplier values (or fears) and who is prepared to have a word in their ear on your behalf. It is usually more difficult for a competitor to interfere with your distribution than your supplies, but it is still worth considering how you might be vulnerable and then to do something about it before your competitor.
- **LEGAL ACTION** There would have to be

FACT FILE

Avoid confrontation, particularly with larger rivals. If you encroach on their perceived territory, which could be geographical, or a range of products or services, they are unlikely to ignore you for long. Until you are established, it is better to seek niches in the market that the larger competitor is ignoring. Keep a low profile; large competitors may ignore you if they think your operation is insignificant.

some pretext, however small, for a competitor even to contemplate some form of legal proceedings. Usually alleged breach of trade name, brand, or logo, or alleged copying of a product, is the type of pretext the other company's lawyers look for. It is not unknown for large companies to start proceedings that are unlikely to be judged in their favor in court. The threat of this course of action lies in obtaining an out-of-court settlement to their advantage. Should any form of legal proceedings be started against you, get competent legal advice at once from a lawyer. It may also be prudent to set aside a fighting fund, just in case.

Never let your competitors know that their actions are hurting you

INDIRECT COMPETITORS

You may focus too much of your attention on direct and indirect competitors in your own industry sector and miss the significance of an outside indirect threat. The subject of indirect competition is also relevant in terms of how a business promotes itself.

Ask yourself what business you are in – the answer is not always obvious. For example, a manufacturer of high-quality jams packaged in attractive jars might carry out an analysis of sales to indicate the types of outlets that are buying their product. The result might show that 80 percent of sales are made to gift shops, rather than food outlets. This reveals that the business is in the gift trade, rather than the food industry, when it comes to thinking about marketing, sales, and competition.

Direct competitors may be all those manufacturers making similar jams, but indirect competitors will be all the other firms that make small desirable gifts that are around the same price point and aimed at similar buyers. Once you have identified your indirect competitors, categorize them as hostile or benign, then act accordingly.

IMITATORS

A particularly irritating form of competition is the "me-too" imitator. Businesses that appear to be doing well and have an easy market entry threshold (see p. 25) are particularly vulnerable to this type of competition. The success rate of such imitators is generally low, however. This is possibly due to their having less market knowledge and the obvious disadvantage of being the second or third in the field. However, especially in the short term, such a competitor is a threat and may take some of your market share. Treat them as a hostile competitor and take the appropriate actions as outlined above.

WHICH BUSINESSES SURVIVE?

Where there is a competitive struggle, it is not necessarily the best or cheapest, or even the most ethical business, that is the ultimate winner. The underlying financial strength of a business and how well it promotes its products or services can count for much more in the long run.

USEFUL information

This section covers the important aspects of business law as they apply to marketing, providing a straightforward, basic grounding in the numerous and complex regulations that are likely to affect you. The Glossary explains key marketing terms, while the Useful Contacts and Suggested Reading sections point you toward other sources of information.

LEGAL MATTERS

There are an increasing number of laws and regulations which businesses, including small businesses, must comply with nationally and in each state. This section provides general guidance, but should not be regarded as a complete or authoritative statement of the law. For more detailed information and advice tailored to your individual business, consult a lawyer or the relevant authorities. Useful contacts and sources for more information are given at the end of this book on pp. 184–7.

The following areas of law and regulation are particularly relevant to selling and marketing goods and services in the United States, but may also apply more widely.

An important feature of our federal system of government is that many aspects of interstate commerce are regulated by federal law, which is often the minimum guarantee of protection. Unless federal law preempts them from doing so, states and localities may add further, and sometimes different, refinements. For that reason, the laws of each state and each locality may differ significantly, and may differ from federal law.

It is important to remember that "interstate commerce" has proven to be a difficult concept to define, and the courts continue to struggle with the concept. In general, any business that uses interstate methods of transporting goods or ideas, such as the postal service, the telephone, or the internet, should expect to be held to federal standards, although state and local laws will also apply.

ADVERTISING AND SALES PROMOTION

Much of the regulation of advertising and promotion is self-regulation, with industry groups largely policing themselves. These groups are usually very influential because their membership is composed of the largest and most prominent companies in the particular industry, and the group's ethical standards become the industry's code.

There are few regulations governing advertising and sales promotion as such in United States. Although federal and state laws do not regulate advertising, they do prohibit the use of false and misleading statements to sell goods.

On a national basis, the Federal Trade Commission administers laws and regulations that prohibit the use of fraudulent, deceptive, and unfair business practices in all manner of trade involving interstate commerce, and state and local laws often supplement the federal rules and regulations. Enforcement actions can be brought by federal, and by state or local authorities for violations of different laws involving the same deceptive scheme. In general, these laws prohibit false advertising, and regulate the use of comparative statements in marketing materials.

ARBITRATION VERSUS LITIGATION

Business agreements should be reviewed carefully as to whether they specify where any claims or disputes must be brought. Also, an increasing number of business agreements require arbitration, or other methods of alternative dispute resolution, rather than litigation. Resolving disputes outside the court system is much faster and less expensive, and is becoming a preferred way to handle many business claims.

BUSINESS AND INTERNET DOMAIN NAMES

The use of business names is regulated by state law. In general, sole proprietors may operate under their own last names, with or without the use of first names or initials, such as W.D. Smith dba ("doing business as") Smith's Gifts. Partnerships may operate under the names of all the partners or under a business name. Corporations may operate under the name of incorporation or under a business name. Business names are generally filed in each county in which the company does business.

Some state laws prohibit the use of certain words or terms in business names, especially names that would be deceptive or misleading.

State laws prohibit two corporations using the same name, or a confusing variation of the same name. Before selecting a business name, check local telephone and relevant business directories to avoid using a name that is the same as or very similar to that of an existing business.

The advent of the internet has created an entirely new problem in the use of domain names, and an entirely new set of regulators. Disputes over the use of domain names involve mandatory arbitration by panelists chosen by one of several international organizations authorized by the Internet Corporation for Assigned Names and Numbers, commonly known as ICANN.

These international arbitrators are not bound by U.S. law or custom, or by state or common-law rules of evidence. The fact that a name is legally registered in a particular state, or a trademark (see below) is registered in the United States, does not guarantee that an arbitrator will not bar the domain name registrant from using that name. The arbitrator can assign the domain name to another business, especially one that has used the name, or a part or variation of the name, under trademark or for a long time. This area of the law is particularly unsettled right now.

CLEAR PRINT AND PLAIN ENGLISH

Many state laws require the use of large, clear print, in some cases bold-faced, in certain contracts and insurance policies. Many state laws encourage, and in some cases require, the use of "plain English," rather than legal or industry terminology, in contracts, especially those involving consumers.

COMMERCIAL DEBTS

Commercial purchases are regulated by state laws, most of which follow the Uniform Commercial Code. Buyers should promptly inspect goods, for quantity, quality, and suitability. Unless they are unconscionable, invoice terms, including discounts and interest, will be upheld. Buyers should also promptly inspect statements of goods sold and delivered, because they may be held liable for accounts stated, to which there has been no protest.

COMPETITION

The Federal Trade Commission and some state regulatory agencies also prohibit anticompetitive agreements, whether written or unwritten, between two or more businesses or trade groups, as well as abusing a dominant position in the market by a business. Examples of such anti-competitive agreements include the fixing of purchase or sales prices, the sharing of markets, or the application of different trading conditions to equivalent transactions.

The agencies have the authority to block mergers and acquisitions, and to force companies to sell divisions, leave markets, or split themselves into several different companies, in order to encourage competition and to punish anticompetitive actions.

CONSUMER CREDIT

The Federal Trade Commission administers the Fair Credit Reporting Act, which gives consumers the right to inspect and challenge information in credit reports that can adversely affect their credit ratings. The act also allows consumers to opt out of marketing lists prepared by credit reporting agencies that are used to solicit customers for credit cards, insurance policies, and other financial products.

The Federal Trade Commission also administers the Truth in Lending Act which, with Regulation Z, requires businesses that offer credit terms in any form to disclose the credit terms and conditions, especially the annual percentage rate of the cost of credit.

The Truth in Lending Act and Regulation Z, which are enforceable under state as well as federal law, prohibit the attempt to disguise a credit transaction through the use of terms such as "budget plan" or "easy monthly payments," and require the disclosure of the true nature of the transaction.

Some state laws also regulate, to varying degrees, the grant or denial of credit, the use of credit reports, the use of marketing lists, and so on.

Interest rates for credit terms and conditions, including credit cards, are set by state law.

Federal and state laws prohibit the use of discriminatory criteria, such as race or religion, to determine creditworthiness.

CONSUMER PROTECTION

The Federal Trade Commission, as well as state and local agencies, regulates many aspects of consumer protection. Federal and state regulations prohibit deceptive business practices in the sale of franchises, network marketing and business opportunity plans, and work-from-home programs. Similar regulations prohibit the use of unfounded claims to promote the sale of diet, health, and fitness products.

Federal regulations prohibit the fraudulent use of "Made in the U.S.A." labels on products, and prohibit deceptive product labeling.

Both federal and state authorities are gearing up to stop the growing problem of identity theft, and the fraudulent use of the identification and credit profile of unsuspecting victims.

The Federal Trade Commission publishes several booklets to educate businesses about the applicable rules, and to encourage compliance, including: *A Business Guide to the Federal Trade Commission's Mail Order Rule*, *A Businessperson's Guide to Federal Warranty Law*, *Complying with the 900-Number Rule: A Business Guide for Pay-per-Call Services*, *Complying with the Telemarketing Sales Rule*, *Guides Against Bait Advertising*, *Guides Against Deceptive Advertising of Guaranties*, *Guides Against Deceptive Pricing*, *Guides Concerning Use of Endorsements and Testimonials in Advertising*, *Guides Concerning the Use of the Word "Free" and Similar Representations*, *Guides for the Use of Environmental Marketing Claims*, and *How to Advertise Consumer Credit: Complying with the Law*.

COOLING-OFF PERIODS

Some state laws give consumers greater protection, such as an extended right of cancellation, for items sold door-to-door. Similar laws extend cancellation rights in certain financial products, such as mortgages.

COPYRIGHTS

The concept of copyright relates to original literary and other creative works, including advertisements and marketing brochures and materials, in all types of media and means of dissemination, including the internet. Often no registration is required other than the use under common law, but legal protection requires being able to prove who created the work, and when. Protection is automatic and immediate, but it is advisable to use the copyright symbol © together with the date the work the work was first created. Registration with the U.S. Copyright Office is strongly advised.

DATA PRIVACY

See Consumer Protection, above. Many states are enacting or considering laws to grant individuals greater control over the use and dissemination of their private data, especially credit and medical information. This area may become subject to greater federal and state regulation, especially with the increasing ability to identify and create databases of genetic or heritable medical conditions.

ENVIRONMENTAL ISSUES

Our precious natural resources are regulated by a network of federal, state, and local authorities, many of which have seemingly overlapping jurisdiction. In addition, the various authorities often have concurrent rights to veto certain projects, or to require environmental impact statements, testing, or cleanups. These issues are far beyond the scope of this book, and are mentioned here for informational purposes only.

Equal Opportunity

Federal and state laws prohibit discrimination in a wide variety of areas, including employment, sales, leasing, and credit decisions.

Financial Services

The sale of financial services is highly regulated by federal or state authorities, or both. In general, the sale of insurance products requires a state license, and the sale of investment products requires licensing by a federally authorized organization, such as the National Association of Security Dealers. Selling other investment-related products, such as real estate and mortgages, generally requires state licenses.

Financing and Guidance

The U.S. Small Business Administration (SBA), a division of the U.S. Department of Commerce, offers several programs providing financing for new businesses, with a particular emphasis on exporting. SBA loans are made by commercial lenders, who are willing to make the loans because most of the principal is guaranteed by the federal government.

The critical element in these loans, as well as most loans to new businesses, is the creditworthiness of the business owner, as well as the business plan.

The SBA also offers a mentoring program of particular interest to new businesses, the Service Corps of Retired Executives (SCORE). These volunteers have a lifetime of experience in business, credit, finance, or marketing, and can help new businesses develop business and marketing plans, loan applications, and grant proposals, at no charge.

SBA staffers and SCORE volunteers can also help new businesses take advantage of other guaranteed and reduced-rate loan programs, industrial development programs, grants, and opportunities for exporting, and for doing business with the government and large corporations.

Food Safety

There are stringent rules, generally set by local authorities, regarding most aspects of food preparation, handling, and marketing. These rules address premises, equipment, refrigeration and storage, cleaning, food handling, work methods and training, labeling, vermin control, and other aspects of the business. In addition to frequent, random, mandatory inspections, many areas require licensing and training certification.

Franchise and Network Marketing

See Consumer Protection, above. Many states are enacting or considering laws to provide greater protection for purchasers of franchises and multilevel marketing plans.

Mail Order and Telemarketing

See Consumer Protection, above. Federal Trade Commission rules prohibit using abusive or deceptive telemarketing methods, such as misrepresenting, or failing to disclose costs, conditions, refund or cancellation policies, the odds of winning a prize or premium, or credit card laundering. Sellers by mail or telephone order must ship within the time specified, or within 30 days.

Patents

The U.S. Patent and Trademark Office grants patents to unique inventions that advance the state of the art. A patent application requires proof that the invention is unique, that the applicant invented it, and how and when it was invented. The office's publications explain the application process, the benefits, and the fees.

Payroll Taxes

Federal law provides a uniform nationwide rate for income and Social Security taxes, and some states and localities have income taxes. States require insurance for on- and off-the job illnesses and injuries, and unemployment. Employers must withhold taxes from employees' salaries and remit the taxes to the appropriate authorities, usually quarterly. All corporate employees, including operators of sole stockholder corporations, are considered employees. Sole proprietors and partners are generally not considered employees, and are responsible for insuring their own health and ability to continue the business.

PRICE MARKING

State laws require goods offered for sale to be clearly marked as to price, but these laws differ markedly as to the specifics, and as to how they are interpreted. Some states require each item to be clearly marked as to the price of that unit. Other states merely require the per-unit price be displayed reasonably near the item. Local ordinances may offer consumers greater protection.

SALES AND USE TAXES

Sales and use taxes are set by state, county, or local law, and the rates, exemptions, and items subject to tax vary from one locality to another. Also, regulations differ as to whether mail, telephone, and internet sales are subject to taxation. In most cases, the business owner is liable for tax whether or not it has been collected from the customers. Local authorities should be consulted as to the applicability of these laws as soon as the business begins operation.

TRADEMARKS

Trademarks and business logos must be unique, and may not be deceptive or misleading. They should be registered with the U.S. Patent and Trademark Office.

WARRANTIES

Federal law does not require a warranty, other than that warranty advertising not be false, misleading, or deceptive. In general, warranty terms are regulated by state law, most of which follows the Uniform Commercial Code, especially in business-to-business sales. Consumers are often given greater protection, including requirements that goods correspond with the description, are of satisfactory quality, and are suitable for the purpose. Consumer services must be performed with reasonable care and skill, within a reasonable time, and for a reasonable charge. Like their rights, consumers' remedies vary from state to state.

WEIGHTS AND MEASURES

The regulation of weights and measures in the sale of food, beverages, household supplies, etc., is generally regulated by state law and administered by local authorities. Enforcement is typically through the use of spot- and random testing, especially during holidays and other peak buying periods.

GLOSSARY

Advertorial
An advertisement that is intended to look like editorial copy.

Body Copy
The main text of an advertisement or leaflet.

Circular
A letter or other document, identical copies of which are sent to many people, usually with a sales motive and not addressed to anyone by name. See also **Mailshot**.

Circulation
The number of copies of each issue that a publication sells or distributes. The number of people who might read the publication will be much higher.

Cross-selling
Selecting customers by their buying patterns in order to sell them related goods or services.

Customer Profile
The details of a customer as they relate to a

market segment.
Depreciation
The loss in value of an item over time. The life of an item for tax purposes is set by the Internal Revenue Service.
Direct Mail
Personally addressed information on products and services sent through the mail.
Direct Marketing
A term describing how a manufacturer or importer sells direct to the end user. Methods of direct marketing include by direct selling, mail order, and direct mail.
Direct Selling
Selling direct to the consumer by personal contact.
E-commerce
The conduct of business transactions over the internet.
Estimate
The approximate price given to a customer in advance for doing a job. See also **Quote**.
Franchising
The right, granted under license, to trade by copying the successful business format of another business, including its name, its products, and its image.
Insert
A leaflet placed inside a publication, either loose or bound in.
Loss Leader
Discounted goods sold at a loss, but highly promoted in order to attract customers.
Mailing List Purge
The removal of duplicate or obsolete names from a mailing list.
Mailshot
A direct mail letter addressed to a named individual, usually with a sales motive. See also **Circular**.
Margin
The profit made on selling goods or services. Usually expressed as a percentage. See also **Markup**.
Market Segmentation
The discipline of considering the total possible market in series of segments or parts. A segment is a group of buyers with similar needs.
Marketing Mix
A phrase used to describe the concept that having the right product (or service) in the right place at the right price and backed up with the right promotion will lead to success in marketing.
Marketing Plan
A written document setting out a business's marketing objectives and how to achieve them. Includes a budget, sales plan, and cash-flow forecast.
Markup
The difference between the cost price and the selling price. Usually expressed as a percentage. Mark-ups tend to be broadly standard within an industry. See also **Margin**.
Network Marketing
A term used in direct selling to describe a multilevel system in which a salesperson receives bonuses based on the performance of those they recruit as salespeople.
Overhead (Fixed Costs)
The regular (often monthly) expenses of keeping a business running; includes rent, electricity, telephone, insurance, and most wages.
Premium Pricing
Supplying goods or services at a premium price. This is usually possible only for exclusive products where demand far outweighs supply.
Press Release
An official statement or news story sent to the media, usually as a typed document, to gain publicity.
Profiling
Grouping customers according to specific characteristics, such as age, gender, and income.
Prospect
An abbreviation for "prospective customer." Used of someone to whom a salesperson is pitching a sale.
Public Relations
The interaction of a business with the public. Often used to refer to the communication of a message via the media.

Quote
The fixed price quoted to a customer in advance for doing a job. If agreed, the quote is normally binding on the seller and the customer. See also **Estimate**.

Rate Card
The advertising costs (called "rates"), technical data, and trading terms of a publication or commercial broadcasting station. Often printed on a card, the information is issued by the advertising department.

Response Rate
The number of replies received as a result of a direct mail campaign, expressed as a percentage of the total number of items sent out.

Return on Investment (ROI)
The amount of profit generated from a marketing campaign, expressed as a percentage of the cost of that campaign.

Run-of-paper (ROP)
A term used to describe placing an advertisement anywhere in a publication.

Strapline
A one-line statement in an advertisement, in addition to the headline, that sums up the key message of that advertisement.

Target Market
The section of the population that could potentially use a product or service.

Telesales
Selling by telephone.

USP (Unique Selling Proposition)
The singular factor that differentiates a product or service from others in the marketplace.

Variable Costs (Direct Costs)
The irregular and changing costs of keeping a business running; these usually vary directly in relation to the level of business.

USEFUL CONTACTS

In addition to these national sites, check the internet and your telephone directory for organizations and government agencies geared to your industry and your locality.

ARTS AND CRAFTS

National Endowment for the Arts
1100 Pennsylvania Avenue, N.W.
Washington, D.C. 20506
Tel: 202-682-5400
www.arts.endow.gov

ADVERTISING AND MARKETING

American Association of Advertising Agencies
405 Lexington Avenue
New York, NY 10174-1801
Tel: 212-682-2500. Fax: 212-682-8391
www.aaaa.org

Direct Marketing Association
1120 Avenue of the Americas
New York, NY 10036-6700
Tel: 212-768-7277. Fax: 212-30-6714
www.the-dma.org

BUSINESS ADVOCACY ORGANIZATIONS

Many business and development groups advance their causes before national and state lawmakers and regulators. Two such national groups, with local affiliates, are:

National Association of Manufacturers
1331 Pennsylvania Avenue, N.W.
Washington, D.C. 20004-1790
Tel: 202-637-3000. Fax: 202-637-3182
www.nam.org

U.S. Chamber of Commerce
1615 H Street
Washington, D.C. 20062-2000
Tel: 202-659-6000
www.uschamber.com

Corporate Information

Corporations must generally register with the Secretary of State of the state, and partnerships with the clerk of the county, in which they are registered. For information on public corporations, contact:

U.S. Securities and Exchange Commission
450 Fifth Street, N.W.
Washington, D.C. 20549-0304
Tel: 202-942-2950
www.sec.gov

Exporting

American Management Association
1601 Broadway
New York, NY 10019
Tel: 212-586-6100. Fax: 212-903-8168
www.amanet.org

U.S. Small Business Administration
409 Third Street
Washington, D.C. 20416
Tel: 800-827-5722
www.sba.gov

Franchising

Federal Trade Commission
Pennsylvania Avenue and Sixth Street, N.W.
Washington, D.C. 20580
Tel: 202-326-2222
www.ftc.gov

Government Business Development Agencies

Department of Commerce
14th Street and Constitution Avenue, N.W.
Washington, D.C. 20230
Tel: 202-482-1850
www.doc.gov

Government Offices

Internal Revenue Service
1111 Constitution Avenue, N.W.
Washington, D.C. 20224
Tel: 202-927-5170
www.irs.ustreas.gov

Occupational Health and Safety Administration (DOL)
Tel: 202-693-1999
www.osha-slc.gov

Social Security Administration
820 First Street, N.W.
Washington, D.C. 20254
Tel: 800-772-6270
www.ssa.gov

Other Useful Websites

Angel Capital Network (Ace-Net)
www.sba.gov/advo
Business Advisor (federal government information)
www.business.gov
Commerce Business Daily (federal government contracts)
cbdnet.access.gpo.gov
Consumer Information Center
www.pueblo.gov
ExpoGuide (trade show information)
www.expoguide.com
Minority Business Development Agency
www.mbda.gov
National Foundation for Women Business Owners
www.nfwbo.org
Service Corps of Retired Executives (SCORE)
www.score.org
State Government and Legal Resource
www.alllaw.com
State Tax Forms
www.taxweb.com/forms
Thomas Register
www.thomasregister.com
University of North Carolina, Charlotte
J. Murrey Atkins Library
libweb.uncc.edu/ref-bus/buselec.htm
Women's Business Center (also young entrepreneurs)
http://onlinewbc.org

U.S. Copyright Office (Library of Congress)
101 Independence Avenue, S.E.
Washington, D.C. 20559-6000
Tel: 202-707-3000
www.loc.gov/copyright

U.S. Department of Labor
200 Constitution Avenue, N.W.
Washington, D.C. 20210
Tel: 202-219-6001
www.dol.gov/elaws

U.S. Patent and Trademark Office
Crystal Plaza 3, Room 2C02
Washington, D.C. 20231
Tel: 800-786-9199
www.uspto.gov

MANUFACTURERS' AGENTS

Manufacturers' Representatives Educational Research Foundation
P.O.B. 247
Geneva, IL 60134
Tel: 630-208-1466. Fax: 630-208-1475
www.mrerf.org

MARKET RESEARCH SOURCES

U.S. Census Bureau
4700 Silver Hill Road
Suitland, MD 20746
Tel: 301-457-4608
www.census.gov

YOUNG ENTREPRENEURS' ASSISTANCE

Many business and development groups promote initiatives by young people. In addition to local groups and universities, you may contact clearinghouses for such information.

Edward Lowe Foundation
P.O. Box 8
Cassapolis, MI 49031
Tel: 800-232-5693
www.lowe.org

The Entrepreneurship Institute
www.tei.net

Initiative for a Competitive Inner City
727 Atlantic Avenue,
Suite 600
Boston, MA 02111
Tel: 617-292-2363
www.icic.org

SUGGESTED READING

The American Marketplace
(New Strategist Publications, 1999)
A survey of how and where we live, what we spend our money on, and what motivates us to do so.

Building a Website
Tim Worsley (Dorling Kindersley, 2000)
An easy-to-follow guide to Microsoft's website building program, FrontPage 2000, aimed at complete beginners to this software. Fully illustrated.

The Complete Idiot's Guide to Online Marketing
Bill Eager and Cathy McCall (Que, 1999)
An easy-to-use and follow guide to using the internet to market and sell products.

The Do-It-Yourself Business Promotions Kit
Jack Griffin (Prentice Hall, 1995)
Using advertising, media planning, and marketing communications to promote your business. Focuses on small-business management.

Do-It-Yourself Direct Marketing
Mark S. Bacon (John Wiley and Sons, 1997)
How to sell using mail order, telemarketing, radio and television commercials, print ads, and the internet, with tips for small businesses with small budgets.

E-Mail Marketing
Jim Sterne and Anthony Priore (John Wiley and Sons, 2000)
Using email to reach a targeted audience, and to build and maintain customer relationships.

Entrepreneur Magazine's How to Start a Network Marketing Business
(Entrepreneur Media, 1997)
A step-by-step guide to building a successful network marketing business.

Essential Manager's Manual
Robert Heller and Tim Hindle (Dorling Kindersley, 1998)
A highly readable reference book with general advice on areas such as giving presentations, communicating, and time management.

ExportAmerica
A monthly magazine from the U.S. Department of Commerce, with practical tips on every step of the business of selling U.S.-made goods abroad, from getting started through getting paid. For details and subscription information, call 202-512-1800, or see http://exportamerica.doc.gov

Getting Started in Export
Roger Bennett (Kogan Page, 1998)
Hands-on advice about researching overseas markets, finding customers, pricing, delivering goods, and the legalities of export.

101 Ways to Promote Your Website
Susan Sweeney (Maximum Press, 1999)
Suggests marketing tips, tools, techniques, and resources to drive traffic to your company's website.

Secrets of Successful Telephone Selling
Robert W. Bly (Henry Holt, 1996)
How to use the telephone to generate leads and referrals, to close sales, and to keep customers.

Selling Successfully
Robert Heller (Dorling Kindersley, 1998)
All you need to know about successful selling.

Small-Business Franchises Made Simple
William Lasher and Carl Hausman (Doubleday, 1994)
A guide to franchising businesses, especially retail operations, throughout the United States.

The Small Business Legal Guide
Lynne Ann Frasier (Sourcebooks, 1998)
A guide to the critical legal matters that can affect your business.

Small Business Legal Smarts
Deborah L. Jacobs (Bloomberg, 1998)
How to establish and protect your business.

Start and Succeed in Multilevel Marketing
Gregory F. Kishel and Patricia Gunter Kishel (John Wiley, 1999)
A guide to building a network sales business.

Starting and Operating a Business in the U.S.
Michael D. Jenkins (Running "R" Media, 1999)
A how-to-guide, with printed forms and a laser optical disc.

Statistical Abstract of the United States, 1999 Issue
(U.S. Census Bureau, 2000)
Updated annually since 1878, this may be the most important fact book on the social, political, and economic aspects of American life. Available in print, CD-ROM, or downloadable (PDF file) format. The 2001 issue should incorporate the results of the 2000 national census.

Streetwise: Do It Yourself Advertising
Sarah White and John Woods (Adams Media, 1997)
How to create ads, and use promotions and direct marketing, with strategies to jump-start sales.

FRANCHISE DIRECTORIES

Franchise Opportunities Handbook
(LaVerne L. Ludden, Park Avenue, 1999)

Franchise World Directory
(Franchise World)

INDEX

A

B

C

ACKNOWLEDGMENTS

AUTHOR'S ACKNOWLEDGMENTS

I would like to thank Charlotte Hingston for reading my manuscript and for her many useful suggestions. I would also like to thank my hard-working editors and designer and, finally, Julie Servante and Stuart Ramsden for their kind assistance.

PUBLISHER'S ACKNOWLEDGMENTS

Grant Laing Partnership would like to thank the following for their help and participation in producing this book:
Special Photography: Mark Hamilton
Advice on websites: Caroline Marklew
Proofreader: Nikky Twyman
Indexer: Kay Ollerenshaw
Models: Nicole Kacajynski, Christine Lacey, Jane Laing, Augustin Luneau, Francis Ritter, Natasha Robertson, Ben Roston, Mario de Souza

Dorling Kindersley would like to thank the following for their help and participation in producing this book:
Editorial: Mary Lindsay, Daphne Richardson, Mark Wallace
Design: Sarah Cowley
DTP: Jason Little, Amanda Peers

The illustration on page 103 is used courtesy of Amazon.co.uk
Clothes featured on pp. 148–9 are by Charlotte Danziger.
Thanks also to Goug Wilcox for allowing us to use her boutique – Keturah Brown, 85 Regents Park Road, London NW1 8UY – for the photoshoot.

PICTURE CREDITS

2: Rex Features; 5 above: The Stock Market; 5 centre above, & centre below: Powerstock/Zefa Photo Library; 5 below: The Image Bank; 8–9: The Stock Market; 13: Rex Features; 18: The Image Bank; 19 Robert Harding Picture Library; 25: The Image Bank; 28: Sally and Richard Greenhill; 33 below: gettyone stone; 38: Courtesy of Mercedes-Benz; 48: Robert Harding Picture Library; 51: The Stock Market; 56: Rex Features; 58: The Image Bank; 61: Environmental Images; 64: Rex Features; 68: gettyone stone; 74: Barry Lewis/Corbis Images; 76–7: Powerstock/Zefa Photo Library; 83: Rex features; 89: Advertising Archives; 91: Robert Harding Picture Library; 93: Garden Picture Library/Ron Sutherland; 98: gettyone stone; 107: gettyone stone; 111: Garden Picture Library/Ron Sutherland; 112: Robert Harding Picture Library; 113: gettyone stone; 118: The Image Bank; 119: Courtesy of BBC Radio Derby; 129: The Stock Market; 134: Powerstock/Zefa Photo Library; 137: Rex Features; 139: The Image Bank; 145: The Stock Market; 156: Rex Features; 158: Rex Features; 160-161: Powerstock/Zefa Photo Library; 163: Robert Harding Picture Library; 168: The Image Bank; 176-7: The Image Bank.

AUTHOR'S BIOGRAPHY

After serving in the RAF, Peter Hingston started his first business in 1979, working with cars near Oxford. He sold this, and later started an electronics manufacturing business in Barbados. Then, with his wife, he launched a fashion shop in Edinburgh, a national trade magazine, and a book publishing business. All traded profitably and were eventually sold, apart from the publishing business, which he runs today. He has written six books on running a small business, some of which have been bestsellers and translated into several different languages. Peter is also a non-executive director of a large retail business in Barbados.